Emerging Trends for Securing Cyber Physical Systems and the Internet of Things

In the past decades, cyber-physical systems (CPSs) have been widely applied to fields such as smart grids, environment monitoring, aerospace, smart transportation, and industrial automation. Great strides have been made in CPSs to improve the computing mechanism, communication, and quality of service by applying optimization algorithms. Currently, these efforts are integrated with the applications of machine learning (ML) and artificial intelligence (AI). To maintain system reliability and stability, CPSs such as smart grids face numerous challenges, including large-scale Internet-of-Things (IoT) device adaptation, ever-increasing demands of electrical energy, and the rise of a wide range of security threats. These challenges bring forth the need to find sustainable and advanced solutions to guarantee reliable and secure operations in these systems.

The goal of this book is to foster transformative, multidisciplinary, and novel approaches that ensure CPS security by taking into consideration the unique security challenges present in the environment. This book attracts contributions in all aspects pertaining to this multidisciplinary paradigm, which includes the development and implementation of Smart CPS, Supervisory Control and Data Acquisition (SCADA) systems, CPS for Industry 4.0, CPS architecture for IoT applications, and CPS forensics.

This book:

- Discusses concepts including wireless sensor networks (WSNs), CPSs, and the IoT in a comprehensive manner.
- Covers routing protocols in sensor networks, attacks, and vulnerabilities in WSNs, the Internet of Cyber-Physical Things, and CPSs for industrial applications.
- Highlights technological advances, practical solutions, emerging trends, and prototypes related to privacy in CPSs and the IoT.
- Presents a pathway and architecture for proactive security schemes in CPSs to counter vulnerabilities, including phishing attacks, malware injection, internal stealing of data, and hacking.
- Discusses the most recent research and development on the enabling technologies for IoT-based CPSs.

Owing to the scope and diversity of topics covered, the book will be of interest not only to researchers and theorists but also to professionals, material developers, technology specialists, and methodologists dealing with the multifarious aspects of data privacy and security enhancement in CPSs. The book will provide these professionals an overview of CPS security and privacy design, as well as enlighten them to promising solutions to research problems such as cyberattacks in CPS, risk identification and management in CPS, ML-based trust computational models for CPSs, nature-inspired algorithms for CPSs, and distributed consensus algorithms for event detection in CPSs. The secondary target audience of this book includes legal practitioners, hackers, cyber law policymakers, cyber forensic analysts, and global security consortiums who may use it to further their research exposure to pertinent topics in cybersecurity.

Future Generation Information Systems
Series editor- Bharat Bhushan

With the evolution of future generation computing systems, it becomes necessary to occasionally take stock, analyze the development of its core theoretical ideas, and adapt to radical innovations. This series will provide a platform to reflect the theoretical progress, and forge emerging theoretical avenues for the future generation information systems. The theoretical progress in the Information Systems field (IS) and the development of associated next generation theories is the need of the hour. This is because Information Technology (IT) has become increasingly infused, interconnected and intelligent in almost all context.

Convergence of Deep Learning and Artificial Intelligence in Internet of Things
Ajay Rana, Arun Rana, Sachin Dhawan, Sharad Sharma and Ahmed A. Elngar

Next Generation Communication Networks for Industrial Internet of Things Systems
Sundresan Perumal, Mujahid Tabassum, Moolchand Sharma and Saju Mohanan

Emerging Trends for Securing Cyber Physical Systems and the Internet of Things
Edited by Bharat Bhushan, Sudhir Kumar Sharma, Parma Nand, Achyut Shankar and Ahmed J. Obaid

Emerging Trends for Securing Cyber Physical Systems and the Internet of Things

Edited by Bharat Bhushan,
Sudhir Kumar Sharma, Parma Nand,
Achyut Shankar and Ahmed J. Obaid

CRC Press
Taylor & Francis Group
Boca Raton London New York

CRC Press is an imprint of the
Taylor & Francis Group, an **informa** business

Designed cover image: Shutterstock

First edition published 2024
by CRC Press
2385 NW Executive Center Drive, Suite 320, Boca Raton FL 33431

and by CRC Press
4 Park Square, Milton Park, Abingdon, Oxon, OX14 4RN

CRC Press is an imprint of Taylor & Francis Group, LLC

ISBN: 978-1-032-39294-3 (hbk)
ISBN: 978-1-032-75470-3 (pbk)
ISBN: 978-1-003-47411-1 (ebk)

DOI: 10.1201/9781003474111

Typeset in Times New Roman
by Apex CoVantage, LLC

Contents

Preface

A cyber-physical system (CPS) refers to an emerging generation of systems with integrated physical and computational capabilities through communication, computation, and control. CPS facilitates bringing forth new applications and services in various fields through its automated decisions and tight interactions. In the past decades, CPS has been widely applied to fields such as smart grids, environment monitoring, aerospace, smart transportation, and industrial automation. Interconnected sensing devices in CPS sense data from the surrounding and send them through the network to the interested nodes. This integration of physical and computing elements in order to create a CPS has opened up numerous potential security problems. Security attacks in CPS may have disruptive consequences and lead to significant economic and social losses. Owing to the variety of attacks that might be launched against these physical components, building a secure CPS is a challenging task. CPS blurs the lines between personal and infrastructural spaces, and this blurring is engineered into the Internet-of-Things (IoT). Advances in CPSs and IoT bring forth the need to find a unified view of security and safety. In order to design an advanced CPS, integration of wireless sensor actuator networks and IoT is of utmost importance. Communication links in such complex, heterogeneous systems must meet stringent requirements on range, latency, and throughput while adhering to the constrained energy budget and providing high levels of security. The goal of this book is to foster transformative, multidisciplinary, and novel approaches that ensure the CPS security by taking into consideration the unique security challenges present in the environment. These security challenges include the full gamut of faults, ranging from an adversary successfully leaking private information to achieving complete control over the system. This may be due to boot process vulnerability, hardware exploitation, chip-level exploitation, backdoors in remote access channels, software exploitation, and a resource-constrained nature. This book attracts contributions in all aspects pertaining to this multidisciplinary paradigm, which includes the development and implementation of Smart CPS, Supervisory Control and Data Acquisition (SCADA) systems, CPS for Industry 4.0, CPS architecture for IoT applications, and CPS forensics.

Editor's Biographies

Bharat Bhushan is an assistant professor in the Department of Computer Science and Engineering (CSE) at the School of Engineering and Technology, Sharda University, Greater Noida, India. He received his undergraduate degree (B.Tech in computer science and engineering), with distinction, in 2012; postgraduate degree (M.Tech in information security), with distinction, in 2015; and doctorate degree (Ph.D. in computer science and engineering) in 2021 from the Birla Institute of Technology, Mesra, India. In 2021 and 2022, Stanford University (USA) listed Dr. Bharat Bhushan in the top 2% of scientists. He has earned numerous international certifications, such as CCNA, MCTS, MCITP, RHCE, and CCNP. He has published more than 150 research papers in various renowned international conferences and SCI-indexed journals, including the *Journal of Network and Computer Applications* (Elsevier), *Wireless Networks* (Springer), *Wireless Personal Communications* (Springer), *Sustainable Cities and Society* (Elsevier), and *Emerging Transactions on Telecommunications* (Wiley). He has contributed more than 30 chapters to various books and has edited 20 books from the most renowned publishers like Elsevier, Springer, Wiley, IOP Press, IGI Global, and CRC Press. He has served as keynote speaker (resource person) in numerous reputed faculty development programs and international conferences held in different countries, including India, Iraq, Morocco, China, Belgium, and Bangladesh. He has served as a reviewer/editorial board member for several reputed international journals. In the past, he has worked as an assistant professor at HMR Institute of Technology and Management, New Delhi, and network engineer at HCL Infosystems Ltd., Noida, India. In addition to being the senior member of IEEE, he is also a member of numerous renowned bodies, including IAENG, CSTA, SCIEI, IAE, and UACEE.

Sudhir Kumar Sharma is Professor and Head of the Department of Computer Science, Institute of Information Technology & Management, Guru Gobind Singh Indraprastha University, New Delhi, India. He has extensive experience spanning over 21 years in the fields of computer science and engineering. He completed his Ph.D. in information technology in 2013 from the University

School of Information, Communication and Technology, Guru Gobind Singh Indraprastha University, New Delhi, India. Dr. Sharma obtained his M.Tech degree in computer science and engineering in 1999 from Guru Jambheshwar University, Hisar, India, and M.Sc. degree in physics from the University of Roorkee (now IIT Roorkee), Roorkee, in 1997. His research interests include machine learning, data mining, and security. He has published more than 60 research papers in various prestigious international journals and international conferences. He is a life member of CSI and IETE. Dr. Sharma is the lead guest editor of the special issue of *Multimedia Tools & Applications* (Springer). He was the convener and volume editor of two international conferences: ICE-TIT-2019 and ICRIHE-2020. He has authored and edited seven books on computer science in the fields of Internet-of-Things, WSN, blockchain, and cyber-physical systems, published by Elsevier, Springer, and CRC Press. He has been a reviewer/editorial board member for several reputed international journals. He has also served as a speaker, session chair, and co-chair at various national and international conferences.

Parma Nand is Dean, School of Engineering Technology, Sharda University Greater Noida, India. He has over 26 years of experience in teaching, industry, and research. He has expertise in wireless and sensor network, cryptography, algorithm, and computer graphics. He has earned his Ph.D. from IIT Roorkee and M.Tech and B.Tech in computer science and engineering from IIT Delhi, India. He has been a head/member of many committees, including the Board of Studies, Faculty and Staff Recruitment Committee, Academic Council, Advisory Committee, Monitoring and Planning Board, Research Advisory Committee, Accreditation Committee, etc. He has also served as President of the National Engineers Organization. He is a senior member of the IEEE (USA). He is a member of the Executive Council of IEEE UP section (R10), a member of the Executive Committee IEEE Computer and Signal Processing Society, a member of the Executive of India Council of Computer Society, member Executive Council Computer Society of India, Noida section, and has acted as an observer in many IEEE conferences. He also has active memberships in ACM, CSI, ACEEE, ISOC, IAENG, and IASCIT. He is a lifetime member of the Soft Computing Research Society (SCRS) and ISTE. He has delivered many invited/keynotes talks at international and national conferences/workshops/seminars in India and abroad. He has published more than 85 papers in peer-reviewed international/national journals and conferences. He has filed two patents. He is an active member of the advisory/technical program committee of reputed international/national conferences and a reviewer of a number of reputed journals, for example, *Computers and Electrical Engineering Journal* (Elsevier).

Achyut Shankar is currently working as an assistant professor at Amity University, Noida, India. He obtained his Ph.D. in computer science and engineering, majoring in wireless sensor networks from VIT University, Vellore,

India. He has published more than 35 research papers in reputed international conferences and journals, of which 17 are in SCI journals. He is a member of ACM and has received research excellence awards in 2016 and 2017. He has organized many special sessions with Scopus Indexed International Conferences worldwide, proceedings of which were published by Springer, IEEE, Elsevier, etc. He is serving as a reviewer for *IEEE Transactions on Intelligent Transportation Systems*, *IEEE Sensors Journal*, *IEEE Internet of Things Journal*, *ACM Transactions on Asian and Low-Resource Language Information Processing*, and other prestigious conferences. His areas of interest include wireless sensor networks, machine learning, Internet-of-Things, blockchain, and cloud computing.

Ahmed J. Obaid is a full assistant professor in the Department of Computer Science, Faculty of Computer Science and Mathematics, University of Kufa, Iraq. He received his B.Sc. degree in information systems from the Faculty of Computer Science, University of Anbar, Iraq, in 2005; M.Tech in computer science and engineering from the School of Information Technology, Jawaharlal Nehru Technological University, India, in 2012; and Ph.D. in web mining and data mining from the University of Babylon, Iraq, in 2017. His main line of research is web mining techniques and applications, image processing on web platforms, image processing, genetic algorithm, and information theory. Dr. Obaid is Associated Editor of the *Brazilian Journal of Operations & Production Management* (ESCI), Guest Editor of *Key Engineering Materials* (Scopus), Guest Editor of *MAICT-19* and *ICMAICT-20* issues of the *Journal of Physics* (IOP), Guest Editor of *JESTEC* (Scopus, WOS), Managing Editor of the *American Journal of Business and Operations Research*, and Associate Editor of *IJAST* (Scopus). Dr. Obaid is also a reviewer of many Scopus Journals (Scientific Publications, Taylor & Francis, ESTA, and many others). He is a leader of ICOITES, MAICT-19, and MAICT-20 EVENTS. He has also supervised several final projects at bachelor and master levels in his main line of work. He has edited several books, such as *Advance Material Science and Engineering* (Scientific.Net) and has authored and coauthored several scientific publications in journals and conferences. He is a frequent reviewer of international journals and international conferences.

Contributors

Joshi A.
Department of Artificial Intelligence
and Data Science
Panimalar Engineering College
Chennai, Tamil Nadu, India

Kameshwaran A.
Department of Information Technology
Dr. M.G.R. Educational and Research
Institute
Chennai, Tamilnadu, India

Qasem Abu Al-Haija
Department of Cybersecurity
Faculty of Computer & Information
Technology
Jordan University of Science and
Technology
PO Box 3030, Irbid 22110, Jordan

Bharat Bhushan
Department of Computer Science and
Engineering
School of Engineering and Technology
Sharda University
Greater Noida, India

Sonia Chhabra
Department of Computer Science and
Engineering
School of Engineering and Technology
Sharda University
Greater Noida, India

P Divyashree
Department of Electronics and
Communication Engineering
Indian Institute of Information
Technology (IIIT)
Sri City, Andra Pradesh, India

Priyanka Dwivedi
Department of Electronics and
Communication Engineering
Indian Institute of Information
Technology (IIIT)
Sri City, Andra Pradesh, India

Md. Ariful Islam
Department of Computer Science and
Engineering
University of Asia Pacific
Dhaka, Bangladesh

Shelbi Joseph
Division of Information
Technology
School of Engineering
Cochin University of Science and
Technology
Kochi, Kerela, India

Jayanthi K.
Department of Computer Science
KGiSL Institute of Information
Management
Coimbatore, Tamilnadu, India

Deepa Kanmani S.
Department of IT
Sri Krishna College of Engineering
    and Technology
Coimbatore, Tamilnadu, India

Manpreet Kaur
Department of Computer Science
    Engineering
Maharishi University of Information
    Technology
Noida, India

Ayasha Malik
Department of Computer Science and
    Engineering
IIMT College of Engineering (AKTU)
Greater Noida, India

Sanand Mishra
Delhi Technical Campus
Guru Gobind Singh Indraprastha
    University
Greater Noida, India

Muhammad Firoz Mridha
American International University
Bangladesh

Sheena N.
Division of Information Technology
School of Engineering
Cochin University of Science &
    Technology
Kochi, Kerala, India

Nandini
Department of Computer Science and
    Engineering
School of Engineering and Technology
Sharda University
Greater Noida, India

Ahmed J. Obaid
Department of Computer Science
Faculty of Computer Science and
    Mathematics
University of Kufa
Kufa, Iraq

Jiby J. Puthiyidam
Division of Information Technology
School of Engineering
Cochin University of Science and
    Technology
Kochi, Kerela, India

Jahir Ibna Rafiq
University of Asia Pacific
Dhaka, Bangladesh

Shailesh S.
Department of Computer Science
Cochin University of Science &
    Technology
Kochi, Kerala, India

Shweta Mayor Sabharwal
Department of computer science and
    engineering
School of computer science and
    engineering
Galgotias University
Greater Noida, India

Aloke Kumar Saha
University of Asia Pacific
Dhaka, Bangladesh

Dahlia Sam
Department of Information
    Technology
Dr. M.G.R. Educational and Research
    Institute
Chennai, Tamilnadu, India

Adlin Sheeba
Department of CSE
St. Joseph's Institute of Technology
Chennai, Tamil Nadu, India

Charanjeet Singh
Department of Computer Applications
Gujranwala Guru Nanak Institute
    of Management and Technology
    (GGNIMT)
Ludhiana, Punjab, India

Edyta Karolina Szczepaniuk
Polish Air Force University
Poland

Hubert Szczepaniuk
Warsaw University of Life
    Sciences
Warszaw, Poland

Shubham Tiwari
KIET Group of Institutions
Delhi-NCR, Ghaziabad

Chapter 1

Transforming Connected World with Cyber-physical System for Smart Life

P Divyashree and Priyanka Dwivedi

1.1 INTRODUCTION

A smart way of living has been incorporated into this new technological era. The entire world is virtually shrinking with the advent of advancement in technology. Thus, massive interconnections in digital space help in the creation of a smart world. One of the gold standard technologies that help in transforming the connected world for smart life is the cyber-physical system (CPS). This chapter introduces the core components of CPS that make up the complete solution for smart life applications. Additionally, various technologies are also merged with CPS, which enhances the utility and performance of deployed smart solutions for real-life applications. The hybrid combination of technologies includes the integration of CPS, Internet-of-Things (IoT), cloud computing (CC), and artificial intelligence (AI). These technologies and the intelligent methodology to combine them in order to reach the target of smart living are emphasized. Moreover, in the connected world scenario, vulnerability to hacking is abundant. Therefore, a secured CPS system is essential. The necessary components for CPS are secured connectivity, confidentiality, data integrity, and availability. In reality, there are several threats in CPS-based technology infrastructure, such as cyber threats, physical threats, and hybrid threats, which need to be addressed judiciously to have a safe system. Finally, the combination of technologies for a secure environment with CPS to build real-world solutions, such as smart healthcare, smart transportation, smart home, and smart agriculture, is presented in this chapter.

Furthermore, the chapter focuses on an introduction to gigantic technologies such as CPS, IoT, CC, and AI that can transform lives to be smart with intelligent systems. The components of technologies and their ability for interconnection to serve a specific purpose in real life are the theme of the entire chapter. These are the next-generation techno innovation for the connected world scenario.

To provide an inclusive understanding of the aforementioned notion of transforming the connected world with CPS for smart life, this chapter is organized as follows. Section 1.1 is the introduction that deals with the general idea of all technologies that can be integrated with CPS for the creation of smart life applications. Section 1.2 elaborates on the CPS technology and its core

DOI: 10.1201/9781003474111-1

components. Section 1.3 discusses emerging technologies such as the IoT, CC, and AI. Moreover, the fusion of advanced technologies such as the CPS and digital twins for the next-generation smart solution is presented. Therefore, the path toward achieving a connected world for smart life applications with CPS is emphasized. Section 1.4 is dedicated to the smart life applications realized using the blends of technologies with CPS. The smart life applications discussed in this chapter comprise smart healthcare, smart transport, smart home, and smart agriculture. Furthermore, Section 1.5 will introduce the security aspects of having a safe connected world for the real-time deployment of smart life applications. Finally, Section 1.6 presents the conclusion for the enhanced smart life using CPS.

1.2 CORE COMPONENTS OF CPS

CPS was coined in 2006 by Hellen Gill at the National Science Foundation (NSF) in the United States [1]. This term is closely related to cyberspace. Both these words originate from the root word "Cybernetics," which was coined by Norbert Weiner in 1948 [2]. Cybernetics deals with the entire theory of control and communication. "Cyber" in CPS indicates the computation in cyber space, and "Physical" in CPS signifies the tangible end actuators for smart automation. CPS is the conjunction of physical processes, computation, and communication. It involves multidisciplinary domains, such as computer engineering, electronics, and mechanical engineering, to realize a real-life solution. CPS is the dynamic and tight integration of physical processes with the virtual environment, such as software, computation, and communication capabilities, to perform a specific smart application [3,4]. Figure 1.1 illustrates the infrastructure in CPS to build applications for smart life. The engineering models and methods are fused with computer science intelligence for the building of CPS-based smart life applications. Through CPS, the quality of life at city standards can be transformed in rural and remote places as well. The following are the core components:

1. *Sensor network:* The set of sensors that are responsible for the capture of useful data from the real world forms a framework of sensor network architecture.
2. *Data transmission and storage:* The humongous real-time data collected is transferred to a storage service for further processing.
3. *Computation to gain intelligence:* Computation is the crucial requirement to acquire intelligence to take a decision on operations for real-time applications.
4. *Communication:* The useful information needs to be communicated to the right person at the right time to take the correct decision at the required instance. Hence, communication is crucial for smart system development.

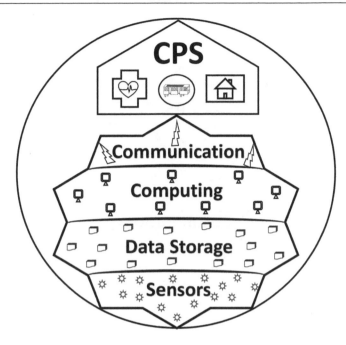

Figure 1.1 Infrastructure for CPS-based connected world applications.

In CPS, there are numerous applications; some of them include smart healthcare, smart transportation, smart home, smart city, smart agriculture, smart military, and Industry 4.0 [4]. The CPS is one of the hybrid technologies with the heterogeneous integration of various technological platforms. Standard communication protocols need to be defined for the integration of various technologies. CPS is expected to have intelligence concerning analyzing the sensor data and communicating the decision. In this component, computation is involved to process the data and interpret the useful information. The end goal is to attain data sharing among various systems integrated to enhance the performance of target action. This aspect is achieved with the collaboration component in CPS. The essential characteristics of the CPS are collaboration, integration, and intelligence [5]. Figure 1.2 graphically represents these characteristics for CPS. The CPS architecture consists of three major parts: the cyber part, the physical part, and the network part. The cyber part is the core element for the computation of data. The physical part is the component responsible for the control of operations to take smart actions. The network part acts as an interface between the cyber and physical parts to efficiently transfer the processed information. Typically, CPS involves the fusion of software-based mathematical analysis to efficiently control physical processes. Each hardware component in CPS is embedded with specific software for performing the purposeful task. The connectivity among all the heterogeneous components is established

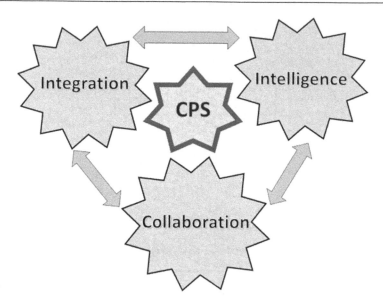

Figure 1.2 Characteristics of CPS.

using networking protocols such as Bluetooth, wireless local-area network, and global system communication. Being adaptive to real-world conditions is one of the requirements for complex CPS systems. Further, the man—machine interface should be strong with an advanced feedback control algorithm. Moreover, for large-scale complex systems, security and reliability are the key factors for efficient CPS system design to deploy in real-life applications [4].

1.3   EMERGING TECHNOLOGIES

The connected world is realized with emerging technologies. CPS is one of the core technologies that involve the integration of the virtual and physical worlds. CPS, AI, IoT, and CC are the major technologies, which are discussed in further sections. The importance of a connected world and these technologies is graphically illustrated in Figure 1.3.

1.3.1   Internet-of-Things

Kevin Aston, in 1999, coined the term "Internet-of-Things" (IoT) at MIT Auto ID, which is the concept of connected devices [6]. The efficient coupling of cyber world with physical world is the essence of CPS. IoT is included in this framework to establish connections [7]. Numerous technologies are emerging with the

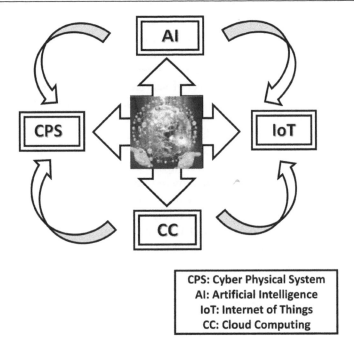

CPS: Cyber Physical System
AI: Artificial Intelligence
IoT: Internet of Things
CC: Cloud Computing

Figure 1.3 Technologies for the connected world.

idea of connected devices such as Machine to Machine (M2M) frequently used in the telecom industry. In this, there is a one-to-one connection established. Industrial IoT consists of interconnection of machines where human interventions are not required. Internet on small scale connects only humans. The Web of Things has a narrow scope that only involves software architecture. The Internet of everything is an emerging technology where the entire ecosystem of smart living can be accomplished. IoT is a broader system of integration with connected machines as well as humans through wearable devices. It is the core technology that has potential utility in many real-world applications. IoT is constructed from three layers, which comprise hardware, communication, and software. The hardware layer consists of chips, sensors, and embedded system. The communication layer possesses a wireless network for transferring information. The software layer is responsible for storing, processing, analyzing the sensor data, and developing front-end applications. Thus, for the development of the specific application in smart living, this IoT architecture forms the basic building block [8].

1.3.2 Cloud Computing

Cloud computing (CC) is a pay-per-use model for enabling available, convenient, on-demand network access to a shared pool of configurable computing resources such as networks, servers, services, applications, and storage. These on-demand computing services are provided under the umbrella of cloud services by companies such as Google, Microsoft, and Amazon. CC offers facilities for computation, storage, and software as a service. Typically, CC consists of three layers as per the abstraction level of services delivered to service seekers. These layers are infrastructure as a service, platform as a service, and software as a service. Among these layers, the bottom layer of CC systems is considered to be infrastructure as a service. This layer manages virtual resources such as computation, communication, and storage when demanded by the end user. A higher level of abstraction is attained from the platform as a service layer. This layer offers developers to build and deploy applications without explicitly knowing the memory or resource requirements. Software as a service includes, for example, Google's G Suits application interfaces where end users access their resources through a web portal [9]. Therefore, the cost-effective, on-demand access to required resources in CC is an energy-efficient and resource-optimized model for smart applications.

1.3.3   Artificial Intelligence

Artificial intelligence (AI) does not mean a technology; perhaps, it comprises a set of technologies continuously emerging to enhance computation capability. AI deals with huge data to get meaningful analysis through its computation. There exist numerous sub-technologies in the umbrella of AI for humongous real-world applications to make life smarter. A few of the AI sub-technologies constitute computer vision, neural networks, speech recognition, image recognition, autonomics, deep learning, virtual agent, chatbot, machine learning (ML), machine reasoning, knowledge representation, natural language processing, and many more [10–12]. These technologies need to be judiciously combined to realize smart applications.

1.3.4   Integrated Technologies

The amalgamation of advanced technologies enhances system integration across diverse smart actions. CPS targets the unification of the cyber and physical worlds with a closed-loop feedback control with seamless integration. Digital twins are another emerging technology that aids CPS integration and focuses on the creation of high-fidelity virtual models for physical entities. This simulation of real-world behavior provides more information for the computation of real-time data to control physical processes. The fusion of these giant technologies – that is, CPS and DT – with IoT opens a new avenue for interfacing physical and virtual worlds. Further, the connected world scenario can be realized, as shown in Figure 1.4. Moreover, technologies such as IoT and digital twin–based CPS can be simulated in virtual space. A few of the software tools to develop digital counterparts of physical models using the IoT and digital twin–based CPS models comprise

Figure 1.4 Integrated technologies for the connected world.

Auto CAD, MATLAB, and ADAMS. The results of digital simulations can be transferred to the physical world. The human–machine interface or direct process control protocols can be provided to carry out physical processes. This way, the control of physical equipment with digital computation is realized with the advent of combining IoT, CC, and CPS with digital twin [7].

1.4 TECHNOLOGIES INTEGRATED WITH CPS FOR SMART LIFE

1.4.1 Smart Healthcare

Secure smart healthcare solution is the emerging demand of the present day. Early disease prediction and continuous monitoring of health conditions are the key components of smart healthcare infrastructure. As graphically illustrated in Figure 1.5, the wearable sensor that can monitor the human body's vital biosignals is integrated into gigantic technological frameworks such as IoT, CPS, and AI to provide a smart solution for healthcare predictions. L.K. Ramasamy et al., in their research contribution, proposed an AI-enabled IoT-CPS architecture to predict diseases such as diabetes, heart disease, and gait disturbances in elderly people with reliable results in accuracy, precision, recall, and F1 score [13]. In the healthcare sector, disease diagnosis and severity estimation are the two major goals. These are achieved with the utilization of advanced intelligent models in the domain of AI computing. The connectivity among the various platforms such as wearable healthcare sensors, data storage, processing, AI algorithms and computing are incorporated in CPS and IoT frameworks. Y. Zhang et al., in their research, introduced the Health-CPS model for managing big data as well as cloud computing. The major issue of handling heterogeneity in healthcare sector is resolved by technology integration. The emerging technologies in the healthcare domain comprise an amalgamation of giant technologies such as big data, IoT, CPS, and AI with wearable healthcare sensors for real-time continuous monitoring of health conditions [14]. The robot-assisted surgeries are operational through these technologies [15]. Thus, complete remote health monitoring can be achieved with the integration of all these technologies for smart healthcare.

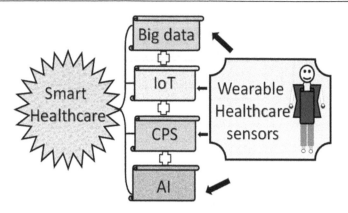

Figure 1.5 Smart healthcare with emerging technologies.

1.4.2   Smart Transport

The person's state of mind and productivity, the country's economy, and the environment's pollution are all influenced by the transportation condition. Smart transportation involves continuous monitoring of vehicular traffic and computing a smart decision for providing quick routes where traffic congestion is low. This intelligent decision also helps in controlling pollution. The police patrolling can be efficiently monitored remotely to take proper control measures. Additionally, road transportation details can be shared with authorities to perform cleaning or sanitization actions to experience safe and smart transportation. To achieve these objectives, the necessary details required are the number of vehicles, the vehicles' locations, the average speed of vehicles, and individual vehicle speed. Thus, this data is acquired through suitable sensory infrastructure. Computation is the key to any smart system; in this context, M. M. U. Rathore et al. in their research developed a graph-based approach in CPS for smart transportation. The proposed system used the integration of Apache Spark GraphX and the Hadoop ecosystem, which gives promising efficiency for smart transportation [16]. Figure 1.6 depicts the pictorial representation of smart transportation with CPS.

Transportation CPS (TCPS) is a technological innovation in the application of transport systems using CPS. In the realm of TCPS, there exist three major instances:

1. *Infrastructure-based TCPS:* This module is responsible for real-time infrastructure monitoring and traffic control with TCPS. This is achieved with the employment of sensors such as cameras, computational components, and wireless communication interfaces for smart traffic management.

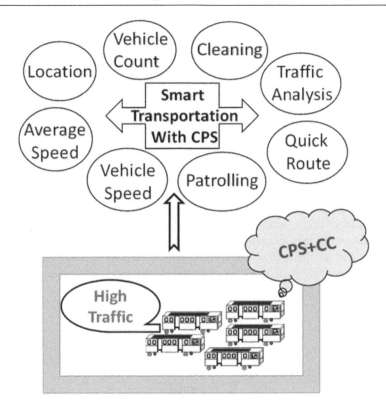

Figure 1.6 Smart transportation with CPS-integrated technologies.

2. *Vehicle-infrastructure coordinated TCPS:* This module involves both vehicles and corresponding sensors like Global Positioning Systems, traffic signals, and computational devices with wireless communication. This has applicability in determining the transit signal priority of traffic signals to smartly guide vehicle movement in the traffic.

3. *Vehicle-based TCPS:* Prevention of accidents is very important to save human lives from dangerous accidents. The vehicle-based TCPS contains sensors, computational units, and actuators like gears, brakes, and ignitors. The electronic control unit is deployed with the wireless communication network. This system can be used for proximity detection and black ice recognition, which can effectively prevent accidents.

Smart transportation with TCPS will try to address major concerns related to the reduction of travel time with smart traffic control, congestion management, monitoring road safety, automated self-driving cars, and prevention of accidents [17]. Therefore, smart living can be attained with the deployment of smart TCPS.

1.4.3   Smart Home

Smart home with CPS is a new technological innovation. Smart living is possible with the transformation of smart homes through advanced technologies. Usually, people spend their relaxing time at home. Thus, the creation of a smart home that is personalized for life will affect cognitive and physical well-being. There are a variety of applications for the smart home environment, as pictorially represented in Figure 1.7. R. Raj et al. proposed a raspberry pi-based sensor-integrated embedded system to identify the voice commands and the intent. A smart home is equipped with automatic light switching, environment monitoring with temperature and humidity measurements, and an air quality monitoring system through interactive voice commands. The diverse integration of CPS, IoT, and real-time data analytics is combined with voice-assisted control system in the smart home [18]. For a smart home, security is an important factor, especially when connected to the Internet. In this scenario, there is a high chance of unauthorized access. M. Alshar'e et al. researched ML techniques for face recognition that can control the door locking system. Hence, secured access to an authorized person can

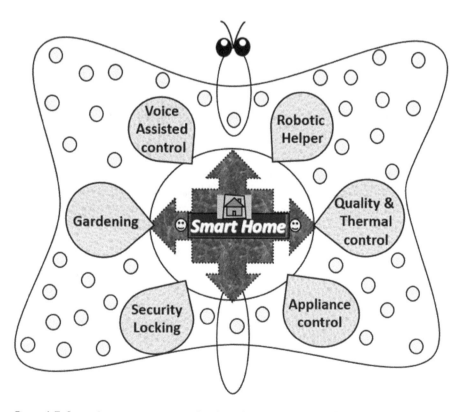

Figure 1.7 Smart home environment developed with advanced technologies.

be provided in the smart home [19]. In smart living, our home needs to be surrounded by various automatic robots to perform smart actions in the home. In this context, D. Lee et al. proposed various smart home robotic companions that emerged and are commercially available. Special robots such as iRobot Roomba, AIBO, Phyno, and Nuvo were employed for cleaning, entertainment, etc. Smart robots were developed for interaction and to perform house-related activities with elderly people to enhance their standard of living [20]. H. M. Do et al. developed a robot-integrated smart home and monitored elderly people's activities [21]. Assistive technology aids in performing smart actions at home. However, the environment of the home should also be set at an optimum level for comfortable living. W. W. Shein et al. built a thermal comfort controller for the available hybrid temperature control system with CPS technology. The air conditioner, window, and curtain were used to maintain the required temperature with efficient consumption of energy [22]. T. Yang et al. proposed cost-effective indoor air management in the smart home. To maintain good indoor air quality, a technological model to control temperature and levels of O_2 and CO_2 at an optimum range was modeled. Further, the external conditions are correlated and mapped to the internal home conditions, effectively regulate energy consumption, and hence save power and money. Markov's decision process and control algorithm were formulated with reinforcement deep learning. The author proposed a novel deep Q network with a prioritized experience relay. This model showed a reduction in average energy cost toward attaining compact indoor air quality and temperature control for smart home deployment [23]. L. Burton et al. developed a smart way of gardening with the monitoring of soil nutrients from a nitrogen-doped polypyrrole ion-selective electrode-based sensor array sheet. The data is communicated through ZigBee to the cloud server, which can be accessed through a smartphone. The proposed system utilizes gardening IoT soil sheets to monitor nitrogen and apply the right quantity of fertilizers in the garden and avoid excess consumption. This in turn improves productivity and reduces the cost of gardening in a smart home environment [24]. Thus, with the utilization of advanced and emerging technologies, a smart life can be accomplished in the smart home environment.

1.4.4 Smart Agriculture

Agriculture is the major sector that plays a substantial role in the growth of the nation. The economy and health of individuals as well as society are influenced by the quality and quantity of food products that are yielded in the agricultural sector. In this era of massive growth in population, with the constraints of the limited land available for agriculture, there is an enormous need for improvement in agricultural yield. The revolution of advanced technologies lends a helping hand that acts as an assistive tool for enhancing the performance of agricultural processes, which in turn gives better yield. A multidisciplinary approach is involved to achieve precision agriculture with technology. The various fields such as information and communication technology (ICT), wireless sensor networks, robotics

AI, big data analytics, CC, and IoT are combined to get the high-value crops [25]. The inclusion of precise farming in traditional agricultural practices will revolutionize the agricultural sector [26]. Precision farming is an information technology–based system that manages crops at the right time and in the right way to get a good yield from minimal resources.

Typically, the smart agriculture process comprises modeling high-value crops with diverse agriculture assistive technologies. Figure 1.8 shows the graphical representation of major aspects of smart and precision agriculture. It is a well-known fact that the right amount of water level in the soil is the major reason for the efficient growth of the crop. If water is in excess, then it will affect the nitrogen absorption in roots. Hence, the moisture level in the soil can be monitored by employing relevant sensors. Moisture measurement and analysis can further guide the autonomous system for demand-oriented irrigation of the crop, which sustains the required water level for the crop. This smart irrigation will provide the right amount of water to the crop to enhance productivity and save a lot of water from being wasted. Ibrahim Mat et al. proposed a wireless moisture sensor network combined with IoT having a feedback control logic in greenhouse crops to provide precision irrigation [27].

Automation is the key to unlocking massive and fast processing of agricultural activities. The speed of harvesting can be drastically magnified with the use of agricultural robots. Driverless tractors can be utilized for smart harvesting in agriculture. Drones employed in the field will monitor the crops. The inspection

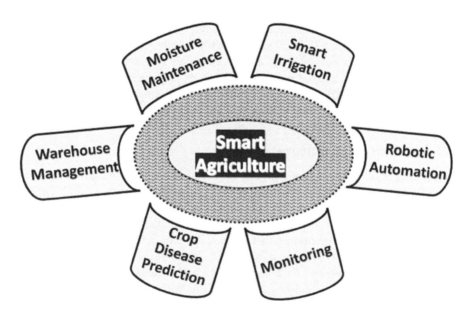

Figure 1.8 Various applications for smart agriculture.

of weeds can be performed with a drone equipped with a camera. Weeds are one of the reasons that negatively affect crop yield, and there is a prime need to control them. I. Rakhmatulin et al. proposed a compact and cost-effective weed control mechanism using a laser. A neural network architecture is utilized to recognize the weeds, and a laser-guided system to estimate the coordinates of the weeds. Further, a laser with different intensities, which include 0.3 W, 1 W, and 5 W, was used to kill the weeds. Parameters such as the intensity of the laser and time of exposure were computed considering the size of the weed. A long exposure time is required for the exposure of low-intensity laser. On the other hand, if high-intensity laser is used, it requires less time to kill the weed. However, it may affect the healthy crop if the laser is split during the weeding process. Therefore, optimal laser intensity should be employed in an efficient weeding process [28]. In the future, the pinpoint firing of weeds with laser should be done autonomously from the data acquired by the drone's camera and image recognition using computer vision algorithms. Weeds can be accurately identified with image recognition. Thus, precise and target-oriented weed control actions can be taken. Therefore, selective weed elimination can be achieved. Fruit and vegetable picking in the agricultural field is one of the most tedious jobs that consume a lot of time and effort. This delay will significantly increase the time to market. However, automation and CPS networking can speed up the process. Z. Wang et al. reviewed various robotic systems for the task of picking fruits and vegetables. The harvesting time can be reduced with automation through agricultural robots and fastening processes to improve the efficiency of crop yield. The vision system, combined with robotic functioning, will guide the picking process. Various techniques such as shear forces and suction are involved in the mechanism of grasping and placing the product. The complete robotic system for smart harvesting includes sensors such as a camera, IR, and proximity. The mechanical robotic system performs the smart actions of plucking, picking, and placing the agricultural product [29].

Monitoring of crops can improve the efficiency of production as necessary preventative and control actions can be taken at the appropriate time to preserve the quality of crops. Disease prediction at an early stage can help the farmer control its spread and save the crop. A. Verma et al. proposed a deep convolution neural network–based novel architecture for the detection and classification of disease in maize leaves. The disease-attacked leaves of maize consist of blight, common rust, and gray leaf spot. Thus, the disease of maize leaves was identified at the initial stage. Then relevant disease control actions can be taken to prevent the further spread of the disease [30].

The incorporation of advanced technologies in agricultural processes yields a better product that needs to be effectively stored and managed in the warehouse to reach consumers. N. Zhang et al. proposed an intelligent storage strategy with deep computing, controlling, and communication protocols for logistics and transportation applications. In IoT and CC-based storage, ant colony-based algorithm was used for path optimization in efficient logistics management [31].

Thus, these techniques can also be incorporated for smart logistic management in agricultural product storage, i.e., for efficient warehouse management.

The evolution of CPS has transformed the entire agriculture processing cycle into smart precision agriculture. W. An et al. presented the applications of agricultural CPS that encompass soil moisture monitoring, smart scheduling of irrigation, monitoring the minerals in the soil to have smart fertilization supply, weather monitoring, crop growth monitoring, and disease prevention. Moreover, unmanned aerial vehicle-based Agricultural CPS (ACPS) and geographic information system-based ACPS manage and analyze spatial information about agronomy and production. ACPS has humongous potential to be used for surveillance, real-time monitoring, tracking, and process management [32]. A healthy life for large masses is achieved by the enhancement of food quality through ACPS.

In this section, various smart life applications with the CPS are discussed. In recent times, the advancement of digital twins has revolutionized the future prospects of technology. The virtual environment created with the sensor hub, IoT connections, CC, and AI will aid in the development of any physical, real-life problem. A prototype of a virtual environment can be created for any complicated task. This enables the optimization of designed models before deploying them in the physical world. Thus, cost minimization and resource optimization are the key advantages of the digital twin–integrated CPS models. The future aspects of any technological innovations are to have an end-to-end solution. This target can be achieved with the heterogeneous integration of advanced technologies through the CPS platform using digital twin–based virtual models. Thus, cost-effective solutions can be realized through virtual simulations.

1.5   SECURITY IN THE CONNECTED WORLD

The approach to revolutionize the interconnected world is possible by integrating technologies in CPS for smart life applications. With this approach, an attempt was made to limit the accessibility of useful and analytical information for anyone, at any time with the unified data access. Since data sharing is global, there exist various security issues that include cyber as well as physical attacks. In the connected world, the major triode essential components for a secured system are *confidentiality, integrity,* and *availability,* often referred to as C-I-A. Preserving *confidentiality* is a required attribute in the connected system to sustain privacy. This feature ensures that data is accessible only to authorized users, which include interconnected systems, processes, applications, or persons. With *confidentiality,* data access is restricted to unauthorized users. However, data manipulation is limited to *integrity.* Additionally, often the denial of service imposed by the hackers and the required data are not available to the concerned person. Thus, for the real-time utilization of the smart system *availability* of the resources and data is very crucial [33–35]. Hence, careful control and monitoring of security are very much essential in CPS systems for secured smart life applications.

There are several kinds of security threats in CPS infrastructure, like cyberattacks, physical attacks, and hybrid attacks. Cybersecurity comprises numerous aspects. These include *Centering Information,* which will protect data across all phases of storage, transmission, and processing. *Oriented function* integrates all the cyber-physical components in the CPS architecture. The oriented threat affects confidentiality, integrity, availability, and accountability. These issues make the CPS vulnerable to wireless exploitation, jamming, reconnaissance, disclosure of information, unauthorized access, interception, and Global Positioning System exploitation that exist under the umbrella of cyber threats. The domain of physical threats in CPS includes physical damage and attack on sensors, computing components, communication devices, and feedback devices [36,37]. Technology to secure this CPS has been researched extensively. Emerging technologies such as cybersecurity and AI can assist in having an authentic and secured CPS-integrated smart life application. K. Sravanthi et al. examined the role of ML in the field of cybersecurity to prevent cyberattacks in CPS-based smart applications [32]. Thus, the transformation of a connected world with CPS for better and smart living can be achieved with secured real-time applications.

1.6 CONCLUSION

In summary, CPS integrated with advanced technologies aids in the development of smart life applications to enhance the quality of life. Various smart life applications with CPS were presented. The smart applications discussed in this chapter comprise smart healthcare, smart transport, smart home, and smart agriculture. Additionally, the chapter presented security threats and measures to safeguard CPS-based smart life applications. Therefore, a complete overview of transforming the connected world for smart life applications with CPS is presented. The current state of the art lacks an end-to-end implementation of virtual model creation for smart real-life applications. A virtual replica of the real-world models can be developed through digital twin–integrated CPS for next-generation smart applications. Therefore, the transformation of the connected world with CPS for smart life could be efficiently developed at an optimized cost.

REFERENCES

[1] N. H. Carreras Guzman, M. Wied, I. Kozine, and M. A. Lundteigen, "Conceptualizing the Key Features of Cyber-Physical Systems in a Multi-layered Representation for Safety and Security Analysis," *Systems Engineering*, vol. 23, no. 2, pp. 189–210, Mar. 2020, doi: 10.1002/sys.21509.
[2] S. C. Suh, U. J. Tanik, J. N. Carbone, and A. Eroglu, "Applied cyber-physical systems," *Applied Cyber-Physical Systems*, vol. 9781461473367, pp. 1–253, 2014, doi: 10.1007/978-1-4614-7336-7.

[3] G. Wu, J. Sun, and J. Chen, "A Survey on the Security of Cyber-Physical Systems," *Control Theory Technology*, vol. 14, no. 1, pp. 2–10, 2016, doi: 10.1007/s11768-016-5123-9.

[4] V. Jirkovsky, M. Obitko, and V. Marik, "Understanding Data Heterogeneity in the Context of Cyber-Physical Systems Integration," *IEEE Transactions on Industrial Informatics*, vol. 13, no. 2, pp. 660–667, 2017, doi: 10.1109/TII.2016.2596101.

[5] A. Napoleone, M. Macchi, and A. Pozzetti, "A Review on the Characteristics of Cyber-Physical Systems for the Future Smart Factories," *Journal of Manufacturing Systems*, vol. 54, pp. 305–335, 2020, doi: 10.1016/j.jmsy.2020.01.007.

[6] P. K. Yadav, S. Pareek, S. Shakeel, J. Kumar, and A. K. Singh, "Advancements and Security Issues of IoT Cyber Physical Systems," *2019 International Conference on Intelligent Computing and Control Systems ICCS 2019*, No. ICICCS, pp. 940–945, 2019, doi: 10.1109/ICCS45141.2019.9065835.

[7] F. Tao, M. Zhang, and A. Y. C. Nee, "Digital Twin, Cyber-Physical System, and Internet of Things," *Digital Twin Driven Smart Manufacturing*, pp. 243–256, 2019, doi: 10.1016/b978-0-12-817630-6.00012-6.

[8] K. L. Lueth, "IoT Basics: Getting Started with the Internet of Things," *white paper*, pp. 0–9, 2015.

[9] W. Voorsluys, J. Broberg, and R. Buyya, "Introduction to Cloud Computing," in *Cloud Computing: Principles and Paradigms*, pp. 1–44, 2011, doi: 10.1002/9780470940105.ch1.

[10] J. Liu *et al.*, "Artificial Intelligence in the 21st Century," *IEEE Access*, vol. 6, pp. 34403–34421, 2018, doi: 10.1109/ACCESS.2018.2819688.

[11] J. D. Rodríguez-García, J. Moreno-León, M. Román-González, and G. Robles, "Introducing Artificial Intelligence Fundamentals with Learning ML: Artificial Intelligence Made Easy," *Eighth International Conference on Technological Ecosystems for Enhancing Multiculturality (TEEM'20)*, pp. 18–20, 2020, doi: 10.1145/3434780.3436705.

[12] N. Berente, B. Gu, J. Recker, and R. Santhanam, "Managing Artificial Intelligence," *MIS Quarterly*, vol. 45, no. 3, pp. 1433–1450, 2021, doi: 10.25300/MISQ/2021/16274.

[13] L. K. Ramasamy, F. Khan, M. Shah, B. V. V. S. Prasad, C. Iwendi, and C. Biamba, "Secure Smart Wearable Computing through Artificial Intelligence-Enabled Internet of Things and Cyber-Physical Systems for Health Monitoring," *Sensors*, vol. 22, no. 3, p. 1076, 2022, doi: 10.3390/s22031076.

[14] Y. Zhang, M. Qiu, C.-W. Tsai, M. M. Hassan, and A. Alamri, "Health-CPS: Healthcare Cyber-Physical System Assisted by Cloud and Big Data," *IEEE Systems Journal*, vol. 11, no. 1, pp. 88–95, 2017, doi: 10.1109/JSYST.2015.2460747.

[15] M. Sony, J. Antony, and O. McDermott, "The Impact of Medical Cyber—Physical Systems on Healthcare Service Delivery," *The TQM Journal*, vol. 34, no. 7, pp. 73–94, 2022, doi: 10.1108/TQM-01-2022-0005.

[16] M. M. U. Rathore, S. A. Shah, A. Awad, D. Shukla, S. Vimal, and A. Paul, "A Cyber-Physical System and Graph-Based Approach for Transportation Management in Smart Cities," *Sustainability*, vol. 13, no. 14, p. 7606, 2021, doi: 10.3390/su13147606.

[17] L. Deka, S. M. Khan, M. Chowdhury, and N. Ayres, "Transportation Cyber-Physical System and Its Importance for Future Mobility," in *Transportation Cyber-Physical Systems*, Elsevier, pp. 1–20, 2018, doi: 10.1016/B978-0-12-814295-0.00001-0.

[18] R. Raj and N. Rai, "Voice Controlled Cyber-Physical System for Smart Home," *In Proceedings of the Workshop Program of the 19th International Conference on Distributed Computing and Networking*, pp. 1–5, 2018, doi: 10.1145/3170521.3170550.

[19] M. Alshar'e, M. R. Al Nasar, R. Kumar, M. Sharma, Dharamvir, and V. Tripathi, "A Face Recognition Method in Machine Learning (ML) for Enhancing Security in Smart Home," in *2022 2nd International Conference on Advance Computing and Innovative Technologies in Engineering (ICACITE)*, pp. 1081–1086, 2022, doi: 10.1109/ICACITE53722.2022.9823833.

[20] D. Lee, T. Yamazaki, and S. Helal, "Robotic Companions for Smart Space Interactions," *IEEE Pervasive Computing*, vol. 8, no. 2, pp. 78–84, 2009, doi: 10.1109/MPRV.2009.34.

[21] H. M. Do, M. Pham, W. Sheng, D. Yang, and M. Liu, "RiSH: A Robot-Integrated Smart Home for Elderly Care," *Robotics and Autonomous Systems*, vol. 101, pp. 74–92, 2018, doi: 10.1016/j.rob ot.2017.12.008.

[22] W. W. Shein, Z. Cheng, Y. Tan, and A. O. Lim, "Study of Temperature Control Using Cyber-Physical System Approach in Home Environment," *2013 IEEE 1st International Conference on Cyber-Physical Systems, Networks and Applications (CPSNA), 2013*, pp. 78–83, 2013, doi: 10.1109/CPSNA.2013.6614250.

[23] T. Yang, L. Zhao, W. Li, J. Wu, and A. Y. Zomaya, "Towards Healthy and Cost-Effective Indoor Environment Management in Smart Homes: A Deep Reinforcement Learning Approach," *Applied Energy*, vol. 300, p. 117335, 2021, doi: 10.1016/j.apenergy.2021.117335.

[24] L. Burton, N. Dave, R. E. Fernandez, K. Jayachandran, and S. Bhansali, "Smart Gardening IoT Soil Sheets for Real-Time Nutrient Analysis," *Journal of the Electrochemical Society*, vol. 165, no. 8, pp. B3157–B3162, 2018, doi: 10.1149/2.0201808jes.

[25] A. Bechar, Ed., *"Innovation in Agricultural Robotics for Precision Agriculture: A Roadmap for Integrating Robots in Precision Agriculture"*, Cham: Springer International Publishing, pp. 1–15, 2021.

[26] R. Gill, "A Review on Various Techniques to Transform Traditional Farming to Precision Agriculture," *Turkish Journal of Computer and Mathematics Education (TURCOMAT)*, vol. 12, no. 2, pp. 131–135, 2021, doi: 10.17762/turcomat.v12i2.690.

[27] I. Mat, M. R. Mohd Kassim, A. N. Harun, and I. Mat Yusoff, "IoT in Precision Agriculture Applications Using Wireless Moisture Sensor Network," *2016 IEEE Conference on Open Systems (ICOS)*, pp. 24–29, 2016, doi: 10.1109/ICOS.2016.7881983.

[28] I. Rakhmatulin and C. Andreasen, "A Concept of a Compact and Inexpensive Device for Controlling Weeds with Laser Beams," *Agronomy*, vol. 10, no. 10, p. 1616, 2020, doi: 10.3390/agronomy10101616.

[29] Z. Wang, Y. Xun, Y. Wang, and Q. Yang, "Review of Smart Robots for Fruit and Vegetable Picking in Agriculture," *International Journal of Agriculture and Biological Engineering*, vol. 15, no. 1, pp. 33–54, 2022, doi: 10.25165/j.ijabe.20221501.7232.

[30] A. Verma and B. Bhowmik, "Automated Detection of Maize Leaf Diseases in Agricultural Cyber-Physical Systems," *In 2022 30th Mediterranean Conference on Control and Automation*, 2022, pp. 841–846, doi: 10.1109/MED54222.2022.9837122.

[31] N. Zhang, "Smart Logistics Path for Cyber-Physical Systems with Internet of Things," *IEEE Access*, vol. 6, pp. 70808–70819, 2018, doi: 10.1109/ACCESS.2 018.2879966.

[32] W. An, D. Wu, S. Ci, H. Luo, V. Adamchuk, and Z. Xu, "Agriculture Cyber-Physical Systems," in *Cyber-Physical System*, pp. 399–417, 2017, doi: 10.1016/B978-0-12-803801-7.00025-0.

[33] M. Zahid, I. Inayat, M. Daneva, and Z. Mehmood, "Security Risks in Cyber Physical Systems-A Systematic Mapping Study," *Journal of Software: Evolution and Process*, vol. 33, no. 9, pp. 1–47, 2021, doi: 10.1002/smr.2346.

[34] G. Wu, J. Sun, and J. Chen, "A Survey on the Security of Cyber-Physical Systems," *Control Theory Technology*, vol. 14, no. 1, pp. 2–10, 2016, doi: 10.1007/s11768-016-5123-9.

[35] K. Sravanthi, M. Shamila, and A. K. Tyagi, "Cyber Physical Systems: The Role of Machine Learning and Cyber Security in Present and Future," *Computer Review Journal*, vol. 4, no. 1, pp. 66–80, 2019.

[36] R. Alguliyev, Y. Imamverdiyev, and L. Sukhostat, "Cyber-Physical Systems and Their Security Issues," *Computers in Industry*, vol. 100, pp. 212–223, 2018, doi: 10.1016/j.compind.2018.04.017.

[37] J.-P. A. Yaacoub, O. Salman, H. N. Noura, N. Kaaniche, A. Chehab, and M. Malli, "Cyber-Physical Systems Security: Limitations, Issues and Future Trends," *Microprocessors and Microsystems*, vol. 77, p. 103201, 2020, doi: 10.1016/j.micpro.2020.103201.

Chapter 2

Lightweight Encryption Algorithms for Resource-constrained Devices for Internet-of-Things Applications

Sheena N., Shelbi Joseph, and Shailesh S.

2.1 INTRODUCTION

2.1.1 Overview of IoT

The Internet-of-Things (IoT) is a cutting-edge technological paradigm that envisions a global network of interconnected technologies and objects. Kevin Ashton first used this rapidly growing technology in this era in 1999 [1]. The physical and digital worlds are connected; everything can be connected anytime, anywhere, with any network service. IoT has many applications in various fields, including environmental [2], industrial, commercial, infrastructural, smart city [3], and healthcare [4,5,6]. IoT features a three- or five-layer architecture [7], as depicted in Figure 2.1, in contrast to the ISO-OSI seven-layer network design.

The perception layer controls the system's intelligent gadgets, which can collect, accept, and process data over the network. The network layer connects all the perception layer's devices to servers and other network hardware and manages all the devices' data transfer needs. User interaction occurs at the application layer, where users receive services tailored to their particular application. In the five-layer architecture, the functions of transport and processing layers do the functions of network layer in the three-layer architecture. The processing layer processes the data throughout the network, and the transport layer controls data transmission.

2.1.2 Requirements and Challenges of IoT

According to the report of [8], connected devices in the IoT are growing exponentially, as shown in Figure 2.2. IoT connects heterogeneous devices like RFID tags, sensors, actuators, smartphones, computers, and servers for data communication via communication protocols.

Adopting open standards and deploying heterogeneous devices and applications create several challenges, such as security, interoperability, energy consumption, adaptability, and scalability, as illustrated in Figure 2.3. Some

DOI: 10.1201/9781003474111-2

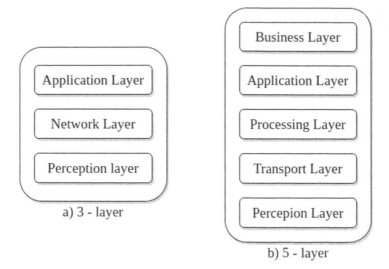

a) 3 - layer

b) 5 - layer

Figure 2.1 Architecture of IoT.

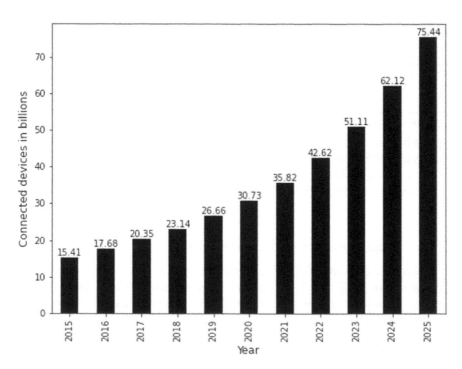

Figure 2.2 Number of connected devices in the Internet-of-Things (2015–2025) [8].

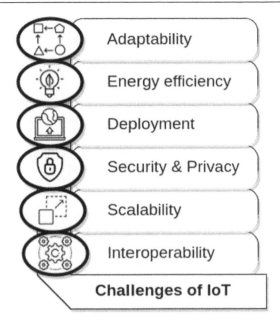

Figure 2.3 Challenges of IoT.

heterogeneous devices are referred to as resource-constrained because they have limited resources, such as low memory, low computing power, low battery power, small physical area, and fast real-time response. The abundant data flow between IoT devices may result in security lapses. Before sharing, data must be encrypted to handle the IoT's security concerns. Conventional cryptography algorithms have trouble dealing with IoT devices due to their limited resource availability, as shown in Figure 2.4. Lightweight cryptographic protocols are used to address this challenge. This chapter discusses the lightweight cryptographic protocols commonly used for resource-constrained devices, mostly in IoT, FPGA, and wireless sensor networks.

2.1.3   Major Contributions

Depending on the number of resources used and security issues, in this chapter, we categorize the lightweight protocols as standard, ultralightweight, hybrid, and multilevel. We performed an extensive survey under each category and further classified the normal lightweight algorithms into key-based, installation-based, cipher-based, and structure-based. A detailed elaboration of protocols under each category gives a better understanding of the classification. As these protocols are vulnerable to various security attacks, we discussed the various types of security

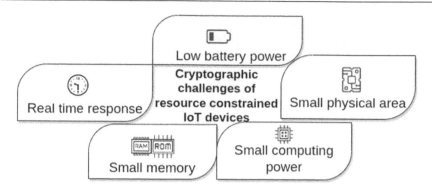

Figure 2.4 Cryptographic challenges of IoT devices.

attacks and how lightweight protocols provide security to these acute attacks. The main highlights of this chapter are as follows:

1. A classification of the lightweight protocols according to resource utilization and security.
2. A comprehensive analysis of lightweight protocols under each category.
3. A detailed explanation of various security attacks and how the lightweight protocols can defend against serious attacks.
4. The issues and challenges of lightweight cryptography are discussed, along with their potential solutions.
5. We proposed a novel, secure, and lightweight protocol to overcome the current shortcomings of lightweight cryptography.

The organization of this chapter is as follows. An extensive discussion of the various categories of lightweight cryptographic protocols is described in Section 2.2. Section 2.3 goes over various security attacks against lightweight encryption systems. The issues and challenges of lightweight cryptography are mentioned in Section 2.4, followed by the conclusion and future directions in Section 2.5.

2.2   LIGHTWEIGHT CRYPTOGRAPHIC PROTOCOLS

There are four categories of lightweight algorithms for cryptographic methods on devices with limited resources: normal, ultra, hybrid, and multilevel algorithms. Ultralightweight algorithms were created to accommodate devices with substantially fewer resources than standard low-weight algorithms. Compared to normal and ultralightweight algorithms, hybrid and multilevel algorithms provide greater security through the combination of normal and ultralightweight algorithms. Figure 2.5 shows the classification of lightweight cryptographic algorithms.

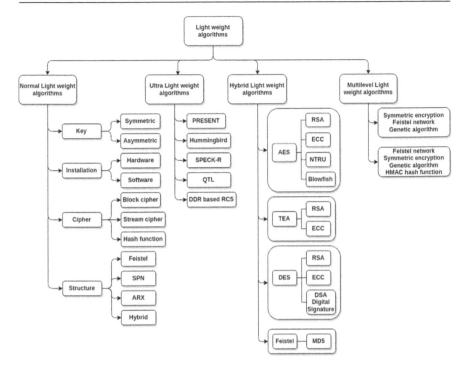

Figure 2.5 Classification of lightweight cryptographic algorithms.

2.2.1   Normal Lightweight Encryption Protocols

Normal lightweight encryption algorithms are classified based on their structure, the types of keys used, where they are installed, and the type of cipher. Table 2.1 lists the key size, block size, number of rounds, and structure of various normal lightweight cryptographic algorithms.

2.2.1.1   Key Based

Lightweight cryptographic algorithms are categorized as symmetric and asymmetric based on the key used in the cryptographic process, just as traditional cryptographic algorithms [36]. Symmetric key encryption is where the sender and the receiver utilize the same secret key for encryption and decryption. Security risks result from using the same pair of keys in symmetric algorithms. But asymmetric encryption offers a very safe approach for data encryption and decryption by providing a different pair of keys, i.e., private and public keys. While the public key can be given to anyone upon request, the private key can only be stored securely by one party and cannot be leaked. The public key is used in asymmetric encryption to encrypt data, whereas the private key is needed to decrypt it [37].

The majority of lightweight cryptographic algorithms such as TEA [9], HEIGHT [21], PRESENT [38,39], AES [18,19,20], RC5 [40,41], and LWE [22] are symmetric algorithms. TEA [9] and its variants such as MTEA [10], XTEA [11], XXTEA [12], and MXXTEA [13] all have the same key length of 128 bits, and only the number of rounds differs. LEA [14], AES [18], RECTANGLE [25], I-Present [26], Speck [31,32], Simon [31,32], and Shadow [35] have varying key sizes. Asymmetric lightweight encryption algorithms are less common because they require larger key sizes and more memory consumption. RSA [42,43] and ECC [44–47] are the most commonly used in this category. The key generation steps in RSA [43] are as follows:

1. Generate any two large prime numbers, say p and q
2. Compute the modulus as $n = p \times q$
3. Calculate $\Phi = (p-1) \times (q-1)$
4. Select an integer e such that $1 \le e \le \Phi$ and $gcd(\Phi(n), e) = 1$
5. Compute $d = e-1 \ mod \ \Phi(n)$
6. Public key is $[e, n]$ and private key is $[d, n]$

RSA keys are very long, typically 1024 or 2048 bits. ECC achieves the same level of security compared to RSA using a smaller key size. In ECC [45], the private key is a cryptographically secure large random number. The public key is a point with x and y coordinates over a certain ECC curve. The degree of security will vary between curves.

2.2.1.2 Installation Based

Hardware or software only or hardware and software installations of lightweight cryptography are available. Hardware lightweight cryptography systems strive to deliver the desired functionality while using the least amount of hardware real estate possible. The complexity of the design, power, and energy consumption, and throughput determine the efficiency of hardware implementation. The difficulty of the implementation is one of the most important variables influencing the design approach. It is defined by the logic gates necessary to construct encryption. The related measure is known as "gate equivalent" (GE). The primary objective of software implementations is to maintain memory and CPU requirements as minimal as feasible to reduce power consumption and device costs. MTEA [10] has only hardware implementation using 0.35 μm CMOS technology and VHDL description language. The compact hardware implementation of SEA [48] consumed 2562 GEs. I-Present [26] required 2467/2783 gate equivalent (GE) for the most compact hardware implementation. The hardware and software performance of the described LWC algorithms such as SFN [33], PRESENT [38,49,39], QTL [50,51], Rectangle [25], SIMON [31,32], SPECK [31,32], SCENARY [34], AES [18,19,20], I-Present [26], HIGHT [21], and LEA [14] was assessed on systems based on 0.09/0.13/0.18/0.35 μm technologies

Table 2.1 Comparison of Lightweight Algorithms

Algorithm	Key Size	Block Size	Structure	Number of Rounds
TEA [9]	128	64	Feistel	1–255
MTEA [10]	128 (for each round)	64	Feistel	1–255
XTEA [11]	128	64	Feistel	64
XXTEA [12]	128	64	Feistel	$6 + \dfrac{5}{n}$
M-XXTEA [13]	128	Multiple of 32 (minimum 64)	Feistel	$6 + \dfrac{5}{n}$
LEA [14]	128/192/256	128	Feistel	24/28/32
Modified-LEA [15]	128/192/256	128	Feistel	64
SEA [16]	96	96	Feistel	93
DESL [17]	54	64	Feistel	16
AES [18,19,20]	128/192/256	128	SPN	10/12/14
HEIGHT [21]	128	64	Feistel	32
LWE [22]	64	64	Hybrid	
RC5 [23,24]	128	32/64/128	ARX	12
RECTANGLE [25]	80/120	64	SPN	25
I-Present [26]	80/128	64	SPN	30
PRESENT-GRP [27]	128	64	Hybrid	31
IDEA [28,29,30]	128	64	ARX	8.5
SPECK [31,32]	64/72/96/ 128/144/ 192/256	32/48/64 /92/128	ARX	22/23/26/27/ 28/29/32/33/34
Simon [31,32]	64/72/96/ 128/144/ 192/256	32/48/64/ 92/128	ARX	32/36/42/44/ 52/54/68/69/72
SFN [33]	96	64	Hybrid	32
SCENERY [34]	80	64	Feistel	28
Shadow [35]	64/128	32/64	ARX	16/32

(hardware implementation) and 8/16/32 bit microcontrollers (software implementation). Table 2.2 compares the hardware implementation of various lightweight protocols at the state-of-the-art level.

2.2.1.3 Cipher Based

When plain text is converted to cipher text, it is categorized as a stream cipher, block cipher, or hash function depending on whether it converts the plain text bit by bit, in blocks, or with an indeterminate data length [52]. The input parts are

Table 2.2 Comparison of Hardware Implementation of Lightweight Block Cipher

Algorithm	Key Size	Block Size	Area/GE	Speed (kbps@100 kHz)	Logic Process (μm)
SEA [48]	96	8	2569	3.29	0.18
PRESENT [38,49,39]	64	80	1570	200	0.18
QTL [50,51]	64	64	1026	200	0.18
SFN [33]	96	64	1877	200	0.18
RECTANGLE [25]	80	64	1467	246	0.13
SIMON [32]	128	64	1751	145.45	0.13
SPECK [32]	128	64	2014	237.04	0.13
SIMON [32]	128	64	1751	145.45	0.13
SCENERY [34]	80	64	1438	228.57	0.18
I-Present [26]	80	64	2783	-	0.18
HEIGHT [21]	128	64	3048	200	0.25
LEA [14]	128	128	3826	-	0.18
TEA [9]	128	64	2355	100	0.18
XTEA [11]	128	64	2355	100	0.18
Shadow [35]	128	64	1688		0.18

continually processed bit by bit (or word by word) in a stream cipher, whereas both encryption and decryption occur on a fixed-size block (64 bits or more) at a time in a block cipher [52]. Claude Shannon introduced confusion and diffusion as two fundamental characteristics of cryptography to make the cipher more effective. Diffusion diffuses the statistical structure of plain text over most cipher text using permutation. In contrast, the confusion uses substitution (S-box) to make the relationship between the cipher text and the key as complicated as possible. As opposed to the block cipher, which has a more straightforward design, and both confusion and diffusion properties than the stream one, the stream cipher merely makes use of the confusion attribute.

TEA [9], MTEA [10], XTEA [11], XXTEA [12], HEIGHT [21], LWE [22], I-Present [26], PRESENT-GRP [27], RECTANGLE [25], IDEA [28,29,30], SFN [33], and SCENERY [34] are normal lightweight algorithms with block size 64 bits, whereas LEA [14], Modified LEA [15], and AES [18,19,20] use 128 bits. M-XXTEA [13], SPECK [31,32], SIMON [31,32], and RC5 [23,24] all allow varying sizes of blocks, but M-XXTEA allows for a multiple of 32. PRESENT [38], SPECK-R [53], QTL [50,51], and DDR-based RC5 [54] are ultralightweight algorithms which have 64-bits block size. Hummingbird [55] has the smallest block size, which is 16 bits.

2.2.1.4 *Structure Based*

Lightweight protocols are divided into SPN (Substitution Permutation Network), FN (Feistel network), ARX (Add-Rotate-XOR), and hybrid categories based on the structure that the plain text takes on throughout the cipher text generation process. SPN transforms plain text by processing it via a sequence of consecutive substitution and permutation boxes, which prepare the data for the following round. S-box performs a one-to-one substitution, which means that a block of input bits is substituted by another block of bits called the output. The lengths of input bits and output bits are the same. The permutation box takes all the S-box output from one round and performs permutation of every bit. The ability to spread the output bits of any S-box to as many S-box inputs as possible is a characteristic of a good P-box. AES [18,19,20], RECTANGLE [25], and I-Present [26] lightweight cryptographic algorithms are under the SPN structure.

For the Feistel structure, plain text is split into two equal-sized blocks. One half is given the round function using a subkey, and the other half is XORed with the output. After that, the two halves are swapped with one another [56]. TEA [9], MTEA [10], XTEA [11], XXTEA [12], M-XXTEA [13], LEA [14], Modified LEA [15], SEA [16], DESL [17], HEIGHT [21], and SCENERY [34] are lightweight algorithms with Feistel structure.

ARX is an abbreviation for Addition/Rotation/XOR, and it was created using only three simple operations: modular addition, bitwise rotation, and exclusive OR. They generate quick and compact implementations, but security features need to be better researched compared to FN and SPN. ARX concepts include RC5 [23,24], IDEA [28,29,30], SPECK [31,32], SIMON [31,32], and Shadow [35]. The hybrid structure integrates ARX, SPN, and Feistel cipher structures to enhance the performance metrics such as throughput, energy, and GE. SFN [33] and LWE [22] have a unique structure that combines an SP network with a Feistel network. In contrast, PRESENT-GRP [27] provides security by combining the S-box of PRESENT and GRP, which yields a smaller version of the PRESENT algorithm. A hybrid combination of ARX and dynamic key-substitution layer provides high security in SPECKR [53] by reducing the number of rounds from 25 to 7 in SPECK.

2.2.2 Ultralightweight Encryption Protocols

The ultralightweight algorithm is a more compact version of the lightweight algorithm that utilizes fewer resources than the lightweight method. Compared to lightweight algorithms, which require more than 2000 GE in hardware, ultralightweight algorithms require less than 1600 GE. Table 2.3 compares the key size, block size, and the number of rounds required for each ultralightweight algorithm. PRESENT [38,49,39], Hummingbird [55], QTL [50,51], Speck-R [53], and DDR-based RC5 [54] are some of the ultralightweight encryption algorithms.

PRESENT [38] is an ultralightweight block cipher that offers high-level security with 64-bit block size and 80-bit key for resource-constrained applications. Each of the 31 rounds passed through AddRoundKey, sBoxlayer, and pLayer. AddRoundKey is the XOR operation of the round key ($K_i = k_{63}^i k_{62}^i \cdots k_0^i$ for $1 \leq i \leq 32$) and the current state ($b_{63} b_{62} \cdots b_0$). sBoxlayer, the non-linear layer where the current state (x) is represented as 16 four-bit words, and the output nibble ($S[x]$)

provides the updated state values. The linear p Layer performed the bit permutation of the state.

Hummingbird [55] first encrypted the plain text with the modulo 2^{16} addition of plain text and the content of the first internal state register. The output is again encrypted by the first block cipher E_{k1} and repeated three times. Each of the four block ciphers used by Hummingbird is a conventional SP network with a 16-bit block size and a 64-bit key. Hummingbird uses these block ciphers in succession.

QTL [50] have the same encryption and decryption processes, which reduce the space to be compatible with resource-constrained devices. Each round of encryption is defined as shown in Equation 2.1.

$$X_{64}.K_0.K_1.K_2.K_3 = Y_{64} \qquad (2.1)$$

Here X is the input, K is the key, and Y is the output. Next, the F-function process consists of AddConstants → AddRoundKey → S-box layer → P permutation layer → S-box layer. Weak block cipher security in Feistel-type structures is improved by the quick diffusion of Substitution Permutation Networks (SPN) structures in QTL.

The key dynamic substitution layer in Speck-R [53] alters in response to the addition of a dynamic key. This change allows for a decrease in the number of rounds from 26 (in Speck) to 7 (in Speck-R). This protocol becomes more resilient to several strong attacks by adding dynamicity. The three steps in the encryption algorithm of Speck-R are encrypting the Nonce, passing across the substitution layer, and XORing the plain text. The seven-round decryption process utilized the same substitution layer. DDR-based RC5 algorithm [54] concentrated on encryption and decryption processes using precomputed enlarged RoundKeys. To launch the encryption process, the user sends a *pause* control signal. The operations in encryption include the XOR operation, left rotation, and addition, whereas decryption consists of subtraction, right rotation, and the XOR operation. After activating the output valid (OV) control signal, the result is recorded.

2.2.3   Hybrid Lightweight Encryption Protocols

While sharing a secret key is challenging, symmetric encryption methods offer efficient and cost-effective ways to safeguard data without sacrificing security.

Table 2.3 Comparison of Ultralightweight Algorithms

Algorithm	Key Size	Block Size	Structure	Number of Rounds
PRESENT [38,49,39]	80/128	64	SPN	31/25
Hummingbird [55]	256	16	SPN	4
Speck-R [53]	96	64	Hybrid	7
QTL [50,51]	64/128	64	Feistel	16/20
DDR-based RC5 [54]	128	64		20

Asymmetric solutions, on the other hand, alleviate the issue of encryption key distribution, although they are slower than symmetric encryption and use more system resources [57]. In light of this, one of the finest encryption options is the complementary use of both symmetric and asymmetric encryption systems in hybrid encryption, with symmetric encryption encrypting data and asymmetric encryption encrypting the shared keys [58]. Combining asymmetric algorithms like RSA, ECC, NTRU, and MD5 with symmetric encryption methods like AES, DES, TEA, and Feistel networks results in highly efficient, lightweight hybrid algorithms.

2.2.3.1   AES with Asymmetric Algorithms

Due to the limited processing resources in IoT devices, computational complexity is a challenge. To address this problem, AES is paired with asymmetric algorithms like RSA [59,60,61], ECC [62], and NTRU [63], as well as the symmetric method Blowfish [64]. Harini et. al. [59] integrated AES, RSA, and MD5 algorithms to enhance the security and integrity of data. The plain text is encrypted using AES, and MD5 creates the hash value. RSA encrypts the hash value to create the digital signature, which is then padded with the cipher text. The existing AES architecture is improved by using hybrid AES-RSA algorithms in [60] and AES-RSA with a digital envelope process using OTP in [61]. This improves the non-linearity of the plain AES, thereby reducing the chance of an algebraic attack. The AES-ECC-MD5 combination in [62] provides better security with very high speed. The HAN algorithm described in [63] is a hybrid method that combines AES with NTRU, which has high speed, less memory, and less fiscal complexity. AbdElminaam's [64] hybrid AES-Blowfish algorithms combined symmetric and symmetric algorithms such as AES and Blowfish rather than combining symmetric and asymmetric algorithms.

2.2.3.2   DES with Asymmetric Algorithms

DES can be paired with asymmetric algorithms RSA and ECC as well as DSA digital signature to ensure the security of IoT devices. The data security of bluetooth technology is strengthened by employing the DES algorithm for data encryption and the RSA method to encrypt the key [65]. Hybrid encryption of DEC and ECC is proposed in Ref. [66] to ensure data security in intelligent transportation systems. Peng et al. [67] suggested a hybrid encryption method incorporating the DES algorithm and DSA digital signature to ensure the security of the equipment management system.

2.2.3.3   TEA with Asymmetric Algorithms

Ragab et al. [68] examined the symmetric ciphers TEA, XTEA, and XXTEA and demonstrated that XXTEA is better suited for IoT devices for data security since it consumes less memory and computes cycles. Furthermore, they studied RSA and ECC asymmetric ciphers and determined that ECC provides a higher level of protection at a smaller key size. So they compared the hybrids of TEA, XTEA, and XXTEA with RSA and ECC algorithms and determined that the XXTEA with ECC hybrid combination outperforms the others. They suggested a hybrid cryptosystem that combines XXTEA, ECC, SHA256, and a chaotic generator to accomplish important cryptographic features such as secrecy, authenticity, integrity, and non-repudiation.

2.2.3.4   Feistel Network with Asymmetric Algorithms

Bismark et al. [69] tackled the issue of data privacy and integrity breaches in IoT devices by proposing a hybrid cryptographic scheme that combines the Feistel cipher and the MD5 to provide greater security for IoT node data. To ensure the integrity of the cipher text, the MD5 cryptographic hash algorithm supplied the hashing mechanism for the cipher text to offer a checksum for each cipher text.

2.2.4   Multilevel Encryption Protocols

Multilevel encryption protocols construct a comprehensive, sophisticated encryption technique by combining the power of several simple encryption algorithms. Efficiency in computing and security are two issues that this method must deal with. Computing efficiency is necessary when sending enormous amounts of data. In contrast, security ensures that combining various encryption algorithms will produce a completely secure system.

Aljawarneh et al. [70] proposed a multilevel protocol for medical multimedia big data that provides security by combining the strengths of a symmetric encryption protocol, a Feistel network, and genetic algorithms. Here, a 256-bit block is divided into two 128-bit blocks, in which the first 128-bit plain text stream is encrypted with the AES algorithm to generate 128-bit ciphered text, and the second 128-bit key stream is computed with the Feistel network. Integrate the two 128-bit ciphers with the help of a genetic algorithm. In addition, before sending the 256-bit cipher text over the network to the recipient, Ahmad Habboush [71] used the HMAC hash function to encrypt it to increase security and address the confidentiality issue.

2.3   SECURITY ATTACKS IN LIGHTWEIGHT ENCRYPTION PROTOCOLS

Data at the application layer, the top layer of the IoT architecture, is vulnerable to various security attacks. The following are some application layer security attacks.

2.3.1   Related Key Attack

A related key attack [72,73] allows the attacker to request plain text encrypted with two or more related keys. The attacker's primary goal is to locate instances of keys for which the encryption procedures use the same or nearly the same permutation. To overcome this threat, PRESENT [38] employed a round-dependent counter to set the subkeys and a non-linear operation to mix the contents of the key register K. TEA is vulnerable to related key attacks. At the same time, XTEA modified the cipher with a better key schedule and a different round function by reordering the processes [74]. In key expansion with S-box, 64-bit round key data can be entirely confused after two rounds, whereas in the Feistel network, it's four rounds. These two cases give the maximum related key differential character in SFN [33]. RECTANGLE [25] needs two consecutive rounds for an 80-bit seed key and four for a 128-bit key. To give the proper diffusion, generalized Feistel transformations were developed. HIGHT [21] resists related key attacks with its key schedule and round function. The key schedule produces two sets of keys: 8 whitening key bytes for the initial and final transformations and 128 subkeys which form 4 subkeys for each round.

2.3.2 Algebraic Attack

In an algebraic attack, the attacker generally solves several multivariate equations to retrieve the key. Solving a multivariate equation to obtain a key becomes an NPHard problem as the number of equations and variables grows. Twenty-one equations and 8 input/output variables in PRESENT [38], QTL [51], and SFN [33] generate a total of $n \times 21$ equations and $n \times 8$ variables, where n is the number of S-boxes. The number of S-boxes is vast, thus achieving resistance to attack.

2.3.3 Linear and Differential Analysis

The complexity of linear and differential analysis depends on the number of active S-boxes from which we derive differential characteristics and linear approximation probabilities. Any three-round differential characteristic and linear approximation of QTL [51] has at least 21 S-boxes to achieve this attack. Count the number of active F-functions involved in the linear and differential active S-boxes in SFN [33]. Out of 32, 16 successive rounds of SFN can have a maximum of 29 F-functions and a minimum of 15 F-functions, confirming the attack's resilience. In PRESENT [38], any five-round differential characteristic has a minimum of ten active S-boxes to resist the attack. I-PRESENT [26] achieved the differential characteristic at round 20 out of 30 rounds to confirm the resistance of the attack.

2.3.4 Meet-in-the-middle Attack

Meet-in-the-middle attacks aim to enhance memory complexity while decreasing time complexity. There are 2^{32} alternative methods to operate due to the differences in 32-bit control keys in SFN [33]. As a result, encrypted and decrypted data cannot be matched in meet-in-the-middle attacks, and attackers cannot estimate incomplete key information.

2.3.5   Integral Attack

The structure of the encryption technique, rather than the algorithm component, is the primary target of an integral attack. The integral attack is particularly suited to block ciphers based on SPN, later extended to a few more ciphers with the Feistel network. The 28-round SCENERY provides enough protection against integral cryptanalysis [34]. However, the entire round of SFN [33] is sufficiently safe against an integral attack when the control key is not set to 32-bit 0 or 1.

2.3.6   Side Channel Attack

Side-channel attacks aim to discover more about a system's implementation than what flaws exist. It mistakenly takes advantage of information that a system has spilled [75].

Table 2.4 depicts the security analysis of various lightweight cryptographic algorithms.

2.4   ISSUES AND CHALLENGES

Key length, number of rounds, and architecture are the three vital factors to consider while designing a lightweight cryptography system to increase performance and security and reduce cost. Figure 2.6 shows these factors' trade-offs. The number of rounds it takes to execute a cipher is the primary metric to assess the system's performance. More rounds would impact system latency since higher computing overhead equals more rounds. This indicates that the delay decreases as the number of rounds falls, but the cipher with more rounds is safer.

However, a processing platform's structural support dynamically impacts the system's speed. Performance increases with the number of simultaneous calculations and processes. Compared to serial architecture, parallel processing improves performance and decreases latency, but the hardware cost rises proportionally. Although serial architecture is the least expensive option, it substantially reduces performance when loops are included. As a result, the parallel architecture and fewer cryptographic rounds improve the performance and response time of the system. The security of lightweight cryptographic network communication is directly correlated with key length. Although larger keys demand more memory and CPU time, they increase network security. This renders the cipher inappropriate for devices with limited resources. A longer key length suggests that an attack will take longer to complete. A shorter key indicates less register and memory demand. The perfect algorithm will strike the right balance between cost, performance, and security. It is simple to maximize either two of them, but it isn't easy to accomplish all three at once. For instance, increasing the number of rounds or

Table 2.4 Security Attacks of Lightweight Algorithms

Algorithm	Linear Cryptanalysis	Differential Cryptanalysis	Relative Key Attack	Algebraic Attack	Meet-in-the-middle Attack	Integral Attack	Side Channel Attack
TEA [74]	—	—	✓	—	—	—	—
XTEA [74]	—	✓	✓	—	—	—	—
XXTEA [13]	—	✓	—	—	—	—	—
M-XXTEA [13]	✓	✓	—	—	—	—	✓
LEA [14]	—	—	—	—	✓	—	✓
AES [18,19,20]	—	✓	✓	—	—	—	—
SPECK [31,32]	—	✓	✓	✓	—	—	—
SIMON [31,32]	—	✓	✓	—	—	—	✓
HIGHT [21]	✓	✓	✓	✓	—	—	✓
PRESENT [38,49,39]	✓	✓	✓	—	—	✓	—
I-PRESENT [26]	✓	✓	—	✓	—	—	—
PRESENT-GRP [27]	✓	✓	✓	—	—	✓	—
RECTANGLE [25]	✓	✓	✓	✓	✓	—	—
QTL [51]	✓	✓	✓	✓	—	✓	—
SFN [33]	✓	✓	✓	✓	✓	✓	—
SCENERY [34]	✓	✓	✓	—	—	✓	✓
Shadow [35]	—	✓	—	—	✓	—	—

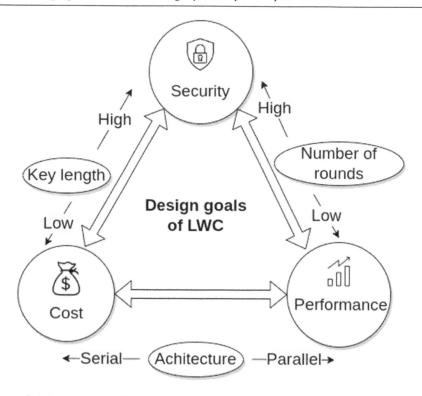

Figure 2.6 Design goals of lightweight cryptography.

the key size causes the algorithm's performance to decline and increases security. This might be accomplished by designing systems with fewer memory and compute requirements, resulting in fewer physical area requirements and lower energy consumption without sacrificing robust security. This leads to the following research questions.

1. How can we improve the security of the system without sacrificing performance?
2. Which method can be adopted to reduce the number of rounds?
3. How can we provide better security by using a key with a smaller size?
4. Is it possible to design an architecture for the cipher with better performance and security?

Considering these research questions, we propose a novel lightweight encryption algorithm at the application layer of the IoT for text data transmission using chaotic theory and machine learning. The chaotic algorithm requires fewer rounds compared to the existing lightweight algorithms.

2.5 CONCLUSION AND FUTURE WORK

IoT security is a significant concern as many IoT devices in many sectors grow exponentially. Because IoT devices have limited resources, conventional encryption approaches are ineffective. As a result, several lightweight cryptographic protocols emerge with a trade-off between cost, performance, and security. In this chapter, we examined lightweight protocols based on normal, ultra, hybrid, and multi-layer protocols. Normal lightweight protocols are examined based on the structure, installation, cipher type, and type of key used. Furthermore, we presented the various types of security threats in lightweight algorithms and how they might be accomplished. The growing attack patterns on IoT networks necessitate research into lightweight ciphers. Key size reduction, the use of a dynamic key, and a reduction in the number of rounds with the high performance of the secure algorithm are potential areas of future research that could be beneficial. We propose a novel, secure, lightweight application layer protocol for text data transmission in the IoT. This method employs a chaotic map encryption strategy, which reduces the number of rounds for encryption compared to state-of-the-art methods. The proposed method compresses the cipher text before transmission, which decreases the amount of data that needs to be communicated.

REFERENCES

1. C. Sobin, "A survey on architecture, protocols and challenges in IoT," *Wireless Personal Communications*, vol. 112, no. 3, pp. 1383–1429, 2020.
2. N. Kansal, B. Bhushan, and S. Sharma, *Architecture, Security Vulnerabilities, and the Proposed Countermeasures in Agriculture-Internet-of-Things (AioT) Systems*, pp. 329–353, Springer, Singapore, 2022.
3. A. B. Haque, B. Bhushan, and G. Dhiman, "Conceptualizing smart city applications: Requirements, architecture, security issues, and emerging trends," *Expert Systems*, vol. 39, no. 5, p. e12753, 2022.
4. A. Khanna and S. Kaur, "Internet of things (IoT), applications and challenges: A comprehensive review," *Wireless Personal Communications*, vol. 114, no. 2, pp. 1687–1762, 2020.
5. J. M. Talavera, L. E. Tobón, J. A. Gómez, M. A. Culman, J. M. Aranda, D. T. Parra, L. A. Quiroz, A. Hoyos, and L. E. Garreta, "Review of IoT applications in agro-industrial and environmental fields," *Computers and Electronics in Agriculture*, vol. 142, pp. 283–297, 2017.
6. P. S. Mathew, A. S. Pillai, and V. Palade, *Applications of IoT in Healthcare*, pp. 263–288. Springer International Publishing, Cham, 2018.
7. M. Burhan, R. A. Rehman, B. Khan, and B.-S. Kim, "IoT elements, layered architectures and security issues: A comprehensive survey," *Sensors*, vol. 18, no. 9, 2018.
8. "2017 roundup of internet of things forecasts." www.forbes.com/sites/louiscolumbus/2017/12/10/2017-roundup-of-internetof-things-forecasts/?sh=512d51b91480187440401480. (Accessed on 02/22/2022).

9.   D. J. Wheeler and R. M. Needham, "Tea, a tiny encryption algorithm," *Fast Software Encryption*, pp. 363–366, 1995.

10. M. B. Abdelhalim, M. El-Mahallawy, and M. Ayyad, "Design and implementation of an encryption algorithm for use in RFID system," *International Journal of RFID Security and Cryptography*, vol. 2, no. 1, pp. 51–57, 2013.

11. J.-P. Kaps, "Chai-tea, cryptographic hardware implementations of XTEA," in *Progress in Cryptology—INDOCRYPT 2008*, pp. 363–375, Springer, Berlin, Heidelberg, 2008.

12. E. Yarrkov, "Cryptanalysis of XXTEA," *Cryptology ePrint Archive*, Paper 2010/254, 2010. https://eprint.iacr.org/2010/254.

13. A. A. M. Ragab, A. Madani, A. Wahdan, and G. M. Selim, "Design, analysis, and implementation of a new lightweight block cipher for protecting IoT smart devices," *Journal of Ambient Intelligence and Humanized Computing*, pp. 1–18, 2021.

14. D. Hong, J.-K. Lee, D.-C. Kim, D. Kwon, K. H. Ryu, and D.-G. Lee, "Lea: A 128bit block cipher for fast encryption on common processors," in *Information Security Applications*, pp. 3–27, Springer International Publishing, Cham, 2014.

15. J. Choi and Y. Kim, "An improved lea block encryption algorithm to prevent sidechannel attack in the IoT system," in *2016 Asia-Pacific Signal and Information Processing Association Annual Summit and Conference (APSIPA)*, pp. 1–4, 2016.

16. F.-X. Standaert, G. Piret, N. Gershenfeld, and J.-J. Quisquater, "Sea: A scalable encryption algorithm for small embedded applications," in *Smart Card Research and Advanced Applications*, pp. 222–236, Springer, Berlin, Heidelberg, 2006.

17. G. Leander, C. Paar, A. Poschmann, and K. Schramm, "New lightweight des variants," in *Fast Software Encryption*, pp. 196–210, Springer, Berlin, Heidelberg, 2007.

18. J. Bos, D. A. Osvik, and D. Stefan, "Fast implementations of AES on various platforms," *IACR Cryptology ePrint Archive*, vol. 2009, p. 501, 2009. https://ia.cr/2009/501.

19. H. Talirongan, A. M. Sison, and R. P. Medina, "Modified advanced encryption standard using butterfly effect," in *2018 IEEE 10th International Conference on Humanoid, Nanotechnology, Information Technology, Communication and Control, Environment and Management (HNICEM)*, pp. 1–6, IEEE, 2018.

20. O. C. Abikoye, A. D. Haruna, A. Abubakar, N. O. Akande, and E. O. Asani, "Modified advanced encryption standard algorithm for information security," *Symmetry*, vol. 11, no. 12, 2019.

21. D. Hong, J. Sung, S. Hong, J. Lim, S. Lee, B.-S. Koo, C. Lee, D. Chang, J. Lee, K. Jeong, H. Kim, J. Kim, and S. Chee, "Hight: A new block cipher suitable for low-resource device," in *Cryptographic Hardware and Embedded Systems—CHES 2006*, pp. 46–59, Springer, Berlin, Heidelberg, 2006.

22. S. Toprak, A. Akbulut, M. A. Aydın, and A. H. Zaim, "Lwe: An energy-efficient lightweight encryption algorithm for medical sensors and IoT devices," *Electrica*, vol. 20, no. 1, pp. 71–80, 2020.

23. R. L. Rivest, "The rc5 encryption algorithm," in *International Workshop on Fast Software Encryption* (B. Preneel, ed.), pp. 86–96, Springer, Berlin, Heidelberg, 1994.

24. B. S. Kaliski and Y. L. Yin, "On the security of the rc5 encryption algorithm," *Tech. Rep., RSA Laboratories Technical Report TR-602. To appear*, 1998.

25. W. Zhang, Z. Bao, D. Lin, V. Rijmen, B. Yang, and I. Verbauwhede, "Rectangle: A bit-slice lightweight block cipher suitable for multiple platforms," *Science China Information Sciences*, vol. 58, no. 12, pp. 1–15, 2015.

26. M. R. Z'aba, N. Jamil, M. E. Rusli, M. Z. Jamaludin, and A. A. M. Yasir, "I-present tm: An involutive lightweight block cipher," *Journal of Information Security*, vol. 2014, 2014.

27. G. Bansod, N. Raval, and N. Pisharoty, "Implementation of a new lightweight encryption design for embedded security," *IEEE Transactions on Information Forensics and Security*, vol. 10, no. 1, pp. 142–151, 2015.

28. X. Lai and J. L. Massey, "A proposal for a new block encryption standard," in *Advances in Cryptology—EUROCRYPT '90* (I. B. Damgard, ed.), pp. 389–404, Springer, Berlin, Heidelberg, 1991.

29. S. Mukherjee and B. Sahoo, "A survey on hardware implementation of idea cryptosystem," *Information Security Journal: A Global Perspective*, vol. 20, no. 4–5, pp. 210–218, 2011.

30. O. Tigli, "Area efficient asic implementation of idea (international data encryption standard)," *Best Design for ASIC Implementation of IDEA, GMU*, 2003.

31. R. Beaulieu, D. Shors, J. Smith, S. Treatman-Clark, B. Weeks, and L. Wingers, "The simon and speck lightweight block ciphers," in *Proceedings of the 52nd Annual Design Automation Conference*, pp. 1–6, 2015.

32. R. Beaulieu, D. Shors, J. Smith, S. Treatman-Clark, B. Weeks, and L. Wingers, "The simon and speck families of lightweight block ciphers." *Cryptology ePrint Archive*, Paper 2013/404, 2013. https://eprint.iacr.org/2013/404.

33. L. Li, B. Liu, Y. Zhou, and Y. Zou, "Sfn: A new lightweight block cipher," *Microprocessors and Microsystems*, vol. 60, pp. 138–150, 2018.

34. J. Feng and L. Li, "Scenery: A lightweight block cipher based on feistel structure," *Frontiers of Computer Science*, vol. 16, no. 3, pp. 1–10, 2022.

35. Y. Guo, L. Li, and B. Liu, "Shadow: A lightweight block cipher for IoT nodes," *IEEE Internet of Things Journal*, vol. 8, no. 16, pp. 13014–13023, 2021.

36. S. Padhiar and K. H. Mori, "A comparative study on symmetric and asymmetric key encryption techniques," in *Implementing Data Analytics and Architectures for Next Generation Wireless Communications*, pp. 132–144, IGI Global, 2022.

37. J. Kapoor and D. Thakur, "Analysis of symmetric and asymmetric key algorithms," in *ICT Analysis and Applications* (S. Fong, N. Dey, and A. Joshi, eds.), pp. 133–143, Springer Nature, Singapore, 2022.

38. A. Bogdanov, L. R. Knudsen, G. Leander, C. Paar, A. Poschmann, M. J. B. Robshaw, Y. Seurin, and C. Vikkelsoe, "Present: An ultra-lightweight block cipher," in *Cryptographic Hardware and Embedded Systems—CHES 2007* (P. Paillier and I. Verbauwhede, eds.), pp. 450–466, Springer, Berlin, Heidelberg, 2007.

39. R. Chatterjee and R. Chakraborty, "A modified lightweight present cipher for IoT security," in *2020 International Conference on Computer Science, Engineering and Applications (ICCSEA)*, pp. 1–6, 2020.

40. Y. A. Birgani, S. Timarchi, and A. Khalid, "Ultra-lightweight FPGA-based rc5 designs via data-dependent rotation block optimization," *Microprocessors and Microsystems*, vol. 93, p. 104588, 2022.

41. R. L. Rivest, "The rc5 encryption algorithm," in *International Workshop on Fast Software Encryption* (B. Preneel, ed.), pp. 86–96, Springer, Berlin, Heidelberg, 1994.

42. C. Thirumalai and H. Kar, "Memory efficient multi key (memk) generation scheme for secure transportation of sensitive data over cloud and IoT devices," in *2017 Innovations in Power and Advanced Computing Technologies (i-PACT)*, pp. 1–6, 2017.

43. H. Yu and Y. Kim, "New RSA encryption mechanism using one-time encryption keys and unpredictable bio-signal for wireless communication devices," *Electronics*, vol. 9, no. 2, 2020.

44. Z. Liu, H. Seo, A. Castiglione, K.-K. R. Choo, and H. Kim, "Memory-efficient implementation of elliptic curve cryptography for the internet-of-things," *IEEE Transactions on Dependable and Secure Computing*, vol. 16, no. 3, pp. 521–529, 2019.

45. S. Kalra and S. K. Sood, "Secure authentication scheme for IoT and cloud servers," *Pervasive and Mobile Computing*, vol. 24, pp. 210–223, 2015. Special Issue on Secure Ubiquitous Computing.

46. S. Kumari, M. Karuppiah, A. K. Das, X. Li, F. Wu, and N. Kumar, "A secure authentication scheme based on elliptic curve cryptography for IoT and cloud servers," *The Journal of Supercomputing*, vol. 74, no. 12, pp. 6428–6453, 2018.

47. D. He and S. Zeadally, "An analysis of RFID authentication schemes for internet of things in healthcare environment using elliptic curve cryptography," *IEEE Internet of Things Journal*, vol. 2, no. 1, pp. 72–83, 2015.

48. T. Plos, C. Dobraunig, M. Hofinger, A. Oprisnik, C. Wiesmeier, and J. Wiesmeier, "Compact hardware implementations of the block ciphers mcrypton, noekeon, and sea," in *International Conference on Cryptology in India*, pp. 358–377, Springer, Berlin, Heidelberg, 2012.

49. E. Gomez, C. Hernández, and F. Martinez, "Performance evaluation of the present cryp-'tographic algorithm over FPGA," *Contemporary Engineering Sciences*, vol. 10, pp. 555–567, 2017.

50. L. Li, B. Liu, and H. Wang, "Qtl: A new ultra-lightweight block cipher," *Microprocessors and Microsystems*, vol. 45, pp. 45–55, 2016.

51. S. Sadeghi, N. Bagheri, and M. A. Abdelraheem, "Cryptanalysis of reduced QTL block cipher," *Microprocessors and Microsystems*, vol. 52, pp. 34–48, 2017.

52. "Cryptography and network security: Principles and practice." https://gacbe.ac.in/images/E (Accessed on 08/17/2022).

53. L. Sleem and R. Couturier, "Speck-r: An ultra light-weight cryptographic scheme for internet of things," *Multimedia Tools and Applications*, vol. 80, no. 11, pp. 17067–17102, 2021.

54. Y. A. Birgani, S. Timarchi, and A. Khalid, "Ultra-lightweight FPGA-based rc5 designs via data-dependent rotation block optimization," *Microprocessors and Microsystems*, vol. 93, p. 104588, 2022.

55. X. Fan, H. Hu, G. Gong, E. M. Smith, and D. Engels, "Lightweight implementation of hummingbird cryptographic algorithm on 4-bit microcontrollers," in *2009 International Conference for Internet Technology and Secured Transactions, (ICITST)*, pp. 1–7, 2009.

56. V. T. Hoang and P. Rogaway, "On generalized feistel networks," in *Advances in Cryptology—CRYPTO 2010* (T. Rabin, ed.), pp. 613–630, Springer, Berlin, Heidelberg, 2010.

57. P. Matta, M. Arora, and D. Sharma, "A comparative survey on data encryption techniques: Big data perspective," *Materials Today: Proceedings*, vol. 46, pp. 11035–11039, 2021. International Conference on Technological Advancements in Materials Science and Manufacturing.

58. Q. Zhang, "An overview and analysis of hybrid encryption: The combination of symmetric encryption and asymmetric encryption," in *2021 2nd International Conference on Computing and Data Science (CDS)*, pp. 616–622, 2021.

59. M. Harini, K. P. Gowri, C. Pavithra, and M. P. Selvarani, "A novel security mechanism using hybrid cryptography algorithms," in *2017 IEEE International Conference on Electrical, Instrumentation and Communication Engineering (ICEICE)*, pp. 1–4, 2017.

60. S. Kuswaha, S. Waghmare, and P. Choudhary, "Data transmission using AES-RSA based hybrid security algorithms," *International Journal on Recent and Innovation Trends in Computing and Communication*, vol. 3, no. 4, pp. 1964–1969, 2015.

61. A. Darwish, M. M. El-Gendy, and A. E. Hassanien, "A new hybrid cryptosystem for internet of things applications," in *Multimedia Forensics and Security*, pp. 365–380, Springer, Cham, 2017.

62. M. Xin, "A mixed encryption algorithm used in internet of things security transmission system," in *2015 International Conference on Cyber-Enabled Distributed Computing and Knowledge Discovery*, pp. 62–65, 2015.

63. A. Safi, "Improving the security of internet of things using encryption algorithms," *International Journal of Computer and Information Engineering*, vol. 11, no. 5, pp. 558–561, 2017.

64. D. S. AbdElminaam, "Improving the security of cloud computing by building new hybrid cryptography algorithms," *International Journal of Electronics and Information Engineering*, vol. 8, no. 1, pp. 40–48, 2018.

65. W. Ren and Z. Miao, "A hybrid encryption algorithm based on DES and RSA in bluetooth communication," in *2010 Second International Conference on Modeling, Simulation and Visualization Methods*, pp. 221–225, 2010.

66. C. Ruan, F. Xiao, and J. Luo, "Design and implementation of mobile payment system for intelligent travel," in *2014 IEEE 3rd International Conference on Cloud Computing and Intelligence Systems*, pp. 547–552, 2014.

67. X. Peng, L. Min, and H. Yu-Jie, "A hybrid encryption algorithm in the application of equipment information management based on internet of things," in *Proceedings of 3rd International Conference on Multimedia Technology (ICMT-13)*, pp. 1116–1122, Atlantis Press, 2013/11.

68. A. Ragab, G. Selim, A. Wahdan, and A. Madani, "Robust hybrid lightweight cryptosystem for protecting IoT smart devices," in *International Conference on Security, Privacy and Anonymity in Computation, Communication and Storage*, pp. 5–19, Springer, Cham 2019.

69. B. T. Asare, K. Quist-Aphetsi, and L. Nana, "A hybrid lightweight cryptographic scheme for securing node data based on the feistel cipher and md5 hash algorithm in a local IoT network," in *2019 International Conference on Mechatronics, Remote Sensing, Information Systems and Industrial Information Technologies (ICMRSISIIT)*, vol. 1, pp. 1–5, 2019.

70. S. Aljawarneh, M. B. Yassein, and W. A. Talafha, "A multithreaded programming approach for multimedia big data: Encryption system," *Multimedia Tools and Applications*, vol. 77, no. 9, pp. 10997–11016, 2018.

71. A. Habboush, "Multi-level encryption framework," *International Journal of Advanced Computer Science and Applications*, vol. 9, no. 4, 2018.

72. E. Biham, "New types of cryptanalytic attacks using related keys," *Journal of Cryptology*, vol. 7, no. 4, pp. 229–246, 1994.

73. E. Biham, O. Dunkelman, and N. Keller, "A unified approach to related-key attacks," in *Fast Software Encryption* (K. Nyberg, ed.), pp. 73–96, Springer, Berlin, Heidelberg, 2008.

74. D. Moon, K. Hwang, W. Lee, S. Lee, and J. Lim, "Impossible differential cryptanalysis of reduced round XTEA and TEA," in *International Workshop on Fast Software Encryption*, pp. 49–60, Springer, Berlin, Heidelberg, 2002.
75. A. Bechtsoudis and N. Sklavos, "Side channel attacks cryptanalysis against block ciphers based on FPGA devices," in *2010 IEEE Computer Society Annual Symposium on VLSI*, pp. 460–461, IEEE, 2010.

Chapter 3

Security Issues in Cyber-physical System

Charanjeet Singh

3.1 CYBER-PHYSICAL SYSTEM: INTRODUCTION

3.1.1 CPS Background

Cyber-physical system (CPS) is the next-generation computational system that amalgamates numerous technologies and subsystems such as computation, control, sensing, and networking and finds its application in real-time environments spanning across healthcare, transport, environment, medicine to manufacturing and agriculture [1]. This term was coined in 2006 by Helen Gill at the National Science Foundation in the United States. CPS integrates both hardware and software components such as machines, sensory devices, IoT-enabled equipment with embedded computational intelligence, and various other communication mechanisms through a networking technology to perform automated tasks that are distributed among multiple agents. CPS combines various interconnected systems and can monitor and manipulate real IoT-based objects and processes. In addition, these systems have the capability to sense the surrounding environment, thereby providing them with the ability to adjust and control the physical world [2].

Thus, a CPS concept is a hybrid system that integrates computer science and engineering communities in several areas, namely embedded computing and mechatronics [3], and encompasses three major C's as its functions: computation, communication, and control. The past two decades have witnessed substantial growth in the development and adoption of CPS in diverse areas such as household appliance, transportation, medical, healthcare, agriculture, military, and many more [4,5,6]. Moreover, advancements in the fields of networking, computing, sensing, and control systems have empowered an extensive range of new devices. In recent times, because of the wider impact of CPS on the economy, society, and environment, it has drawn the attention of government, industry, and academia [7].

3.1.2 Problem Statement

Although CPS has numerous benefits and widespread acceptance in distinct domains, it has to deal with numerous security issues, threats, vulnerabilities, and attacks due to its heterogeneity, dependence on data from multiple sources, and

DOI: 10.1201/9781003474111-3

large-scale deployment. In such a case it is indispensable that these issues and problems must be properly identified and dealt with.

3.1.3   Motivation

The major objective behind this work is to review and understand distinct cybersecurity issues, threats, vulnerabilities, and attacks and discuss the various security solutions for the same.

Amalgamation of Internet-of-Things (IoT) with CPS has raised security concerns not only against cyber threats but also for physical devices and infrastructure that form part of IoT. The prime purpose of this chapter is to review various cybersecurity issues, threats, vulnerabilities, and attacks and discuss the distinct cybersecurity solutions.

3.1.4   Contribution

This work highlights the importance of security in CPS, discusses various CPS security issues, categorizes CPS security threats into cyber threats, physical threats, and cyber-physical threats. It further presents the classification of CPS vulnerabilities as cyber, physical, and cyber-physical threats. The various CPS attacks have been presented under two categories, namely, physical and cyberattacks. It finally details numerous cryptographic and non-cryptographic CPS security solutions. It also outlines CPS security solutions for distinct CPS layers.

3.1.5   Chapter Organization

The chapter has been organized into eight sections, namely, Cyber-physical System: Introduction, Security in Cyber-physical System (CPS), Security Issues in CPS, Security Threats in CPS, CPS Vulnerabilities, CPS Attacks, CPS Security Solutions, and finally the chapter ends with a Conclusion.

3.2   SECURITY IN CYBER-PHYSICAL SYSTEM

The swift growth of CPS applications has given rise to numerous problems with security and confidentiality that are attributed not only to the heterogeneous nature of CPS, its dependence on sensitive data, but also to its large-scale deployment.

The CPS architecture has two layers, namely cyber and physical [8]. Wang et al. attributed that with the increase in the interaction between physical and cyber systems, the physical systems are more prone to the security vulnerabilities of cyber system [9].

The security issues in CPS can be related to cyber, physical, or both cyber and physical (hybrid) space [10]. The security requirement of CPS encompasses the following aspects [11,12]:

1. *Data confidentiality*: It ensures that data is secure from unauthorized access both during transit from one system to another as well as in database (data at rest). An authorized person should not be able to eavesdrop communication flow both between sensors and controller as well as between controller and actuator [13].
2. *Integrity:* It guarantees accuracy/correctness of the data. An unauthorized or adversary may modify or delete the sensitive data that may supply false information to an authorized user. In CPS, integrity can be enforced by preventing, detecting, or blocking deception attacks on the data sent and received by the controller, actuator, and sensors [14].
3. *Availability*: It ensures that the services of CPS components are accessible to authorized users at all times. CPS must ensure that there is no corruption in communication, control, and computing systems due to failure in hardware, system upgradation, power failure, or DoS attack [15].
4. *Authentication*: It ensures that the two parties involved in communication process have validated each other's identity by verifying the credentials supplied to each other.
5. *Non-repudiation*: It ensures that none of the parties involved in the communication or data access deny the receipt of transaction.

Humayed et al. [10] categorize attacks in CPS on the basis of three aspects: cyber-attacks, physical attacks, and cyber-physical attack. The physical components, such as sensors that interface with the physical world, are included in the physical aspect, whereas computations, communication processes, and monitoring activities are included in cyber and cyber-physical aspects.

3.3 SECURITY ISSUES IN CPS

The heterogeneous nature of CPS poses a big security challenge as it is composed of a diverse range of physical devices, hardware components, protocols, and architectures [16]. In addition, monitoring and controlling processes also involve different forms of software products. This diversity and complication in their integration expose CPS to several security attacks.

Besides security concerns, CPS privacy is another serious issue [17]. Cyber-physical systems are often distributed systems that span across diverse geographic locations. It typically employs sophisticated machine learning algorithms for data analysis and decision-making. These algorithms analyze the collected data that help in the decision-making process. In such a system, the data breach may happen at different stages that range from data collection, transmission, operation to data storage.

The cyber-physical system usually has huge computational and storage needs. In order to fulfill these needs at a lower cost, cloud computing offers a promising solution that ensures access to unlimited resources in a virtualized and scalable manner, thereby creating a cloud cyber-physical system (CCPS). Moreover, cloud computing not only provides on-demand access to different networks but also makes various computational resources available to users with minimal managerial effort or with little or no interaction from the service providers [18]. In CCPS, security issues like real-time monitoring, rootkits, data management issues, and cyberattacks may creep up that pose new challenges in addition to security issues of traditional cyber-physical systems [19].

3.4   CPS SECURITY THREATS

It is imperative to understand from what we need to protect a CPS, in addition to having knowledge of various threats, weaknesses, and the attack mechanisms. Charles P. Pfleeger [20] defines threat as "*a set of circumstances that has the potential to cause loss or harm.*" A threat is identified by five major factors:

1. *Source*: It refers to the originator of an attack. Threat sources are further categorized into three types: *adversarial* threats, which pose malicious intentions from individuals, groups organizations, or states/nations; *accidental* threats are the ones that have been caused accidentally or through legitimate CPS components; *environmental* threats, which include natural or human-caused disasters such as cyclones, floods, earthquakes, fire or explosion, and failures of supporting infrastructure such as power outage or telecommunications failure [21].
2. *Target*: It includes CPS applications and their specific components or users that are being affected by the attack.
3. *Motive*: It refers to the reasons behind the attack that may be criminal, spying, terroristic, political, or cyberwar [22,23].
4. *Attack vector*: It refers to the mechanism used for attack, namely, interception, interruption, modification, or fabrication.
5. *Consequence*: It includes the aspect of CPS security affected by the attack, namely, confidentiality, integrity, availability, privacy, or safety.

Security threats in CPS are categorized as cyber threats, physical threats, and cyber-physical threats. Cyber threats are usually scalable in nature as they are automated and replicated and are distributed freely via unreliable domains. Cyber-physical threats originate in cyberspace but affect the physical space of the system.

3.4.1   Cyber Threats in CPS

In order to delineate various cyber threats of CPS, several different perspectives need to be considered. One of the first perspectives is protecting data in transit, during processing as well as in storage (these are termed as *entering function*). The second is integrating cyber-physical components into CPS. The third includes the oriented threat that affects CIA aspects of security.

The various threats that the CPS system is prone to are the following:

1. *Unauthorized access:* It is a kind of privacy breach where an unauthorized person tries to gain entry through either a logical or a physical network breach [24].
2. *Disclosure of information*: It is a privacy and confidentiality breach [25] where an unauthorized person discloses personal information through the interception of communication traffic with the help of wireless hacking tools.
3. *Remote access*: When an unauthorized person tries to gain access to a CPS resource through a remote location with the intent of causing financial loss, disturbance, or blackout.
4. *Interception*: It is another king of privacy and confidentiality breach where an attacker tries to intercept private conversations through the manipulation of existing or new weaknesses in the CPS system [26].
5. *Information gathering*: It is a kind of privacy breach where users' information collected from various devices is illegally sold for marketing and commercial purposes.
6. *Jamming*: It is a kind of attack where an authorized user is denied of a specific service or access to a device by changing the device's state and expected operations either by wireless jamming or by launching a wave of de-authentication [27].
7. *GPS exploitation*: It is at kind of attack where location privacy of a user is violated by tracking a device or GPS navigation system of a user. Hackers can track a device or even a car by exploiting (GPS) navigation systems, resulting in a location privacy violation [28].
8. *Wireless exploitation*: This attack aims at either disrupting the system operation or gaining access to a remote system by exploiting wireless capabilities of CPS [29].

3.4.2 Physical Threats in CPS

The classification of physical threats is done on the basis of three prime factors: physical damage, loss, and ability of self-repair. The various physical threats to CPS are as follows:

1. *Spoofing:* In this, a malicious unknown source masquerades the identity of trusted entity. In spoofing attack, attackers spoof sensors by sending misleading and/or false measurements to the control center.
2. *Sabotage*: In this, an attacker disrupts the communication process or intercepts traffic between two parties and redirects it to unauthorized third party. For instance, an unauthorized person sabotages physically exposed CPS

components across the power grid, causing either a service disruption or denial of service. This can lead to total or partial blackout.

3. *Service disruption or denial*: An unauthorized person can tamper any device that can disrupt a service or changes its configuration. In CPS, it usually has serious effects, especially in the case of medical applications.

4. *Tracking*: An unauthorized person can track a legal CPS device. He can gain illegal access to a CPS device or can also attach another malicious device to the system.

3.5 CPS VULNERABILITIES

A vulnerability is defined as a gap or a weakness in the security of a system that can be exploited for unauthorized access either for reconnaissance or active attacks. This can be extended to stealing a sensitive data or installing a malware in the system and even running a malicious code. In CPS, a vulnerability can be present in cyber, cyber-physical, or in physical state.

CPS vulnerabilities can be categorized into three main types: network-based, platform-based, and management-related. Network vulnerabilities relate to hardware, its configuration, and problems related to its monitoring. It also includes compromised open wired and wireless communication and connections and encompasses a wide range of attacks, such as eavesdropping, man-in-the-middle attack, replay spoofing, sniffing backdoor [30], DoS, DdoS, packet manipulation attacks [31], and communication-stack (network/transport/application layer) [32]. Platform-based vulnerabilities are associated with database [33], hardware, software, and configuration. It also includes deficiencies of protection measures. Management vulnerabilities relate to the lack of security policies, procedures, and guidelines. The CPS vulnerabilities are attributed to several different causes:

1. Isolated assumption of the engineers that the systems are isolated from the outside world and the monitoring, control operations are performed locally.
2. Increased connectivity of CPS with the addition of several open network and wireless technologies such as Bluetooth, cellular, satellite radio communications, etc.
3. Heterogeneity due to the usage of third party and proprietary components [34].
4. Usage of USB affected with malware may spread malware across numerous devices through exploitation and replication upon plugging.
5. Bad or weak coding skills may cause a code to execute infinite loops or may provide gaps to attackers.
6. A spyware or malware may expose a CPS system to spying or surveillance attack. Such a malicious code may get into system unnoticed for several years and can steal or eavesdrop sensitive data of different users.
7. Homogeneity is another vulnerability issue that CPS of similar types suffer from. A prime example is the Stuxnet worm attack on Iranian nuclear power plants [35].

Another classification of CPS vulnerabilities is done as cyber, physical, and cyber-physical threat. The details of each have been discussed in subsequent subsections.

3.5.1   Cyber Vulnerabilities

Cyber vulnerabilities have been grouped as follows:

1. *Protocol vulnerabilities*: The open standard protocols of CPS such as Transmission Control Protocol/Internet Protocol (TCP/IP) and Inter-Control Center Communications Protocol (ICCP) suffer from certain issues. ICCP has critical buffer overflow vulnerability [36].
2. *Wired/wireless/open system vulnerabilities*: Ethernet is prone to a variety of attacks as wiretapping interception, sniffing, eavesdropping and wardriving attacks [37,38], and meet-in-the-middle attacks. A malicious insider can manipulate, damage, delete, capture, or analyze short-range wireless communications [39]. Even long-range wireless communications are prone to eavesdropping, replay attacks, and unauthorized access attacks. Owing to the lack of encryption, wireless communications are also subjected to variety of wireless attacks such as jamming, modification, and replay attacks.

3.5.2   Physical Vulnerabilities

Physical vulnerabilities arise due to the insufficient physical security provided to the components of CPS. The absence of such a measure may result in tampering and produce misleading data in cyber-physical components. MacDonald et al. [40] have discussed the physical attacks with their cyber impact. CPS field devices such as smart grids, power grids, supply chains, etc. are usually susceptible to these vulnerabilities as a large number of physical components do not have sufficient physical security, thereby making them prone to physical destruction. Thus, detecting and preventing such issues is the only solution [41]. In medical CPS, the devices are prone to physical access. Consequently, the probability of installing malware into them and modifying their configurations is a common issue [10]. In such cases, even targeted attacks are easily launched as unauthorized person can easily access the device's serial number [42].

For a CPS to deliver services effectively and efficiently, it is indispensable that identification and analysis of CPS weaknesses must be done. This vulnerability assessment helps in the identification of corrective and preventive actions with the objective to mitigate, reduce, and remove these weaknesses [43].

3.6   CPS ATTACKS

Cyber-physical system attacks can be cyber base or physical ones. This section discusses varied forms of attacks under these two categories.

3.6.1   Physical Attacks

Al-Mhiqani et al. [44] outlined distinct range of these attacks:

1. *Fake identity*: In this, an unauthorized person/attacker masquerades as a legitimate user. These attacks are common in cloud environments and include credential stuffing, phishing, and password spraying. The solution to contain these issues is their rapid detection and stopping an attack from progressing further.
2. *Stalking*: This includes disgruntled employees who try to acquire credentials of other authorized employees by being on their shoulder with an intent to either harm the organization or to sell the information to competitors for financial gains.
3. *Wiretapping*: An intruder may cut the wires of CPS headquarters or wiretap into them to capture the communicated data.
4. *Malicious software*: An attacker employs malicious third-party software with an aim to replace legitimate files with a malware that compromises the system or provides remote access capabilities to an attacker. A classic example of this type of attack is case of the Georgia Nuclear Power Plant Shutdown in 2008 [45].
5. *Infected devices*: An attack that employs the usage of infected CDs, USBs, and other devices or drivers that install a malicious software into the devices of CPS. Example, the Stuxnet worm [46].
6. *Interception of surveillance devices*: An attacker may distort the camera signals, cut off communication lines, delete CCTV footage by intercepting CCTV cameras of certain entry points or key areas of the CPS.
7. *Physical breach*: An attacker may damage or shut down network-connected manufacturing systems and CPS devices, thereby causing loss of availability and productivity. Examples of physical breach include Springfield Pumping Station in 2011 [47] and US Georgia Water Treatment Plant in 2013 [48].
8. *Privilege abuse*: A disgruntled insider may help an unauthorized person to launch an attack by disclosing information about CPS system as these insiders have access to server rooms or installation areas in CPS domains. Such an abuse can be in the form of physical tampering where CPS devices can be mishandled or in the form of unauthorized activity such as increasing or decreasing power voltage in grids.

3.6.2   Cyberattacks

CPS is prone to varied forms of cyberattacks. This section summarizes these attacks:

1. *DoS and DdoS*: In this attack, the authorized user is denied access to the system. The legal flow of data between the two communicating computers/devices is blocked in such a manner that the authorized user does not

get the required service. As a result, the requested service is denied to the legitimate user [49]. In DdoS attack, the illegitimate requests for a specific resource are launched from multiple (distributed) locations at the same time in order to overwhelm the server. This is can be done by means of worms that multiply on several computers and attack the target. DoS attacks can be in the form of blackhole [50] or teardrop [51]. DdoS can be in the form of ping-of-death [52].

TCP handshake process can be exploited where requests are sent to the server constantly without sending response. In this way, the server keeps on waiting for reply and keeps on allocating space, causing buffer overflow [53]. This may cause a CPS to crash.

2. *Eavesdropping*: An attacker can steal sensitive information such as passwords by intercepting the CPS network traffic. This may be in the form of active attack or passive attack.

3. *Password cracking*: An attacker can employ brute-force [54], password guessing [55], rainbow table [56], and dictionary [57] attack to capture the authorized CPS user's password. the attacker may gain access to the database or to the network traffic.

4. *Replay:* The real-time operations of CPS and their availability is adversely affected when an attacker impersonates and intercepts incoming and outgoing packets between ICSs, RTUs, and PLCs.

5. *Cross-site scripting*: A malicious script is run in the targeted victim's browser using a third-party web resource. A malicious coding script is injected into a website's database.

6. *SQL injections*: This attack aims at capturing (read and/or modify) sensitive data from CPS database-driven websites. In SQL-based data management system, it may be fatal as this attack can also be used to execute administrative operations such as database shutdown [58].

7. *Malware*: This malicious software can compromise CPS devices and steal or damage sensitive information/data and even CPS devices. Several different types of malwares that effect CPS are the follows:

    a. *Spyware*: A malicious software is installed secretly on a CPS device without the user's knowledge or the authorizer's knowledge. This code then spies the system.

    b. *Trojan horse*: It is a malicious code that hides dangerous code and usually appears like a legitimate program that the user is willing to run [59]. Once downloaded, it infects the CPS devices and provides a remote access to attacker for stealing data credentials and monitoring users' activities.

    c. *Virus*: This malicious code replicates itself and spreads to other devices via human or non-human intervention. A virus attaches itself to various executable codes and programs and harms distinct CPS devices.

    d. *Worms*: It is an autonomous system program that exploits OS vulnerabilities and harms host network and regenerates itself by copying from one computer to another in the network [60].

e. *Botnets*: Botnets are the electronic soldiers [61] that are installed secretly on the target system and allows illegitimate users to remotely control the system. It can be used to perform a variety of tasks, such as distributing malwares, spam, and steal messages. Botnet exploits CPS devices' vulnerabilities to conduct DdoS attacks.

f. *Logic bomb*: It is a type of attack where a malicious code is executed when a specific condition is met in a program. Such a condition may be a specific date, time, or count of a specific transaction [62].

g. *Ransomware*: It is a malicious software that exploits CPS vulnerabilities in order to get hold of important CPS data or encrypts it and later on demands ransom from genuine users to either decrypt it or to provide its access. Some of the instances of such attacks are targeting oil refineries and power grids [63].

h. *Rootkit*: In this, an illegitimate user can remotely access files or steal information from a CPS and can also change system configuration. An example of this attack is Blackhole exploit kit (2012) [64].

i. *Polymorphic malware*: This kind of malware frequently keeps on changing its form, such as filename and keys for encryption in order to evade the detection process.

3.7   CPS SECURITY SOLUTIONS

CPS is vulnerable to various types of networks, and cyber and cryptographic attacks. Therefore, it is indispensable to employ robust cybersecurity techniques, tools, processes, and protocols to provide sufficient protection to CPS. Moreover, adequate user training is also essential to protect and prevent attacks on networks, resources, and channels against illegitimate access, modification, and destruction of both data and CPS resources.

Although the deployment of various security options help in protecting CPS resources but it has a toll on CPS in terms of additional costs, higher power consumption, reduced performance, and transmission delay.

CPS security can be augmented by employing varied cryptographic and noncryptographic solutions.

3.7.1   Cryptographic CPS Security Solutions

The constraints of power and size restricts the usage of hash function and cipher-based traditional cryptography techniques in CPS. However, these approaches help in securing communication channels from passive and active attacks against unauthorized access and interception [66]. Zhang et al. [67] used a compression technique before encrypting the traffic to ensure confidentiality of data in transit, thereby securing CPS communication lines. For real-time requirement in CPS such as the vehicular ad hoc networks (VANETs), Zhou et al. [68] presented a novel lightweight encryption scheme. For CPS communications, Vegh et al. [69] suggested a hierarchical cryptosystem method using the ElGamal algorithm. A blockchain-based algorithm called Secure Pub-Sub (SPS) was proposed by Zhao et al. [70].

The security of CPS can be augmented by strengthening the authentication process using cryptographic methods. A public key-exchange-based authentication scheme by Halperin et al. [71] that uses external radio frequency instead of batteries as an energy source prevents an unauthorized person from gaining access. Usage of addition authentication channels (out of band authentication) in certain wearable devices increases the security to manifold [72].

The techniques like differential privacy and homomorphic encryption are used to preserve the privacy of users' data in CPS.

3.7.2   Non-cryptographic CPS Security Solutions

The non-cryptographic security solution for CPS includes the usage of firewalls, honeypots, and intrusion detection systems (IDS) that helps in evading cyberattack and malicious events. IDS that can detect unusual and malicious activity in the network can be sited at the border router of any IoT network, hosts, or in every physical object. The three main methods of IDS placement in a network as cited by Zarpelao et al. [73] include distributed, centralized, and hybrid. They further classified the intrusion detection methods in four main categories as signature-based, anomaly-based, behavior-based, and hybrid-based.

Due to rapid advancements in IDS and AI-based systems, firewalls have limited applications in CPS. However, Jiang et al. [74] proposed a method of enhancing cybersecurity by using paired firewalls between enterprise and manufacturing zones. Usage of Iptables for SCADA systems was suggested by Nivethan et al. [75] that inspects and filters SCADA protocol messages.

Honeypots are deceptive systems that work by providing something that seems to be desirable to the attacker [76]. In CPS, the deployment of honeypot to enhance protection against cyberattacks is a common practice. Irvene et al. [77] employed software hybrid interaction honeypot for robotic systems that was named HoneyBot. A honeypot system by Fraunholz et al. [78] based on Secure Shell (SSH) and telnet helps in capturing the data. The analysis of data captured during attack session further helps in classifying the attacker types.

3.7.3   CPS Security Solutions for Distinct CPS Layers

Zhang and Li [65] also suggested several approaches to enhance CPS security by using specific security measure at each CPS layer.

1. *Session layer security*: It is vital to contemplate security of sensor networks at this layer. This layer requires lightweight password algorithms and protocols due to its weak storage capacity. Node authentication and data integrity

are two important functions that must be performed at this layer in order to prevent node tampering and stealing.

2. *Network layer security*: Due to the involvement of heterogeneous networks at this layer, it is imperative to provide network layer identity authentication, network resource access control, confidentiality and integrity of data, routing security, and remote access security. Network layer security tasks include data transmission confidentiality and integrity, remote access security, and routing system security. Network layer must ensure point-to-point security, i.e., between various node along the path and end-to-end security, i.e., between source and destination. The point-to-point security is offered using mutual authentication between nodes, hop-by-hop encryption, and cross-network authentication, etc. The end-to-end security is provided using cryptographic algorithms, hierarchical architecture, and employing detection and defense services for DoS and DdoS attacks.

3. *Collaborative solution security*: Since this layer deals with data collection, analysis, and processing, it is important that the malicious information in the data source is identified and deleted, and the effective information is collected and kept on the basis of the security it requires. This layer requires several security measures as secure cloud computing, efficient data mining techniques, virus detection, and confident data source.

4. *Application control layer security*: This layer requires targeted security measure considering the type of application being used. Users' data privacy preservation and prohibition of unauthorized access is provided using access control, privacy protection mechanisms, security software, and varied authentication methods, including multifactor authentication (MFA).

3.8 CONCLUSION

CPS has potential technological impact on varied industries as well as organizations to develop smart cyber systems for the benefit of society, community, and individuals. However, if proper security policies and methods are not deployed in CPS, it can target physical devices, infrastructural networks, and organizational data as well. Such a security lapse not only hinders its deployment but also degrades the reliability, safety, and efficiency of CPS. Thus, it is important that these security lapses are properly identified, understood, and appropriately dealt with. In this chapter, various CPS security issues have been discussed. The CPS security threats have been categorized into cyber threats, physical threats, and cyber-physical threats. Further, the classifications of CPS vulnerabilities have been presented as cyber, physical, and cyber-physical threats. The numerous CPS attacks have been outlined under physical and cyberattacks. Finally, cryptographic and non-cryptographic CPS security solutions for distinct CPS layers have been highlighted.

REFERENCES

[1] Rajkumar R., Lee I., Sha L., Stankovic J. Proceedings of the 47th Design Automation Conference. IEE, Anaheim, CA; 2010. Cyber-physical systems: The next computing revolution, pp. 731–736. https://ieeexplore.ieee.org/document/5523280.

[2] Gries S., Hesenius M., Gruhn V. Proceedings of the 11th ACM International Conference on Distributed and Event-Based Systems. ACM; 2017. Cascading data corruption: About dependencies in cyber-physical systems: Poster, pp. 345–346.

[3] Greer C., Burns M., Wollman D., Griffor E. Cyber-physical systems and internet of things. NST Special Publication, no. 202, p. 52, 1900 [online]. https://doi.org/10.6028/NIST.SP.1900-202.

[4] Oks S.J., Jalowski M., Lechner M., et al. Cyber-physical systems in the context of industry 4.0: A review, categorization and outlook. Inf. Syst. Front. 2022. https://doi.org/10.1007/s10796-022-10252-x.

[5] Siddappaji B., Akhilesh K. Smart Technologies. Springer; 2020. Role of cyber security in drone technology. In: Akhilesh, K., Möller, D. (eds) Smart Technologies. Springer, Singapore. pp. 169–178.

[6] Yaacoub J.-P.A., Noura M., Noura H.N., Salman O., Yaacoub E., Couturier R., Chehab A. Securing internet of medical things systems: Limitations, issues and recommendations. Future Generation Computer System. 2020;105: pp. 581–606.

[7] Kim K.-D., Kumar P.R. Cyber-physical systems: A perspective at the centennial. Proceedings of the IEEE. 2012;100(Special Centennial Issue): pp. 1287–1308.

[8] Hahn A., Thomas R.K., Lozano I., Cardenas A. A multi-layered and kill-chain based security analysis framework for cyber-physical systems. International Journal Critical Infrastructure Protection, Elsevier. 2015;11: pp. 39–50.

[9] Wang E.K., Ye Y.M., Xu X., Yiu S., Hui L.C., Chow K.P. IEEE/ACM Int'l Conference on Green Computing and Communications & Int'l Conference on Cyber, Physical and Social Computing. 2010. Security issues and challenges for cyber physical system, pp. 733–738.

[10] Humayed A., Lin J., Li F., Luo B. Cyber-physical systems security—A survey. IEEE Internet of Things Journal. 2017 Dec;4(6): pp. 1802–1831. doi: 10.1109/JIOT.2017.2703172.

[11] Govindarasu M., Hann A., Sauer P. Cyber-Physical Systems Security for Smart Grid. PSERC Publication, New York, 2012.

[12] Venkatasubramanian K. Security Solutions for Cyber-Physical Systems [PhD Dissertation]. Tempe: Arizona State University, 2009.

[13] Alguliyev R., Imamverdiyev Y., Sukhostat L. Cyber-physical systems and their security issues. Comput. Ind. 2018;100: pp. 212–223. doi: 10.1016/j.compind.2018.04.017.

[14] Madden J., McMillin B., Sinha A. Workshop on 34th Annual IEEE Computer Software and Applications Conference. 2010. Environmental obfuscation of a cyber physical system—Vehicle example.

[15] Wang E.K., Ye Y., Xu X., Yiu S.M., Hui L.C.K., Chow K.P. 2010 IEEE/ACM Int'l Conference on Green Computing and Communications & Int'l Conference on Cyber, Physical and Social Computing. 2010. Security issues and challenges for cyber physical system, pp. 733–738. doi: 10.1109/GreenCom-CPSCom.2010.36.

[16] Yaacoub J.A., Salman O., Noura H.N., Kaaniche N., Chehab A., Malli M. Cyber-physical systems security: Limitations, issues and future trends. Microprocess

Microsystem. 2020 Sep;77: p. 103201. doi: 10.1016/j.micpro.2020.103201. Epub 2020 Jul 8. PMID: 32834204; PMCID: PMC7340599.

[17] Konstantinou C., Maniatakos M., Saqib F., Hu S., Plusquellic J., Jin Y. 2015 20th IEEE European Test Symposium (ETS). 2015. Cyber-physical systems: A security perspective, pp. 1–8. doi: 10.1109/ETS.2015.7138763.

[18] Orumwense E.F., Abo-Al-Ez, Khaled M. AIUE Proceedings of the 18th Industrial and Commercial Use of Energy Conference 2020. 2020 Nov 24. The role of cloud computing in energy cyber-physical systems. SSRN. https://ssrn.com/abstract=3740717 or http://dx.doi.org/10.2139/ssrn.3740717.

[19] Borse Y., Shaikh M.S. Cloud based cyber physical systems security issues: A survey. International Journal of Computer Applications. 2019;177(9): pp. 38–40.

[20] Charles P. Pfleeger and Shari Lawrence Pfleeger: Security in Computing (4th Edition). Prentice Hall PTR, Upper Saddle River, NJ, USA, 2006.

[21] Nicholson A., Webber S., Dyer S., Patel T., Janicke H. Scada security in the light of cyber-warfare. Computers & Security. 2012;31(4): pp. 418–436.

[22] US-CERT. Cyber Threat Source Descriptions. https://ics-cert.us-cert.gov/content/cyber-threat-source-descriptions, 2009.

[23] Setola R. Cyber Threats to SCADA Systems. http://panzieri.dia.uniroma3.it/MICIE/docs/Setola%20WS%20Micie%202011.pdf, 2011.

[24] Lee I., Sokolsky O., Chen S., Hatcliff J., Jee E., Kim B., King A., Mullen-Fortino M., Park S., Roederer A., Venkatasubramanian K. K. Challenges and research directions in medical cyber-physical systems. Proceedings of the IEEE. 2012;100(1): pp. 75–90. Article 6051465. https://doi.org/10.1109/JPROC.2011.2165270

[25] Halperin D., Heydt-Benjamin T.S., Fu K., Kohno T., Maisel W.H. Security and privacy for implantable medical devices. IEEE Perv. Comput. 2008;(1): pp. 30–39.

[26] Checkoway S., McCoy D., Kantor B., Anderson D., Shacham H., Savage S., Koscher K., Czeskis A., Roesner F., Kohno T. USENIX Security Symposium. San Francisco; 2011. Comprehensive experimental analyses of automotive attack surfaces, pp. 77–92.

[27] Rushanan M., Rubin A.D., Kune D.F., Swanson C.M. 2014 IEEE Symposium on Security and Privacy (SP). IEEE; 2014. Sok: Security and privacy in implantable medical devices and body area networks, pp. 524–539.

[28] Brooks R., Sander S., Deng J., Taiber J. Proceedings of the 4th Annual Workshop on Cyber Security and Information Intelligence Research: Developing Strategies to Meet the Cyber Security and Information Intelligence Challenges Ahead. ACM; 2008. Automotive system security: Challenges and state-of-the-art, p. 26.

[29] Checkoway S., McCoy D., Kantor B., Anderson D., Shacham H., Savage S., Koscher K., Czeskis A., Roesner F., Kohno T. USENIX Security Symposium. San Francisco; 2011. Comprehensive experimental analyses of automotive attack surfaces, pp. 77–92.

[30] Nash T. Backdoors and Holes in Network Perimeters. [Google Scholar Online]. http://ics-cert.us-cert.gov/controlsystems, 2005.

[31] Amin S., Litrico X., Sastry S., Bayen A.M. Cyber security of water SCADA systems-part I: Analysis and experimentation of stealthy deception attacks. IEEE Transaction Control System Technology. 2012;21(5): pp. 1963–1970.

[32] Zhu B., Joseph A., Sastry S. 2011 International Conference on Internet of Things and 4th International Conference on Cyber, Physical and Social Computing. IEEE; 2011. A taxonomy of cyber-attacks on SCADA systems, pp. 380–388.

[33] Sridharan V. Cyber Security in Power Systems [Ph.D. thesis]. Georgia Institute of Technology, 2012. https://repository.gatech.edu/entities/publication/9d559d85-5d61-4714-9166-fa4218e7b3b5

[34] Amin S., Schwartz G.A., Hussain A. In quest of benchmarking security risks to cyber-physical systems. IEEE Network. 2013;27(1): pp. 19–24.

[35] Iasiello E. 2013 5th International Conference on Cyber Conflict (CYCON 2013). IEEE; 2013. Cyber attack: A dull tool to shape foreign policy, pp. 1–18.

[36] Zhu B., Joseph A., Sastry S. 2011 International Conference on Internet of Things and 4th International Conference on Cyber, Physical and Social Computing. IEEE; 2011. A taxonomy of cyber attacks on SCADA systems, pp. 380–388.

[37] Simmonds A., Sandilands P., Van Ekert L. Asian Applied Computing Conference. Springer; 2004. An ontology for network security attacks, pp. 317–323.

[38] Francia G., III, Thornton D., Brookshire T. Proc. 16th Colloquium Inf. Syst. Security Educ. 2012. Cyberattacks on SCADA systems, pp. 9–14.

[39] D'Amico A., Verderosa C., Horn C., Imhof T. Technologies for Homeland Security (HST), 2011 IEEE International Conference on. IEEE; 2011. Integrating physical and cyber security resources to detect wireless threats to critical infrastructure, pp. 494–500.

[40] MacDonald D., Clements S.L., Patrick S.W., Perkins C., Muller G., Lancaster M.J., Hutton W. Innovative Smart Grid Technologies (ISGT), 2013 IEEE PES. IEEE; 2013. Cyber/physical security vulnerability assessment integration, pp. 1–6.

[41] Mo Y., Kim T.H.-J., Brancik K., Dickinson D., Lee H., Perrig A., Sinopoli B. Cyber—Physical security of a smart grid infrastructure. Proceedings IEEE. 2012;100(1): pp. 195–209.

[42] Radcliffe J. Black Hat Conference Presentation Slides. Vol. 2011. 2011. Hacking medical devices for fun and insulin: Breaking the human SCADA system.

[43] Moteff, J. Library of Congress Washington DC Congressional Research Service. 2005 Feb. Risk management and critical infrastructure protection: Assessing, integrating, and managing threats, vulnerabilities and consequences.

[44] Al-Mhiqani M.N., Ahmad R., Yassin W., Hassan A., Abidin Z.Z., Ali N.S., Abdulkareem K.H. Cyber-security incidents: A review cases in cyber-physical systems. International Journal of Advanced Computer Science and Applications. 2018;9(1): pp. 499–508.

[45] Krebs B. Cyber incident blamed for nuclear power plant shutdown. Washington Post. 2008 Jun;5.

[46] Albright D., Brannan P., Walrond C. Stuxnet malware and natanz: Update of isis December 22, 2010 report. Institute for Science and International Security. 2011;15: pp. 739883–739893.

[47] Fillatre L., Nikiforov I., Willett P. Security of SCADA systems against cyber—Physical attacks. IEEE Aerospace Electronic System Magazine. 2017;32(5): pp. 28–45.

[48] Credeur M.J. Fbi Probes Georgia Water Plant Break-In on Terror Concern, 2013. https://www.bloomberg.com/news/articles/2013-04-30/fbi-probes-georgia-water-plant-break-in-on-terror-concern

[49] Topping C., Dwyer A., Michalec O., Craggs B., Rashid A. Beware suppliers bearing gifts!: Analysing coverage of supply chain cyber security in critical national infrastructure sectorial and cross-sectorial frameworks. Computers & Security. 2021; 108: p. 102324.

[50] Al-Shurman M., Yoo S.-M., Park S. Proceedings of the 42nd Annual Southeast Regional Conference. 2004. Black hole attack in mobile ad hoc networks, pp. 96–97.

[51] Solankar P., Pingale S., Parihar R. Denial of service attack and classification techniques for attack detection. International Journal of Computer Science Information Technology. 2015;6(2): pp. 1096–1099.

[52] Yihunie F., Abdelfattah E., Odeh A. 2018 IEEE Long Island Systems, Applications and Technology Conference (LISAT). IEEE; 2018. Analysis of ping of death DoS and DdoS attacks, pp. 1–4.

[53] Lemon J. BSDCon. Vol. 2002. 2002. Resisting SYN flood DoS attacks with a SYN cache, pp. 89–97.

[54] Owens J., Matthews J. USENIX Workshop on Large-Scale Exploits and Emergent Threats (LEET). 2008. A study of passwords and methods used in brute-force SSH attacks.

[55] Kelley P.G., Komanduri S., Mazurek M.L., Shay R., Vidas T., Bauer L., Christin N., Cranor L.F., Lopez J. 2012 IEEE Symposium on Security and Privacy. IEEE; 2012. Guess again (and again and again): Measuring password strength by simulating password-cracking algorithms, pp. 523–537.

[56] Papantonakis P., Pnevmatikatos D., Papaefstathiou I., Manifavas C. 2013 23rd International Conference on Field programmable Logic and Applications. IEEE; 2013. Fast, FPGA-based rainbow table creation for attacking encrypted mobile communications, pp. 1–6.

[57] Narayanan A., Shmatikov V. Proceedings of the 12th ACM Conference on Computer and Communications Security. ACM; 2005. Fast dictionary attacks on passwords using time-space tradeoff, pp. 364–372.

[58] Gudivada V.N., Ramaswamy S., Srinivasan S. Transportation Cyber-Physical Systems. Elsevier; 2018. Data management issues in cyber-physical systems, pp. 173–200.

[59] Al Shaer D., Al Musaimi O., Beatriz G., Albericio F. Hydroxamate siderophores: Natural occurrence, chemical synthesis, iron binding affinity and use as Trojan horses against pathogens. European Journal of Medicinal Chemistry. 2020;208: p. 112791.

[60] Aziz A.A., Amtul Z. Developing Trojan horses to induce, diagnose and suppress Alzheimer's pathology. Pharmacological Research. 2019;149: p. 104471.

[61] Kharlamova N., Hashemi S., Træholt C. Data-driven approaches for cyber defense of battery energy storage systems. Energy and AI. 2021;5: p. 100095.

[62] Li J., Sun C., Su Q. Analysis of cascading failures of power cyber-physical systems considering false data injection attacks. Global Energy Interconnection. 2021;4(2): pp. 204–213.

[63] Sullivan J.E., Kamensky D. How cyber-attacks in Ukraine show the vulnerability of the U.S. power grid. The Electricity Journal. 2017;30(3): pp. 30–35.

[64] Desai D., Haq T. Malware Research Team Technical Paper. 2012. Blackhole exploit kit: Rise & evolution.

[65] Li B., Zhang L. Security analysis of cyber-physical system. AIP Conference Proceedings. May 2017;1839.

[66] Association A.G. Technical Report. AGA Report; 2005. Cryptographic protection of SCADA communications part 1: Background, policies and test plan.

[67] Zhang M., Raghunathan A., Jha N.K. Trustworthiness of medical devices and body area networks. Proceedings of the IEEE. 2014;102(8): pp. 1174–1188.

[68] Zhou T., Shen J., Li X., Wang C., Tan H. Logarithmic encryption scheme for cyber—Physical systems employing fibonacci Q-matrix. Future Generation Computer System. 2018: pp. 1307–1313.

[69] Vegh L., Miclea L. 2016 International Conference on Communications (COMM). IEEE; 2016. Secure and efficient communication in cyber-physical systems through cryptography and complex event processing, pp. 273–276.

[70] Zhao Y., Li Y., Mu Q., Yang B., Yu Y. Secure pub-sub: Blockchain-based fair payment with reputation for reliable cyber physical systems. Special Section on Research Challenges and Opportunities in Security and Privacy of Blockchain Technologies, IEEE Access. 2018;6: pp. 12295–12303.

[71] Halperin D., Heydt-Benjamin T.S., Ransford B., Clark S.S., Defend B., Morgan W., Fu K., Kohno T., Maisel W.H. Security and Privacy, 2008. SP 2008. IEEE Symposium on. IEEE; 2008. Pacemakers and implantable cardiac defibrillators: Software radio attacks and zero-power defenses, pp. 129–142.

[72] Rushanan M., Rubin A.D., Kune D.F., Swanson C.M. 2014 IEEE Symposium on Security and Privacy (SP). IEEE; 2014. Sok: Security and privacy in implantable medical devices and body area networks, pp. 524–539.

[73] Zarpelão B.B., Miani R.S., Kawakani C.T., de Alvarenga S.C. A survey of intrusion detection in internet of things. Journal of Network and Computer Applications. 2017;84: pp. 25–37.

[74] Jiang N., Lin H., Yin Z., Xi C. 2017 IEEE International Conference on Information and Automation (ICIA). IEEE; 2017. Research of paired industrial firewalls in defense-in-depth architecture of integrated manufacturing or production system, pp. 523–526.

[75] Nivethan J., Papa M. On the use of open-source firewalls in ICS/SCADA systems. Information Security Journal: A Global Perspective. 2016;25(1–3): pp. 83–93.

[76] Cohen F. The use of deception techniques: Honeypots and decoys. Handbook of Information Security. 2006;3(1): pp. 646–655.

[77] Irvene C., Formby D., Litchfield S., Beyah R. Honeybot: A honeypot for robotic systems. Proceedings of the IEEE. 2017;106(1): pp. 61–70.

[78] Fraunholz D., Krohmer D., Anton S.D., Schotten H.D. 2017 International Conference on Cyber Security and Protection of Digital Services (Cyber Security). IEEE; 2017. Investigation of cyber crime conducted by abusing weak or default passwords with a medium interaction honeypot, pp. 1–7.

Chapter 4

Programmability and Virtualization in Next-generation Networks for Cybersecurity of Cyber-physical Systems and Internet of Medical Things

Hubert Szczepaniuk

4.1 INTRODUCTION

Progressive and dynamic digitization has led to the development of the smart healthcare concept. From a technical point of view, smart healthcare involves using various technologies and devices of the Internet of Medical Things (IoMT) integrated with cyber-physical systems (CPSs) to support medical processes. Thanks to this, medical processes can be implemented more effectively, e.g., by automating and reducing the time of medical activities, real-time remote supervision of the patient by monitoring health parameters, intelligent medical data analysis, and ensuring constant access to the results of diagnostic tests and other medical data for doctors, medical staff, and patients. Implementing smart healthcare systems (SHSs) may translate into improving the quality of medical services and contribute to health promotion through prophylaxis, prevention, early detection of disease entities, and rapid development of adequate treatment strategies.

Nowadays, cybersecurity is one of the fundamental research problems of computer science. Numerous cybersecurity studies are available in the scientific literature (see, e.g., [1–5]). Therefore, when considering the issues of IoMT architecture, one should also consider many cybersecurity threats related to the digitization of medical processes. First of all, patients' health data should be subject to special protection due to their exceptional importance and privacy. For this reason, the issue of cybersecurity in the area of the Internet of Medical Things is of fundamental importance for the successful implementation of the smart healthcare concept.

Practical implementations of IoT ecosystems, including IoMT, broadly use wireless connectivity. The specific requirements of IoT and IoMT encourage the development of modern standards of wireless transmission media that will be able to safely carry out data transfer, taking into account the limited computing power of end devices and the pro-ecological focus on energy saving. Currently,

DOI: 10.1201/9781003474111-4

work is underway in the world on developing and implementing next-generation networks, which offer, among other things, higher transmission speed, lower data link latency, more stable connection, and reduced energy consumption per gigabyte of data transferred. Considering the above-mentioned features, next-generation networks can be used as the primary transmission medium for SHSs. The essential requirement for implementing a new-generation network in the smart healthcare environment is a multi-criteria analysis of cybersecurity conditions.

The chapter structure includes an introduction, five substantive sections, conclusion, and a reference list. The introduction defines the background of the research and explains the significance of the issues under consideration. The next point concerns related works in which selected research results available in the literature were analyzed. In particular, the research results discussed concerned the cybersecurity of IoMT, CPS, and next-generation networks. The next section deals with the research methodology used in this chapter. Among other things, the research subject, goals, and applied research methods were defined. The following section examines the architecture of SHSs in the context of the IoMT and Medical Cyber-physical Systems (MCPSs). Layer models were analyzed, and universal components were distinguished. The following section deals with analyzing the technical architecture of generation networks. In particular, the concepts of software-defined networking and virtualization of network functions were discussed. The next section presents the framework for implementing IoMT and MCPSs in the NG-RAN environment, taking into account cybersecurity requirements. The chapter ends with conclusion and a reference list.

4.2 RELATED WORKS

Scientific studies on various aspects of smart healthcare, IoMT, CPSs, and next-generation networks are available in the literature on the subject. For the purposes of this chapter, selected research results related to the above categories will be analyzed in terms of cybersecurity issues.

The literature review was organized according to the following categories:

- Cybersecurity conditions for SHSs, IoMT, and MCPSs
- Cybersecurity conditions for next-generation networks
- Research on SHSs cybersecurity in next-generation networks.

Algarni [6] analyzed the state of research on the security and privacy of smart healthcare systems. Based on the analysis carried out in the cited article, it was indicated that attacks on SHS can be divided into four main categories: attacks on healthcare devices, attacks on communication between devices, attacks on service providers and equipment manufacturers, and attacks on patients [6]. The presented division of attacks shows a broad spectrum of threats to SHS. It is also crucial that SHS can be implemented using devices derived from different vendors, which can work according to different communication protocols and collect heterogeneous data in various formats. It is therefore legitimate to analyze the related work on the state of cybersecurity research for both IoMT and CPSs.

Alsubaei et al. [7] published studies on developing an IoMT security assessment framework based on ontological scenarios. The platform presented in the above-mentioned article enables the assessment of the security level of IoMT systems and identifies potential problems together with a proposal of remedial measures [7]. Within the framework developed, three types of IoMT system vulnerabilities were adopted, i.e., user, system, and hardware [7]. The authors also distinguished the main threats to medical data, which include interception, inaccessibility, modification, fabrication, and replication [7]. The presented platform is an essential contribution to the systematization and formalization of the security assessment of IoMT systems.

Sun et al. [8] published IoMT security and privacy review. In the publication cited, the authors defined the following key requirements for the security and privacy of IoMT systems: data integrity, data usability, data audit, and patient information privacy [8]. As regards the existing solutions used to ensure security and privacy, the following were indicated in particular: data encryption, access control techniques, trusted third-party auditing, encrypted data search mechanisms, and data animation [8]. The article also indicates future challenges for the security and privacy of IoMT, including unsecured wireless computer networks, lightweight protocols for devices, and problems related to data sharing [8]. The discussed research is an essential contribution to the theory of cybersecurity of IT systems.

The technical architecture of SHSs can also include CPSs. Therefore, it is justified to analyze selected scientific studies in the field of CPS security. Alguliyev et al. [9] addressed the issues of CPSs and their security. In the cited publication, the existing research on CPS security was analyzed in relation to the key attributes of information security, and a tree of attacks on CSP systems was presented [9]. The authors distinguished the following tree branches that represent the various types of attacks on CPSs: attacks on sensor devices, attacks on actuators, attacks on computing components, attacks on communication, and feedback attacks [9]. The main research areas covered by the literature analyzed in the article were derived from the conducted analysis: the consequence of cyberattacks, CPS attack modeling, attack detection, and development of security architecture [9]. This chapter also identifies key research challenges for CPS cybersecurity, including developing methods for authenticating CPS components and methods to ensure the security of personal data, developing CPS security architecture and protocols, and minimizing security vulnerabilities [9]. The cited studies illustrate the complexity and multidimensionality of the CPS cybersecurity issues.

Ashibani and Mahmoud [10] also published a detailed review and analysis of CPS security issues. The chapter refers to the three-tier CPS architecture covering the application, transport, and perception layers [10]. The authors rightly pointed out that implementing IT security measures in CPSs may affect the response and lag of the physical parts of the system that may require real-time response [10]. The chapter also identifies a number of open security challenges for CPSs. One of the important issues in this respect is the heterogeneity of data from different devices, which can lead to problems with compliance with the data format and communication protocols [10]. The cited research also highlights important issues related to user privacy. The authors point out that the fundamental mechanisms in this regard are contextual privacy protection, encryption schemes, and contextual mutual authentication protocols [10].

The literature recognizes that developing next-generation networks, in particular NG-RAN networks, can find wide application in IoMT systems. Tarikere et al. [11] rightly note that IoMT devices using next-generation mobile transmission will generate personal health data at an unprecedented level. Therefore, it is important to recognize the cybersecurity issues related to developing next-generation networks. In the last stage of the literature review, selected research results related to the key areas of cybersecurity of next-generation mobile networks were analyzed. Khan et al. [12] researched the issues related to, among other things, building a security model in 5G networks, network software security, and the physical layer, with particular emphasis on authentication, access control, and encryption. The results of the cited research identified potential security threats to technologies related to 5G networks, in particular in the areas of Software-Defined Networking (SDN), Network Function Virtualization (NFV), cloud computing, Multi-Access Edge Computing, and Network Slicing [12]. The set of potential threats and attack vectors for next-generation mobile networks is broad and must be considered when designing IoMT systems. For example, selected threats of 5G mobile networks in various functional areas include DoS/DdoS cyberattacks, Message Insertion Attack, TLS/SSL Attacks, SDN Scanner, Mobile Malware Attacks, Botnet, Microcell Attacks, VM escape attack, VNF Manipulation Attacks [12]. The cited research provides an overview of threats to next-generation mobile networks and illustrates the consequences of different threats and attacks.

Mamolar et al. [13] note that 5G cellular networks require developing new methods for detecting and mitigating DdoS cyberattacks. The authors of the cited studies developed mechanisms to protect the 5G infrastructure against DdoS attacks without human intervention, based, among other things, on the extension of the current IDS sensors to ensure the analysis of flows in 5G networks [13]. The results of the research indicate that the current methods of protecting computer networks will not always be able to ensure a sufficient level of security in the next-generation network environment. This is especially important in the context of emerging new network concepts such as Network Function Virtualization, Software-Defined Networking, and self-organizing networks.

Research is also available on the cybersecurity of IoMT systems embedded in next-generation mobile networks. In particular, Tarikere et al. [11] indicate many key security areas in the implementation of IoMT systems in the 5G network environment, which include primarily the following:

- IoMT device supply chain vulnerabilities that may be degraded, which may lead to the use of faulty, damaged, or counterfeit hardware and devices.
- Threats to network security, taking into account the fact that 5G networks can increase the area of attack.
- Privacy threats are also related to legal regulations on cybersecurity, sensitive data, and data owners' rights.

Chen et al. [14] proposed a safety awareness and protection system design for smart healthcare based on the Zero-Trust architecture. The above-mentioned article highlights the main safety requirements of smart healthcare resulting from the specificity of next-generation mobile networks, in particular: the possibility of signaling storms and DdoS attacks; difficulties in implementing network traffic protection mechanisms due to high network capacity; ineffectiveness of a centralized monitoring system when using device-to-device and edge cloud protocols [14]. According to the presented analysis of selected research results, the issue of SHS cybersecurity using IoMT, CPSs, and next-generation networks is a complex and interdisciplinary scientific issue and should be considered systemically.

4.3 RESEARCH METHODOLOGY

The contribution of this chapter to the theory and practice of computer science is as follows:

- Defining cybersecurity conditions for next-generation networks in the context of medical data security attributes
- Defining the concept of architecture for the implementation of virtualization and programmability mechanisms in new-generation networks for SHSs
- Vulnerability analysis and proposed actions to prevent threats in the presented architecture.

The subject of the research are SHSs based on IoMT and CPS architecture, taking into account cybersecurity in next-generation networks. The main goal of the research is to develop a framework for SHS cybersecurity based on virtualization protocols and programmability mechanisms in next-generation networks.

The chapter defines the following specific research objectives:

- Analysis of the architecture of IoMT and MCPSs in a layered approach
- Analysis of the technical architecture of next-generation networks in terms of the NFV and SDN concepts

- Defining the framework for the implementation of IoMT and MCPSs based on the NFV and SDN concepts
- Analysis of the cybersecurity conditions of the proposed framework in terms of confidentiality, availability, and integrity of medical data.

The chapter deals with research on modeling information systems for the medical industry. In theoretical research, the method of literature analysis and synthesis as well as the method of technical architecture analysis of information systems were used. In the model part, the method of designing information systems was used, referring to the principles defined by software engineering.

4.4 ARCHITECTURE OF SMART HEALTHCARE SYSTEMS

Conceptually, SHSs are based on using the IoT and CPSs to support medical processes. The growing popularity of IoT solutions in the medical industry has led to the emergence of a new term in the literature, the Internet of Medical Things. In technical terms, IoT systems (including IoMT) are often considered in the scientific literature in a layered perspective (see, e.g., [15–17]). The layered models of the IoT architecture (including IoMT) available in the literature differ in assumptions and the number of layers. In particular, three-layer, four-layer, and five-layer models can be distinguished. Mohamad Noor and Hassan [18] distinguished a three-tier model of IoT architecture to analyze security conditions. The cited research distinguished the application, network, and perception layers [18]. The adopted model is justified and corresponds to the logic of the actual functioning of IoT ecosystems. The application layer is responsible for implementing business logic and IoT application services in the cited studies. The network layer carries out data transmission using various transmission media. The perception layer is responsible for handling IoT end devices [18]. Considering architecture in the approach presented above allows for analyzing cybersecurity aspects in a systemic and holistic approach. In turn, Xu et al. [19] proposed a four-layer architecture model of an IoT-based system in big data processing and visualization in the medical area. The above article distinguishes the application, network, analysis, and sensing layers. The application layer provides an access interface for medical personnel via personal computers and mobile devices in the cited studies. The network layer is responsible for the implementation of data transmission. The analysis layer includes data processing and visualization algorithms to implement medical processes. In turn, the lowest sensing layer is responsible for the registration of patient data obtained, e.g., as a result of computed tomography and magnetic resonance imaging [19]. The above architecture emphasizes the layer responsible for processing and analyzing data obtained from diagnostic devices. Distinguishing the analysis layer in IoMT ecosystems is of key importance due to the added value of the effective extraction of knowledge from big data sets generated by medical end devices. Liu et al. [20] presented a five-layer IoMT model designed to integrate with iPv6 technology. The article distinguishes the application, integration, network, communication, auxiliary, and detection layers [20]. The layer model has been validly developed, inter alia, to analyze the IoMT architecture based on the iPv6 protocol.

By synthesizing the above analysis of layered models available in the literature, it is possible to distinguish universal components of the IoMT architecture:

- Medical equipment responsible for recording patients' health parameters.
- Transmission media, network devices, protocols, and communication standards: in practice, it is possible to use any network technologies, including Ethernet networks, wireless transmission technologies (NFC, Z-Wave, Zigbee), Low-Power Wide Area Networks (LoRaWAN, NB-IoT, LTE-M), and GSM mobile transmission (3G, 4G, 5G).
- Medical data processing and storage services.
- Access interface for medical process stakeholders, including patients, doctors, medical personnel, insurance companies, and other IoMT systems.

CPSs are also defined and analyzed in many dimensions in the literature. Ashibani and Mahmoud [10] defined CPSs in general terms as networked systems of cyber and physical components that interact in a feedback loop with possible human interactions. Alguliyev et al. [9] emphasize the definitions of CPSs from the point of view of automation technology as well as computer science. Many architectural models of the CPS have been proposed in the literature. The general architecture model of CPSs can be presented in a layered approach. Ashibani and Mahmoud [10] described the three-tier architecture of CPSs, which includes the application, transmission, and perception layers. It can be seen that, in general terms, the layered architecture of IoT and CPS is similar. However, the literature indicates that CPSs mainly refer to real-time systems (see, e.g., [10,21]). As in the case of IoT systems, the interest in the world of science in CPSs in the medical field led to the concept of MCPSs (see, e.g., [22,23]), which also includes the cyber and physical dimensions.

Regardless of the approach in CPSs in the medical industry, the following universal components can be distinguished:

- Real-time operation-oriented medical devices and apparatus
- Transmission media
- Protocols
- Control software and processing services.

Both IoT and CPSs are dynamically developing in the smart healthcare environment. The development of these systems leads to the emergence of a new logic of medical processes, new types of devices, new communication protocols, but also new requirements related to cybersecurity. An important issue in the field of security is the implementation of virtualization protocols in next-generation mobile networks.

4.5   TECHNICAL ARCHITECTURE OF NEXT-GENERATION NETWORKS IN THE CONTEXT OF VIRTUALIZATION PROTOCOLS AND PROGRAMMABILITY MECHANISMS

For the assumed research purposes, it is necessary to perform a technical analysis of the new Next-Generation Radio Access Network (NG-RAN) concept in terms of software virtualization protocols and network service programmability mechanisms. Virtualization is increasingly being used when building the technology stack of information systems architecture. The primary assumption of virtualization is the abstract separation of the hardware resource layer (processor, memory and mass memory, input–output operations, including a computer network) and making these resources available to sovereign environments, i.e., virtual machines (VM). The concept of virtualization allows for more effective use of hardware resources, including computing power, and easier management of IT infrastructure.

The next-generation network architecture supports virtualization in terms of implementing the functionality of individual modules by the software layer. The main assumptions include enabling, among others, the implementation of improved mobile broadband communication (eMBB), mass communication between machines (eMTC), and low-latency communication [24].

NG-RAN architecture introduced a number of new technical components (see, e.g., [25]). In a general perspective, the architecture may include a collection of base stations (gNBs) or ng-eNB stations that are connected to each other and to the 5G core network via respective NG and Xn interfaces [26]. The gNB base stations contain three key components: a central unit (CU), a distributed unit (DU), and a radio unit (RU) [27]. The listed components have the following functionalities:

- *gNB centralized unit*: It represents a logical node supporting RRC, SDAP, and PDCP protocols (for gNB) or RRC and PDCP (for en-gNB) and controls the operation of one or more gNB-DU [28].
- *gNB distributed unit*: It represents a logical node containing the RLC, MAC, and PHY layers of the gNB or en-gNB network, and its operation is partially controlled by gNB-CU [28].
- *Radio unit (RU)*: It represents a radio hardware unit.

The interface between gNB-CU and gNB-DU is called F1 [26,28]. One of the key aspects of next-generation network design is virtualization services for RAN functionality. The concept of virtualization ensures more efficient use of mobile network resources, as many virtual services can be run on the same network hardware, fulfilling different functional requirements. In reference to the above-described approach in the area of computer networks, the concepts of Network Functions Virtualization (NFV) and Software-Defined Networking (SDF) were created (see, e.g., [29–33]).

The above concepts respond to the growing demands of information-oriented computer networks. In general, the SDN assumes the improvement of network management by separating the control plane from the data plane [34]. The network programmability orientation means it is possible to control and use network resources more efficiently through the software. Basu et al. [31] define the following layered structure of the SDN:

- *Application layer*: It fulfills the requirements of business applications.
- *Control layer*: It performs, among other things, Network Operating System (NOS) functions and communicates with the application layer via Application Programming Interface (API).
- *Transfer (data) layer*: It is responsible for delivering data from source to destination.

The presented SDN layered model will enable the implementation of various software functional requirements in a network environment. It is also possible to better implement cybersecurity requirements at the application level. The dissemination of the SDN concept is also carried out by developing dedicated high-level programming languages supporting network management and service implementation in network environments (see, e.g., [34]).

In turn, the NFV technology related to SDN introduces many new network functions which, through server virtualization, ensure flexible network infrastructure management [34]. In particular, NFV enables the virtualization of various network services and functions, including, e.g., DNS, NAT, and firewalls [31]. By synthesizing the literature, the key NFV components can be distinguished [35,36]:

- *Virtualized Network Functions (VNFs)*: It runs on one or more virtual machines and provide network services with defined interfaces.
- *NFV Infrastructure (NFVI)*: It is the hardware and software environment providing a virtual execution layer allowing for the implementation and launch of Virtualized Network Functions.
- *NFV Management and Orchestration (MANO)*: It controls and manages NFVs and NFVI resources, in particular responsible for resource allocation, function virtualization, and authorization of NFVI resource requests.

It can be expected that future 5G projects will be implemented based on the SDN/NFV architecture (see, e.g., [37]). The SDN/NFV architecture principles allow the opportunity to implement advanced cybersecurity mechanisms necessary to ensure the appropriate level of security for medical data and processes in IoMT systems.

It is also worth recalling the limitations of next-generation networks. In particular, it is necessary to take into account the difficulties with the penetration of waves through some building materials and the need to compact the transmitting and to receive installations in the field (see, e.g., [38,39]). These limits can create potential problems in IoMT systems that operate in a similar regime to real-time systems. In such a case, the difficulties and delays associated with limiting the penetration of waves may be disqualifying.

4.6 IOMT AND MCPS FRAMEWORK MODEL USING NG-RAN

Based on the conducted analyses, it is possible to develop a framework for implementing IoMT and MCPSs using next-generation networks, considering cybersecurity requirements. In the first step, the model's assumptions were defined in the context of the multidimensional security of medical data. Next, the concept of a layered model of IoMT and MCPSs embedded in the NG-RAN network based on service virtualization and hardware abstraction of virtual machines was presented. In the last step, the cybersecurity conditions of the presented model were defined with regard to ensuring the confidentiality, availability, and integrity of medical data.

4.6.1 Model Assumptions

During the implementation of medical processes, digital data containing patients' health parameters are generated. In the available research results, digitized patient data collected, processed, and sent in IoMT systems is called Electronic Medical Records (EMR) (see, e.g., [40,41]). In particular, EMRs may include a variety of data sets generated from a variety of clinical and laboratory studies, measurements made by diagnostic devices, treatment histories, strategies, etc. (see, e.g., [42]). The unique nature of the above-mentioned medical data requires specific protection methods.

The scientific literature defines three main attributes of information security: confidentiality, availability, and integrity (see, e.g., [43,44]). With reference to the adopted research goals and based on the definitions available in the literature, in this chapter, confidentiality is understood as ensuring access to EHRs only for authorized stakeholders of medical processes. Availability is understood as ensuring that all SHS services and data contained in EHRs are available to authorized stakeholders at a defined and required time. Integrity is understood as the certainty that all SHS elements function properly and that the data has not been an unauthorized modification.

4.6.2 The Layered Model

The above analysis shows that it is possible to consider the IoMT architecture in multidimensional and layered models, depending on the adopted research objective. In this chapter, research goals focus on developing cybersecurity mechanisms in IoMT ecosystems using next-generation networking technology. Figure 4.1 shows the generic layered model framework for IoMT and MCPS in next-generation networks.

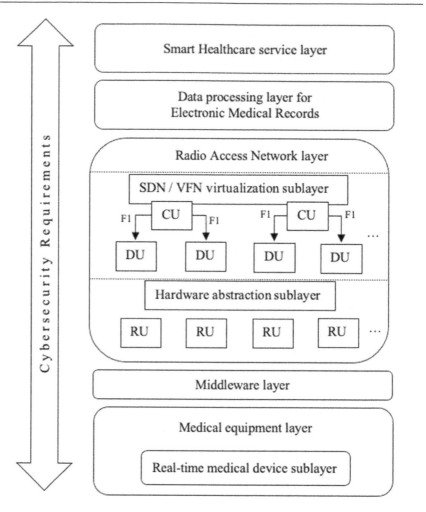

Figure 4.1 Generic layered model framework for IoMT and MCPS in next-generation networks.
Source: Own work.

In the model shown in Figure 4.1, individual layers are used as follows:

- *Smart healthcare service layer:* It ensures the implementation of the functional logic of medical processes. The service layer is also responsible for the access interface for all participants and stakeholders in medical processes: in particular for patients, doctors, medical personnel, insurance companies, and other IoMT systems. The layer supports SHS interoperability through data exchange and sharing.

- *Data processing layer:* It ensures medical data must be securely stored and efficiently processed to support ongoing medical processes. The analysis of medical data with adequate tools can significantly contribute to the improvement of medical processes, particularly in the field of faster diagnosis of disease entities, selection of effective treatment strategies, and faster response to various threats. The diverse structure and volume of data processed in IoMT systems often mean the need to use advanced data analysis methods in big data conditions.
- *Radio Access Network layer:* It carries out data transmissions and refers to the NG-RAN network protocol stack and is implemented in accordance with the principles of the SDN/VFN architecture. The model's assumption is based on virtualization that allows the separation of dedicated NFVs responsible for implementing programmable network services as part of smart healthcare systems. The layer has two sublayers:

  - *SDN/VFN virtualization sublayer:* It is responsible for the implementation of the centralized unit (CU) and distributed unit (DU) functions on the virtual machines (VM) provided by the hardware abstraction sublayer.
  - *Hardware abstraction sublayer:* It provides a virtualization interface based on the abstraction of the physical hardware and makes resources available for individual virtual machines. This layer also includes Radio Hardware Units (RU).

- *Middleware layer:* It provides an interface between medical devices and the Radio Access Network layer. Medical devices installed within internal ecosystems can use various transmission media and communication protocols. It is necessary to implement intermediary interfaces for next-generation networks. The layer is also responsible for implementing device authentication mechanisms in IoMT and MCPS.
- *Medical equipment layer:* It includes all kinds of medical equipment necessary for implementing medical processes, in particular: hospital devices, clinical grade wearables, and remote patient monitoring devices. At the level of this layer, logging of diagnostic data and, in some cases, the implementation of medical procedures by connected devices takes place. There is one sublayer in the medical equipment layer:

  - *Real-time medical device sublayer:* This layer is responsible for implementing devices included in MCPSs with real-time requirements.

- *Vertical layer of cybersecurity requirements*: It ensures the implementation and enforcement of cybersecurity procedures at the organizational and technical level regarding confidentiality, availability, and data integrity. In accordance with the software engineering guidelines, cybersecurity requirements should be defined at the IoMT design stage in the context of the functional and non-functional requirements of the system.

The model presented in Figure 4.1 contains the general framework of the layered architecture of IoMT systems design using the concept of virtualization, referring to the SDN/NFV principles. Further research is required at the level of the distinguished model layers in implementing cybersecurity methods, both on the organizational and technical levels.

4.6.3   Cybersecurity Conditions

In computer science, cybersecurity often refers to the fundamental attributes of information security, i.e., confidentiality, availability, and integrity (see, e.g., [45,46]). For the presented IoMT- and MCPS-layered model embedded in a new-generation network environment, cybersecurity requirements were defined in terms of medical data security attributes. Detailed cybersecurity requirements for the presented model are presented in Table 4.1.

The cybersecurity requirements for the presented layered model indicated in Table 4.1 constitute only a part of the research area that requires further studies and should be taken into account at an early stage of designing IoMT systems.

Table 4.1 Cybersecurity Requirements for the Presented Model

Cybersecurity Attributes	Cybersecurity Determinants for the Proposed Smart Health Systems Framework
Confidentiality of medical data	1. Critical vulnerabilities to attacks of obtaining unauthorized access to SHS and EHR can occur in the service layer as it provides an access interface for users 2. The service access interface should include strong user authentication security at the stage of defining functional requirements 3. Login security can be based on two-factor and biometric authentication 4. An important issue is raising users' awareness of cyber threats, as a significant proportion of attacks are based on social engineering 5. The Radio Access Network layer may be a critical area of attack vectors against SHSs 6. In order to support data confidentiality, it is possible to use strong transmission encryption algorithms and support for the encryption of IMSI (International Mobile Subscriber Identity) numbers by mobile end devices 7. Implementing mechanisms to counteract attacks based on network traffic tracking based on GUTI (Globally Unique Temporary Identifier) is of key importance 8. In the medical equipment layer, scenarios of attacks on the confidentiality attribute are also possible 9. It is possible to implement the mechanisms of restrictive authentication of end devices based on the EAP (Extensible Authentication Protocol) protocol

Cybersecurity Attributes	Cybersecurity Determinants for the Proposed Smart Health Systems Framework
Availability of medical data	1. Typical attack vectors on the availability attribute are based primarily on DDoS attacks 2. In terms of DdoS attacks prevention in the service layer, it is possible to use mechanisms of active routing management, flow control, and analysis of trends in network traffic 3. IDS/IPS class intrusion and anomaly detection systems extended with components supporting the next-generation network architecture may be of key importance 4. Cloud solutions are also worth considering, as they significantly hinder the implementation of DdoS attacks due to the transfer of data storage and analysis to external highly accessible websites 5. At the Radio Access Layer, the virtualization of security functions can support protection against DdoS attacks
Integrity of medical data	1. Attack on the integrity attribute may lead to inconsistency of entries in Electronic Medical Records with ongoing medical processes 2. The key methods of ensuring the integrity of information on all layers of the model will be primarily the verification of the correctness of the input data 3. In particular, cryptographic hash functions and MAC codes may be used to support the integrity of medical data 4. In order to support data integrity, it is also crucial to prevent data redundancy, planned and cyclical audits of IoMT, and MCPSs

Source: Own work.

4.7 CONCLUSION

Developing next-generation networks is still an open research challenge in various areas of computer science. Scenarios for the use of IoMT and MCPSs in the medical sector are evolving along with the development of information technology.

This chapter provides a framework for virtualization and programmability in next-generation networks for SHSs. The presented model was developed to support the cybersecurity requirements of medical data. The main assumptions of the developed model are based on a layered approach, virtualization, and network services' programmability to implement medical processes in IoMT and MCPSs. The presented solution has been analyzed regarding cybersecurity determinants for confidentiality, availability, and integrity of medical information. In addition, the feature of the presented concept is to facilitate the service management process by virtualizing them, which enables easy transfer of services between different virtual machines and their safe restoration.

Research may continue in many directions. The encapsulation of virtual services in next-generation networks requires research for implementation in SHSs. Important directions for further research include the development of cryptographic evidence-based security mechanisms in the IoMT and MCPS environment.

REFERENCES

[1] Bhushan, B. (2022). Middleware and Security Requirements for Internet of Things. In D.K. Sharma, S.L. Peng, R. Sharma, & D.A. Zaitsev (Eds.). *Micro-Electronics and Telecommunication Engineering: Lecture Notes in Networks and Systems* (pp. 309–321). Springer, Singapore. https://doi.org/10.1007/978-981-16-8721-1_30

[2] Szczepaniuk, H., & Szczepaniuk, E. (2021). Cybersecurity Management within the Internet of Things. In S.K. Sharma, B. Bharat, & N.C. Debnath (Eds.). *IoT Security Paradigms and Applications: Research and Practices* (pp. 25–42). CRC Press, Taylor & Francis Group. https://doi.org/10.1201/9781003054115

[3] Sharma, S.K., Bhushan, B., Khamparia, A., Astya, P.N., & Debnath, N.C. (Eds.) (2021). *Blockchain Technology for Data Privacy Management* (1st ed.). CRC Press, Taylor & Francis Group. https://doi.org/10.1201/9781003133391

[4] Szczepaniuk, E.K., Szczepaniuk, H., Rokicki, T., & Klepacki, B. (2020). Information Security Assessment in Public Administration. *Computers & Security, 90,* 101709. https://doi.org/10.1016/j.cose.2019.101709

[5] Sharma, S.K., Bhushan, B., & Debnath, N.C. (2021). *Security and Privacy Issues in IoT Devices and Sensor Networks.* Academic Press, London, UK. https://doi.org/10.1016/C2019-0-03189-5

[6] Algarni, A. (2019). A Survey and Classification of Security and Privacy Research in Smart Healthcare Systems. *IEEE Access: Practical Innovations, Open Solutions, 7,* 101879–101894. https://doi.org/10.1109/access.2019.2930962

[7] Alsubaei, F., Abuhussein, A., Shandilya, V., & Shiva, S. (2019). IoMT-SAF: Internet of Medical Things Security Assessment Framework. *Internet of Things, 8,* 100123. https://doi.org/10.1016/j.iot.2019.100123

[8] Sun, W., Cai, Z., Li, Y., Liu, F., Fang, S., & Wang, G. (2018). Security and Privacy in the Medical Internet of Things: A Review. *Security and Communication Networks, 2018,* 5978636. https://doi.org/10.1155/2018/5978636

[9] Alguliyev, A., Imamverdiyev, Y., & Sukhostat, L. (2018). Cyber-Physical Systems and Their Security Issues. *Computers in Industry, 100,* 212–223. https://doi.org/10.1016/j.compind.2018.04.017

[10] Ashibani, Y., & Mahmoud, Q.H. (2017). Cyber Physical Systems Security: Analysis, Challenges and Solutions. *Computers & Security, 68,* 81–97. https://doi.org/10.1016/j.cose.2017.04.005

[11] Tarikere, S., Donner, I., & Woods, D. (2021). Diagnosing a Healthcare Cybersecurity Crisis: The Impact of IoMT Advancements and 5G. *Business Horizons, 64*(6), 799–807. https://doi.org/10.1016/j.bushor.2021.07.015

[12] Khan, R., Kumar, P., Jayakody, D.N.K., & Liyanage, M. (2020). A Survey on Security and Privacy of 5G Technologies: Potential Solutions, Recent Advancements, and Future Directions. *IEEE Communications Surveys & Tutorials, 22*(1), 196–248. https://doi.org/10.1109/COMST.2019.2933899

[13] Mamolar, A.S., Salvá-García, P., Chirivella-Perez, E., Pervez, Z., Alcaraz Calero, J.M., & Wang, Q. (2019). Autonomic Protection of Multi-Tenant 5G Mobile Networks against UDP Flooding DdoS Attacks. *Journal of Network and Computer Applications, 145,* 102416. https://doi.org/10.1016/j.jnca.2019.102416

[14] Chen, B., Qiao, S., Zhao, J., Liu, D., Shi, X., Lyu, M., Chen, H., Lu, H., & Zhai, Y. (2021). A Security Awareness and Protection System for 5G Smart Healthcare Based

on Zero-Trust Architecture. *IEEE Internet of Things Journal*, *8*(13), 10248–10263. https://doi.org/10.1109/JIOT.2020.3041042

[15] Aman, A.H.M., Hassan, W.H., Sameen, S., Attarbashi, Z.S., Alizadeh, M., & Latiff, A.Z. (2021). IoMT Amid COVID-19 Pandemic: Application, Architecture, Technology, and Security. *Journal of Network and Computer Applications*, *174*, 102886. https://doi.org/10.1016/j.jnca.2020.102886

[16] Dilibal, Ç. (2020). Development of Edge-IoMT Computing Architecture for Smart Healthcare Monitoring Platform. *2020 4th International Symposium on Multidisciplinary Studies and Innovative Technologies (ISMSIT)*. Istanbul, Turkey. https://doi.org/10.1109/ISMSIT50672.2020.9254501

[17] Razdan, S., & Sharma, S. (2022). Internet of Medical Things (IoMT): Overview, Emerging Technologies, and Case Studies. *IETE Technical Review*, *39*(4), 775–788. https://doi.org/10.1080/02564602.2021.1927863

[18] Mohamad Noor, M.B., & Hassan, W.H. (2019). Current Research on Internet of Things (IoT) Security: A Survey. *Computer Networks*, *148*, 283–294. https://doi.org/10.1016/j.comnet.2018.11.025

[19] Xu, G., Lan, Y., Zhou, W., Huang, C., Li, W., Zhang, W., Zhang, G., Ng, E.Y.K., Cheng, Y., Peng, Y., & Che, W. (2019). An IoT-Based Framework of Webvr Visualization for Medical Big Data in Connected Health. *IEEE Access*, *7*, 173866–173874. https://doi.org/10.1109/ACCESS.2019.2957149

[20] Liu, C., Chen, F., Zhao, C., Wang, T., Zhang, C., & Zhang, Z. (2018). Ipv6-Based Architecture of Community Medical Internet of Things. *IEEE Access*, *6*, 7897–7910. https://doi.org/10.1109/ACCESS.2018.2801563

[21] Suo, H., Wan, J., Zou, C., & Liu, J. (2012). Security in the Internet of Things: A Review. *2012 International Conference on Computer Science and Electronics Engineering*. Hangzhou, China. https://doi.org/10.1109/ICCSEE.2012.373

[22] Dey, N., Ashour, A.S., Shi, F., Fong, S.J., & Tavares, J.M.R.S. (2018). Medical Cyber-Physical Systems: A Survey. *Journal of Medical Systems*, *42*(4), 74. https://doi.org/10.1007/s10916-018-0921-x

[23] Chen, F., Tang, Y., Wang, C., Huang, J., Huang, C., Xie, D., Wang, T., & Zhao C. (2022). Medical Cyber—Physical Systems: A Solution to Smart Health and the State of the Art. *IEEE Transactions on Computational Social Systems*, *9*(5), 1359–1386. https://doi.org/10.1109/tcss.2021.3122807

[24] Pateromichelakis, E., Moggio, F., Mannweiler, C., Arnold, P., Shariat, M., Einhaus, M., Wei, Q., Bulakci, Ö., & De Domenico, A. (2019). End-to-End Data Analytics Framework for 5G Architecture. *IEEE Access*, *7*, 40295–40312. https://doi.org/10.1109/ACCESS.2019.2902984

[25] 3GPP. (2021). *NG-RAN Architecture*. www.3gpp.org/news-events/2160-ng_ran_architecture (accessed September 21, 2022).

[26] Bertenyi, B., Burbidge, R., Masini, G., Sirotkin, S., & Gao Y. (2018). NG Radio Access Network (NG-RAN). *Journal of ICT Standardization*, *6*(combined Special Issue 1 & 2), 59–76. https://doi.org/10.13052/jicts2245-800x.614

[27] Giannone, F., Kondepu, K., Gupta, H., Civerchia, F., Castoldi, P., Franklin, A.A., & Valcarenghi, L. (2019). Impact of Virtualization Technologies on Virtualized RAN Midhaul Latency Budget: A Quantitative Experimental Evaluation. *IEEE Communications Letters*, *23*(4), 604–607. https://doi.org/10.1109/LCOMM.2019.2899308

[28] ETSI. (2020). *Technical Specification ETSI TS 138 401 V15.7.0*. www.etsi.org/deliver/etsi_ts/138400_138499/138401/15.07.00_60/ts_138401v150700p.pdf

[29] Abdelwahab, S., Hamdaoui, B., Guizani, M., & Znati, T. (2016). Network Function Virtualization in 5G. *IEEE Communications Magazine, 54*(4), 84–91. https://doi.org/10.1109/mcom.2016.7452271

[30] Liang, C., Yu, F.R., & Zhang, X. (2015). Information-Centric Network Function Virtualization Over 5g Mobile Wireless Networks. *IEEE Network, 29*(3), 68–74. https://doi.org/10.1109/mnet.2015.7113228

[31] Basu, D., Datta, R., & Ghosh, U. (2020). Softwarized Network Function Virtualization for 5G: Challenges and Opportunities. In U. Ghosh, D.B. Rawat, R. Datta, & A.S.K. Pathan (Eds.). *Internet of Things and Secure Smart Environments: Successes and Pitfalls* (1st ed., pp. 145–193). Chapman and Hall/CRC, New York.

[32] Al-Quzweeni, A., El-Gorashi, T.E.H., Nonde, L., & Elmirghani, J.M.H. (2015). Energy Efficient Network Function Virtualization in 5G Networks. *2015 17th International Conference on Transparent Optical Networks (ICTON)*. Budapest, Hungary. https://doi.org/10.1109/ICTON.2015.7193559

[33] Robertazzi, T.G. (2017). *Introduction to Computer Networking*. Springer, Cham.

[34] Masoudi, R. & Ghaffari, A. (2016). Software Defined Networks: A Survey. *Journal of Network and Computer Applications, 67*, 1–25. https://doi.org/10.1016/j.jnca.2016.03.016

[35] Leonhardt, A. (2019). Defining the Elements of NFV Architectures. *Equinix*. https://blog.equinix.com/blog/2019/10/17/networking-for-nerds-defining-the-elements-of-nfv-architectures/ (accessed September 11, 2022).

[36] Yi, B., Wang, X., Li, K., Das, S.K., & Huang, M. (2018). A Comprehensive Survey of Network Function Virtualization. *Computer Networks, 133*, 212–262. https://doi.org/10.1016/j.comnet.2018.01.021

[37] Barakabitze, A.A., Ahmad, A., Mijumbi, R., & Hines, A. (2020). 5G Network Slicing Using SDN and NFV: A Survey of Taxonomy, Architectures and Future Challenges. *Computer Networks, 167*, 106984. https://doi.org/10.1016/j.comnet.2019.106984

[38] El-Shorbagy, A. (2021). 5G Technology and the Future of Architecture. *Procedia Computer Science, 182*, 121–131. https://doi.org/10.1016/j.procs.2021.02.017

[39] Zhan, H. (2019). 5G Will Hit a Wall, Literally, In 2019. *Networkcomputing*. www.networkcomputing.com/networking/5g-will-hit-wall-literally-2019 (accessed September 15, 2022).

[40] Kruse, C.S., Stein, A., Thomas, H., & Kaur, H. (2018). The Use of Electronic Health Records to Support Population Health: A Systematic Review of the Literature. *Journal of Medical Systems, 42*, 214. https://doi.org/10.1007/s10916-018-1075-6

[41] Kruse, C.S., Smith, B., Vanderlinden, H., & Nealand, A. (2017). Security Techniques for the Electronic Health Records. *Journal of Medical Systems, 41*, 127. https://doi.org/10.1007/s10916-017-0778-4

[42] Tomar, D., Bhati, J.P., Tomar, P., & Kaur, G. (2019). Migration of Healthcare Relational Database to NoSQL Cloud Database for Healthcare Analytics and Management. In N. Dey, A.S. Ashour, C. Bhatt, & S.J. Fong (Eds.). *Advances in Ubiquitous Sensing Applications for Healthcare, Healthcare Data Analytics and Management* (pp. 59–87). Academic Press. https://doi.org/10.1016/B978-0-12-815368-0.00002-6

[43] Tchernykh, A., Schwiegelsohn, U., Talbi, E., & Babenko, M. (2019). Towards Understanding Uncertainty in Cloud Computing With Risks of Confidentiality, Integrity, and

Availability. *Journal of Computational Science, 36*, 100581. https://doi.org/10.1016/j.jocs.2016.11.011

[44] Aminzade, M. (2018). Confidentiality, Integrity and Availability—Finding a Balanced IT Framework. *Network Security, 2018*(5), 9–11. https://doi.org/10.1016/S1353-4858(18)30043-6

[45] Aminzade, M. (2018). Confidentiality, Integrity and Availability—Finding a Balanced IT Framework. *Network Security, 2018*(5), 9–11. https://doi.org/10.1016/s1353-4858(18)30043-6

[46] Tchernykh, A., Schwiegelsohn, U., Talbi, E.-G., & Babenko, M. (2019). Towards Understanding Uncertainty in Cloud Computing With Risks of Confidentiality, Integrity, and Availability. *Journal of Computational Science, 36*, 100581. https://doi.org/10.1016/j.jocs.2016.11.011

Chapter 5

Techniques to Prioritize Messages in MQTT Communication Protocol

Jiby J. Puthiyidam and Shelbi Joseph

5.1 INTRODUCTION

Nowadays Internet-of-Things (IoT) rules the Internet world. IoT integrates the physical world with the virtual world. IoT refers to the countless devices connected to the Internet to collect and share information. This technology uses the Internet as a communication medium to exchange information. The IoT architecture provides all objects with identification, detection, networking, and processing capabilities, and these objects can generate and share information [1]. IoT proposes an enhanced technology that enables everyday devices such as home appliances, furniture, and electronic devices to access, generate, and share information through the Internet. In other words, IoT transforms everyday objects smarter by exploiting technologies such as ubiquitous and pervasive computing, embedded devices, communication technologies, and sensor networks [2]. The smart IoT devices can be classified into three application groups: consumer, enterprise, and industrial. Smart TV and wearable smart devices form user-connected devices. The devices used for monitoring traffic and climate conditions are examples of enterprise and industrial IoT devices [3]. The application domains of IoT include smart cities, smart homes, agriculture, healthcare systems, smart water and energy management, vehicular traffic, and industrial automation, to name a few [4]. Figure 5.1 explains general IoT characteristics.

The Hypertext Transfer Protocol (HTTP) is the widely used communication protocol for the Internet [5]. Since HTTP is operated over TCP/IP, reliable communication is ensured. However, connections established by TCP are released on every access [6]. The communication completes after the establishment and release of the connection many times. IoT applications use devices with limited memory capacity, low processing power, and limited battery backup. When HTTP is used for IoT communication, it causes severe protocol overhead and consumption of network resources and hence is not suitable for IoT applications [7]. Specialized communication protocols are required to handle communications in IoT networks with constrained devices.

Several communication protocols are available for IoT applications. Popular among them are Constrained Application Protocol (CoAP) [8], Message Queuing

DOI: 10.1201/9781003474111-5

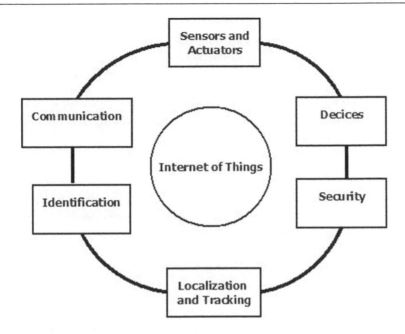

Figure 5.1 Characteristics of IoT.

Source: Based on Lova Raju, K., & Vijayaraghavan, V. (2020).

Telemetry Transport (MQTT) [9], Advanced Message Queuing Protocol (AMQP) [10], Data Distribution Service (DDS) [11], Extensible Messaging and Presence Protocol (XMPP) [12], etc. MQTT is the most widely accepted standard for the Industrial Internet-of-Things.

5.1.1   Message Queue Telemetry Transport Protocol

The Message Queue Telemetry Transport Protocol (MQTT) protocol is the most widely used communication protocol in the Internet-of-Things applications [15]. It is a lightweight connectivity protocol and uses the publish/subscribe method for the transportation of data. MQTT is built over the TCP/IP protocol, making it suitable for unreliable communication networks. Payload size does not affect throughput rate of MQTT protocol [13]. The minimal resource requirement and reduced network bandwidth make the MQTT protocol well-positioned for machine-to-machine (M2M) communications, a critical aspect of the IoT. Big public clouds like Amazon Web Services, Microsoft Azure, and Google Cloud Platform use the power of the MQTT protocol [14].

The MQTT architecture has two main participants: clients and a message broker. There are two types of participating clients in MQTT applications: publishers and subscribers. The broker is the server that receives all messages from publishing clients and then routes these messages to relevant subscriber clients. A client interacts with the broker to send and receive messages. A client could be an IoT sensor in the field or an application in a data center that processes IoT data. MQTT protocol decouples publishers and subscribers [16]. Clients are unaware of the presence of each other. There is no direct communication between MQTT clients. Clients interact through MQTT broker. A subscriber client expresses willingness to receive messages by specifying a topic name with its connection request to the broker. The publishing clients publish messages on a topic to the broker server. The broker filter messages based on the topic name and forward the messages to the clients subscribed to that topic. The general architecture of the MQTT protocol is given in Figure 5.2.

At the same time, MQTT is lightweight and well-suited for battery-powered constrained IoT devices. It has a simple header to specify the message type, a text-based topic, and an arbitrary binary payload. Hence, it is easy to implement in software and fast in data transmission. MQTT uses minimized data packets resulting in low network usage. It has a low power requirement, and as a result, it saves the connected device's battery.

MQTT has a 2-byte fixed message header, the smallest among the IoT communication protocols. It also has a variable header field to specify the size of the message and the actual payload, if available. The structure of the MQTT message header is described in Figure 5.3.

The first 4 bits in byte 1 of the message fixed header specify the message type. There are 14 standard message types for the MQTT protocol. The remaining 4 bits represent flag bits such as Retain flag, Quality of Service (QoS), and Duplicate flag. If the Retain flag is set, the MQTT broker retains the last message received for a topic and forwards this message when a new subscriber establishes

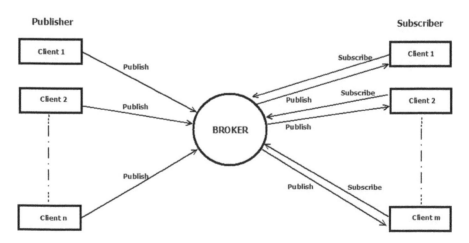

Figure 5.2 MQTT protocol architecture.

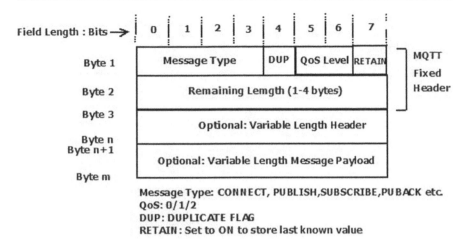

Figure 5.3 MQTT message format.

Source: Mishra, Biswajeeban (2018).

a connection. QoS flag denotes the reliability level of the message, and the Duplicate flag is set when the publisher resends a message when it does not receive an acknowledgement from the subscriber. Byte 2 indicates the remaining size or packet length, which indicates the size of the variable header and actual message. The 14 standard message types specified with the MQTT protocol is shown in Table 5.1. Message type values 0 and 15 are reserved for future expansion.

In order to ensure reliable message delivery, MQTT clients are configured with different Quality of Services (QoS). MQTT offers three levels of QoS:

(a) QoS 0: At most once delivery
(b) QoS 1: At least once delivery
(c) QoS 2: Exactly once delivery

QoS 0 is the default Quality of Service MQTT protocol offers. It does not guarantee message delivery. QoS 0 is preferred when the communication network is reliable and losing messages is acceptable. For example, atmospheric pressure or temperature sensor data. QoS 1 ensure message delivery. Subscribers should acknowledge the receipt of messages. The message is delivered to the subscriber at least once. The message is retransmitted if there is no acknowledgement within a pre-specified period. QoS 1 is used with applications where guaranteed message delivery is essential and can handle duplicate messages. Reporting machine health data to ensure maintenance at the right time is an example of QoS 1 message delivery. QoS 2 is the highest and most expensive quality of service MQTT offers. This QoS has been used in mission-critical scenarios that neither accept

Table 5.1 MQTT Message Types

Message Type	Value	Description
Reserved	0	Reserved
CONNECT	1	Client request to connect to server
CONNACK	2	Connect acknowledgment
PUBLISH	3	Publish message
PUBACK	4	Publish acknowledgment
PUBREC	5	Publish received
PUBREL	6	Publish release
PUBCOMB	7	Publish complete
SUBSCRIBE	8	Client subscribe request
SUBACK	9	Subscribe acknowledgment
UNSUBSCRIBE	10	Unsubscribe request
UNSUBACK	11	Unsubscribe acknowledgment
PINGREQ	12	PING request
PINGRESP	13	PING response
DISCONNECT	14	Client is disconnecting
Reserved	15	Reserved

the loss of messages nor duplicate messages. Examples are billing and invoicing systems where duplicate entries are not accepted. Each message should properly be delivered exactly once. Figure 5.4 depicts MQTT protocol QoS interactions.

MQTT broker does not support the prioritization of messages. The message broker forwards the messages from publishing clients to the subscriber client in the order in which it receives, in the first-in, first-out (FIFO) order. Since MQTT supports many-to-many communications, the broker can accept messages from multiple publishers. Data from some publishing clients may be more important than other sources. If any publisher has critical data, it must be immediately available to the subscribers. For example, the data gathered from the fire alarm system is more critical than atmospheric temperature or pressure sensor data. Any delay in passing such crucial data may cause severe damage to the system. It must be available to the receiver immediately, without waiting for the earlier-generated data to be sent to the subscribers. For that, the prioritization of messages is required. This feature is not available in the standard MQTT broker architecture. Efforts from specific authors are traced in the literature to address this problem. This chapter's core content is an analysis of the various techniques proposed to address the message priority problem of the MQTT protocol. This chapter is a preparation for the future work in which we discuss a novel approach for prioritizing MQTT messages.

This chapter is organized as follows. A survey on related research work in prioritizing MQTT messages is presented in Section 5.2. Section 5.3 discusses the results of the survey performed. The future expansion plan based on the survey result is given in Section 5.4. Finally, Section 5.5 concludes the chapter.

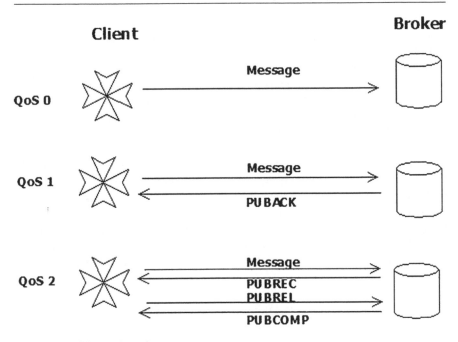

Figure 5.4 MQTT quality of services.

5.2 RELATED WORKS ON ASSIGNING PRIORITY TO MQTT MESSAGES

The MQTT broker server can receive messages from multiple sources. The broker forwards these incoming messages in a First Come, First Serve (FCFS) manner. In the standard MQTT protocol, there is no provision for forwarding critical information immediately to subscribers. Delay in delivering crucial information may result in catastrophic effects. Multiple factors need to be taken into account while selecting the priority criteria. The importance of fulfilling the requirement, the penalty for not having it, implementation cost, time, risk, and volatility are a few examples. A survey on some existing research in prioritizing MQTT messages is presented in this section.

5.2.1 A New Back-off Algorithm with Priority Scheduling for MQTT Protocol and IoT Protocols [17]

Exponential Back-off is a prominent algorithm used in computer networks to avoid the repeated retransmission of messages or data. It is helpful to eliminate network congestion by setting a random delay time depending on the slot time. This algorithm organizes the retransmission of packets in the CSMA/CD after a collision is detected. After detecting a collision based on the number of collisions and time slots, this algorithm determines the waiting time for collisional stations.

Enany et al. [17] proposed a new back-off algorithm with priority scheduling for MQTT and IoT protocols in their work. The proposed algorithm aims to reduce network congestion by slowing down the transmission rate of suspicious devices. The broker calculates the average frequent rate for publishing messages for each client by analyzing the time interval between every two consecutive messages for the first N messages. When a new message arrives, the broker compares the current publishing frequency rate with that publisher's initial average frequent rate. If the current rate is higher than the initial rate, it indicates some problem with the publisher or may be under attack. The broker computes a delay factor for the publisher based on the current frequent rate. Receiving messages from the publisher is delayed until the calculated delay time. The exponential back-off algorithm is activated for this purpose. The exponential delay continues until the publisher reaches its actual frequent publishing rate.

$FR_{avg} = 1/((\sum_{i=1}^{N} I_{(Mi,Mi+1)})/(N-1))$ //computing average frequent rate
$FR_{new} = (1/I_{(Mi,Mi+1)})$ // new frequent rate
$Df = e^{(FRnew)}$ // Delay factor computation

Based on the calculated average frequent rate, the publishers can be classified into different priority levels. The higher the frequent rate of a publisher, the lower the priority level; and the lower the frequent rate, the higher the priority level.

$PRL = MiN \{p_1FRavg, p_2FRavg, p_3FRavg, \dots p_KFRavg\}$ // Low priority messages
$PRH = MAx \{ p_1FRavg, p_2FRavg, p_3FRavg, \dots p_KFRavg\}$ // High priority messages

This procedure assumes that a sensor that sends one message every 24 hours has a higher priority than a sensor that sends a message every second. Depending on the original publishing frequency rate factor, the arrived messages are arranged in a queue for processing based on the assigned priority level. The main goal of this algorithm is to assign priority to the connected devices from the broker's side, not from the client's side, where any hacker can assign himself a high priority. This algorithm was implemented using the Mosquitto broker. The experimental results showed less latency for the new high-priority publisher in the back-off broker than the original MQTT broker. The proposed Back-off and priority scheduling algorithm showed an acceptable result for RAM and CPU consumption with a minimum traffic load that leads to the ability to be employed in constrained resource devices.

5.2.2 Method of Message Processing According to Priority in MQTT Broker [18]

In their work [18], Kim et al. proposed a method to assign priority to MQTT messages by modifying the message header of MQTT messages. The fixed header part is not affected by this approach. To set the priority, a 2-bit priority-QoS flag is defined in byte 3 of the MQTT message header. With the 2-bit priority flag, we can specify four different priority levels (priority levels 0, 1, 2, and 3). Priority level 0 is assigned to the lowest priority data, and priority level 3 is set to the most urgent messages. In this method, the priority of a message is set by the publisher while publishing the message. Before sending the message, the priority level should be specified in the message header. Authors claim that their experiments' delivery time of high-priority messages is better than low-priority messages. Figure 5.5 shows the message header modified for this experiment.

5.2.3 A Study on MQTT Based on Priority Topic for IoT [19]

A different approach is proposed in [19] by Oh et al. This method selects a rarely used character as the prioritization character. This character is used as the first character of the topic name of the priority message. For example, suppose the rarely used "^" character is selected to denote high-priority messages. In that case, messages in a topic name that begins with the "^" character are assumed with the highest priority, and if "_" is the character denoting messages with the next highest priority, then messages in the topic begin with "_" is assigned with the following priority. If any other character is the first character of the topic, it is considered a normal priority topic. The authors claim that this method is simple and reliable and can send the priority of the corresponding topic within the PUBLISH packet

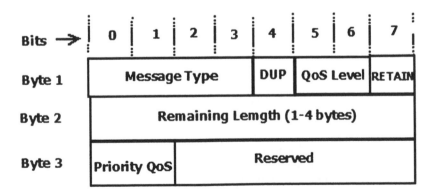

Figure 5.5 Modified message header.

Source: Data from Kim, Sung-jin, and Chang-heon Oh (2017).

while complying with the existing MQTT standard. This approach maintains a separate queue for each priority level. Only if the queue for the highest priority level is empty will the messages for the following priority level be executed. The authors claim that their experiments proved that the average processing time for high-priority messages is lower than that required for normal messages.

5.2.4   Prioritized Data Transmission Mechanism for IoT [20]

The study in Ref. [20] proposed a novel priority assignment scheme. It also reduces the number of packet transmissions in the resource-constrained network. Two threshold values are adopted to categorize packets with priorities. If a packet from a sensor belongs to the external range of the two threshold values, it is assigned the highest priority (priority 0). Contrarily, if the measured sensor value is within the two threshold values, it is considered a packet with normal priority (priority 1). In addition, a tolerance value is also identified to control the message transfer frequency rate. Suppose the difference between the previously measured data (di) and the newly measured data (di + 1) is within the tolerance range. Then, the proposed scheme considers the newest data as the previously measured value and assigns the lowest priority (priority 2) to that data. This algorithm maintains a keep-alive timeout variable to minimize packet transmission. If the lowest priority messages arrive continuously, this method skips messages until a specified keep-alive timeout value is reached. The packet prioritization scheme proposed in this method is explained in Figure 5.6.

The proposed method reduces the packet transmission rate. This method also showed improved performance in bandwidth consumption, less energy usage, and packet drop rate due to the decreased packet transmission. The transmission delay of high-priority messages is almost identical in any actual situation.

5.2.5   Message Queue Telemetry Transport Broker with Priority Support for Emergency Events in Internet-of-Things [21]

The technique proposed by Lee et al. in [21], p-MQTT, consists of three components: classification, virtual queue, and priority control mechanism. The p-MQTT broker maintains three virtual queues: urgent, critical, and normal. The urgent queue stores the most important messages that should be transmitted before any other message. The critical queue stores less urgent messages than the urgent ones but still requires high reliability. Messages with no specific priority are stored in the normal queue. P-MQTT architecture is shown Figure 5.7.

The classification component classifies the messages into different virtual queues based on their message type. MQTT uses 4 bits in the fixed message header to specify the message type. MQTT specifications include 14 standard message types (1–14), and message types 0 and 15 are reserved. P-MQTT uses reserved message type 0 to denote urgent messages and message type 15 to denote critical events. If the message type is any standard MQTT message (message types 1–14),

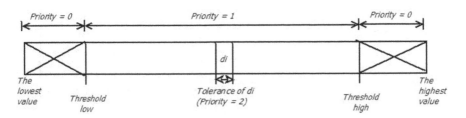

Figure 5.6 Packet prioritization.

Source: Data from Jung and Changsu (2017).

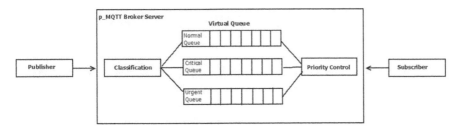

Figure 5.7 p-MQTT system architecture.

Source: Data from Kim, Yong-Seong, et al. (2018).

the p-MQTT broker identifies it as a standard message. The publisher assigns the message type value before sending the message, and based on this value, the message is placed in the appropriate virtual queue by the classification component. The priority control mechanism determines the forwarding priority of each virtual queue. The messages in the urgent queue are forwarded first. The messages in the critical queue are forwarded if the urgent queue is empty, and messages in the normal queue are forwarded only when both the urgent and critical queues are empty. The results show that this method experiences lower latency and message loss rates for urgent messages than standard MQTT broker performance. The p-MQTT is implemented using Mosquitto broker and standard paho MQTT clients.

5.2.6 Priority-based Multilevel MQTT System to Provide Differentiated IoT Services [22]

The proposed method in [22] inserts priority information in the fixed header of the existing MQTT message packet. A 2-bit priority flag is set in byte 2 of the MQTT message header. Hence, four priority levels (levels 0 to 3) can be assigned. The higher the priority flag value, the higher the message's priority. The modified MQTT message fixed header structure for this method is given in Figure 5.8.

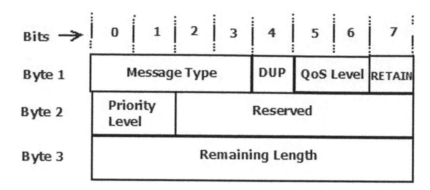

Figure 5.8 Modified MQTT message fixed header.

Source: Data from Kim, Geonwoo, Jiwoo Park, and Kwangsue Chung (2018).

This approach uses a classifier component that classifies messages based on priority flag value and assigns them to the specific queue. This system maintains four independent message queues for four different levels of priority. This approach also uses a weighted round-robin (WRR) scheduler to schedule messages in different queues. In order to prevent the indefinite postponement of processing of low-priority messages, the weighted round-robin scheduling algorithm assigns weight to each priority queue. It decreases the weight of the queue once a message from the queue is published. Figure 5.9 depicts the system architecture of the proposed method.

The authors claim that their method reduces the latency of high-priority messages and improves message throughput. Moreover, the number of messages in the high-priority queue will always be less than in other queues.

5.2.7   Modification of Mosquitto Broker for Delivery of Urgent MQTT Messages [23]

In the method explained in [23], Hwang K. et al. modify the Mosquitto broker to treat urgent messages with high priority. Mosquitto broker maintains a subscription list of the connected subscribers and their subscribed topics. The main_loop() of the Mosquitto broker calls a poll() system call, inset a newly connected subscriber into the subscription list, and if a message arrives from a publisher, inserts the message into the message queue with a topic. The message topic in the message queue is compared with the topics stored in the subscription list. If the two topics match, the message is copied to the message buffer, and the matched subscriber's message pointer is linked to this copied message in the message buffer. Then the messages are forwarded to the subscriber.

In the proposed approach, U-Mosquitto adds an urgent message list to store urgent messages and the message buffer and subscription list used in the standard

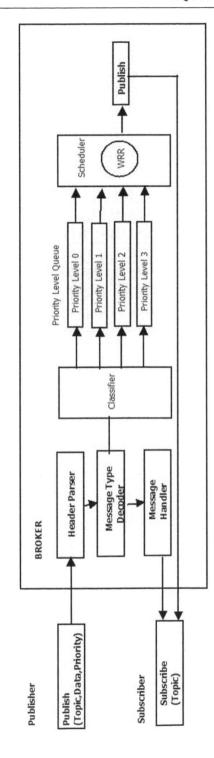

Figure 5.9 System architecture.

Source: Data from Kim, Geonwoo, Jiwoo Park, and Kwangsue Chung (2018).

Value	Description
1	EMERGENCY
2	CONNECT
3	CONNACK
4	PUBACK
5	PUBREC
6	PUBREL
7	PUBCOMP
8	SUBSCRIBE
9	SUBACK
10	UNSUBSCRIBE
11	UNSUBACK
12	PINGREQ
13	PINGRESP
14	DISCONNECT
15	RESERVED

Figure 5.10 Emerg-MQ message types.

Source: Hidalgo, Wilfredo A. Tovar, and Marwan Ghalib (2020).

Mosquitto broker. Only the first message from each publisher is selected and assigned to an urgent or normal list based on their message type. U-Mosquitto processes the urgent message list before the subscription list. The message distribution and forwarding is depicted in Figure 5.10. In order to maintain the required load, the experimental environment was set up with multiple laptops to run publisher clients and threads to control multiple clients. This method checks the delivery time of messages to analyze the performance of the modified Mosquitto broker. As the publisher size increased, urgent messages were delivered faster than normal messages under the U-Mosquitto broker.

5.2.8 An Efficient Multiclass Message Scheduling Scheme for Healthcare IoT Systems [24]

Park et al. [24] propose an efficient multiclass message scheduling algorithm for healthcare IoT environments. Messages are classified into three groups based on their characteristics: unconditional messages (UNC), real-time (RT) messages, and delay-tolerant (DT) messages. Each message class has its message queue. UNC messages should be sent immediately. Whenever an RT message is sent, the priority of the RT message queue is decreased by 10%, and the priority of the DT message queue is increased by 10%. Whenever a DT message is sent, the priority of the DT message queue is decreased by 30% and the priority of the RT message queue is increased by 30%. The algorithm ensures that the transmission of DT messages is not blocked indefinitely. Figure 5.10 gives the message types used with Emerg-MQTT.

The experiments show that the proposed scheduling algorithm performs better than the MQL scheduling algorithm in most cases. It is mainly because the proposed algorithm uses a more straightforward priority calculation than the MQL algorithm. It also schedules more messages for a given time than MQL.

5.2.9 Examination of Vulnerabilities in Message Queuing Telemetry Transport in IoT Systems and Implementation of Countermeasures [25]

Hidalgo et al. proposed an MQTT broker with priority assistance for emergency messages in IoT applications, aiming to ensure the delivery of emergency messages in a timely and reliable manner. The proposed Emerg-MQTT broker contains classification/distribution, virtual queue, and priority control modules. The classification/distribution segment classifies the collected messages into two types, normal and emergency, by examining the message type section in the header of the incoming message. Then store the message in the assigned virtual queue according to its priority. The priority control module designates the forwarding preference to each virtual queue. This method classifies incoming messages into two priority levels: emergency and normal messages. The message type field of the MQTT header is used to determine the priority type of the message. MQTT standard protocol, by default, reserves two values, 0 and 15, in the message type header. This method uses one of the reserved fields, 0, to mark emergency messages. If the incoming message type is 0, it is considered an emergency message and placed in the virtual emergency queue. If the message type is 1–15, it is a standard message and is placed in the normal virtual queue. The elements in the emergency message queue are forwarded first, irrespective of the number of messages in the normal queue.

The experimental evaluation shows that the Emerg-MQTT achieves 35.3% lower latencies for emergency messages than the existing MQTT. Moreover, on average, the Emerg-MQTT achieves 51.8% lower message loss for critical messages and mitigates potential DoS attacks more effectively than the standard MQTT Architecture.

5.3 RESULTS AND DISCUSSION

Standard MQTT brokers treat messages from all sources uniformly. The broker cannot distinguish incoming messages based on importance or priority, and all incoming messages are forwarded to the subscribers in the same order as they are received. However, messages from some sources may be more critical in real-life applications. For example, a warning message from a fire alarm or gas leak sensor may be more crucial than a regular temperature or atmospheric pressure sensor reading. Such messages must be treated urgently or forwarded immediately to the subscriber without waiting for the previous messages to deliver. Any delay in dealing with such critical data may lead to catastrophic damage to the system. Therefore, in this work, we have decided to conduct a detailed survey on existing research to prioritize incoming messages in an IoT environment. As our first observation, it is revealed that the prioritization of MQTT messages is a rarely explored research area. Only a little related work exists in the focused research area. We could identify hardly ten related works in the literature survey. We have made a detailed analysis of these works, and the findings are summarized as follows.

The related works we have in the literature use different approaches to assign priority to incoming messages in the MQTT protocol. Many approaches determine the priority of a message by altering the structure of the MQTT message header. For example, Refs. [18] and [22] add a 2-bit priority flag field in the message header of an MQTT PUBLISH message to specify the priority of the message. The higher the flag value, the higher will be the priority. This approach consequently increases the MQTT fixed header size from two to three. Some other research in this area used reserved message types (message type 0 and message type 15) to denote high-priority messages [21,25]. The message type field is supposed to specify the message type value, and how this field can also be used to mention the priority needs to be clearly explained in these works. In another attempt, the first character of a message topic is used to denote critical messages [19]. If the message topic begins with a rarely used special character, the broker can distinguish that the message is urgent. In [24], messages are prioritized based on their characteristics. How to specify message characteristics needs to be explained in this chapter. The message priority is determined at the client side (publisher side) in all the cases mentioned above. In other words, messages from certain publishers are preassigned as priority messages. Hence, the publisher client nodes need to assign priority to messages generated. MQTT clients are constrained devices with limited processing, storage, and communication capabilities. Overloading such devices with the responsibility of prioritizing their messages at the time of packet generation and publishing is not advisable.

A different approach is given in Ref. [17]. It assigns priority to messages by calculating each publisher's average frequent rate of incoming messages. A message from a publisher with a higher frequency rate is assigned with lower priority, and messages from low frequent rate publishers (publishers generating messages less frequently) are assigned with higher priority. The most popular MQTT broker, the Mosquitto broker, is modified in Ref. [23] to deliver urgent messages. An urgent message list is constructed in the Mosquitto broker to store urgent messages in addition to the message buffer and subscription list for normal messages. The research work in Ref. [20] tries to put the responsibility of identifying and processing priority messages to the broker. Two threshold values are used to identify the messages needed urgent treatment, and a tolerance value is used to reduce the number of packets transmitted. This approach treats critical messages immediately as well as reduces network traffic. The survey results are summarized in Table 5.2.

Most of the existing research on prioritizing MQTT messages claims that they improve the latency of delivering priority messages, reduce the CPU and RAM resources, improve the throughput, etc. However, it is found that most of the works were proposals only. Details of actual implementation and experimental evaluation should be included in many works. Many of the works put the responsibility of assigning/identifying priority to messages to the constrained publishing clients. In IoT applications, the input clients are devices with limited sensing, processing, and memory capacity. Hence, it is not desirable to add the extra burden of prioritization of messages to such input devices. Some other works propose using reserved message types in MQTT message format for assigning priority to messages. The 4-bit message type field is supposed to specify the message type, such as CONNECT, PUBLISH, SUBSCRIBE, etc. It is still being determined how the same 4 bits can also be used to denote the priority of messages. In all the proposals discussed, some modification/updation is required by the broker. However, the implementation details need to be included in most works. For example, in the technique that uses the first character of the topic name to determine the priority of messages, how the broker identifies priority character is not mentioned. Some proposals indicate that a classification component classifies incoming messages into different priority queues. Nevertheless, in many cases, the criteria used by the classification component to categorize messages need to be clearly explained. Our analysis concludes that dealing with emergency messages in the Internet-of-Things scenario is a yet to explore research area. We could not identify more works in this area, and most of the works examined were only proposals. The actual implementation details are missing in most of the experiments. Hence, prioritization of incoming messages in the Internet-of-Things applications is an open research area with much research scope.

5.4 FUTURE RESEARCH DIRECTION

As future expansion of our work, we can design and develop an improved method for treating urgent messages in IoT communication protocols. Message Queue Telemetry Transport (MQTT) is the most popular communication protocol in an IoT environment. Hence, MQTT may be selected for future implementation of message priority in IoT networks. In our future work, we expect the clients, publishers, and subscribers to work normally. No additional overhead is assigned to them for prioritizing MQTT messages. Publisher clients generate and forward messages in the usual way. The responsibility for identifying important messages, assigning priority, and forwarding messages based on priority lies with the powerful broker server. We plan to implement the work using HBMQTT, the broker written in Python. HBMQTT broker may be modified to incorporate the priority

Table 5.2 Survey Findings on Prioritizing MQTT Messages

References	Priority Method	Evaluation Environment	Evaluation Parameters	Evaluation Result
[17]	Frequent rate of publishing messages	Mosquitto Broker Intel i7 Processor Windows 10 64-bit 16 GB RAM	1. Network Traffic 2. CPU Load 3. Consumed RAM 4. Latency	1. Less network traffic 2. Slightly increased but manageable CPU load 3. RAM consumption at par with standard broker 4. Improved latency
[18]	Set a 2-bit priority flag at byte 3 of message header	Mosquitto Broker Paho Client Library Intel i7 Processor 16 GB RAM	1. End-to-end delay with different QoS 2. Latency under different priority levels	1. Reduced end-to-end delay for priority nodes 2. Lowest delay when QoS is 0
[19]	Using a rarely used character as the first character of priority topic	Mosquitto Broker Intel i5 Processor Windows 10 64-bit Raspberry pi as MQTT broker Paho MQTT client	1. Latency with varying message sizes	1. Reduced processing time for priority messages 2. Fast processing of high-priority messages 3. Use relatively less CPU resources
[20]	Use threshold values	Raspberry Pi 3 Arduino board Linux-based computer with JDK installed	1. Packet transmission rate 2. Energy consumption 3. Bandwidth utilization 4. Packet loss rate 5. Transmission delay	1. 40% reduced packet transmission rate 2. Reduced energy consumption 3. Less bandwidth utilization 4. Reduced packet loss rate 5. Improved transmission delay
[21]	Use reserved message types to set priority	Mosquitto 1.4.13 Ubuntu 16.04.2 Paho MQTT library	1. Latency of urgent messages 2. Message loss rate	1. 35.3% lower latency for urgent messages 2. Slightly higher loss rate for urgent messages

Ref	Method	Setup	Metrics	Results
[22]	Priority flag set in the fixed message header		1. Latency with different priority levels 2. Message throughput	1. Reduced latency 2. Improved throughput
[23]	Maintain an urgent list to store priority messages	11 PC's used as clients (10 publishers and 1 subscriber) Mosquitto on Raspberry pi board as broker	1. Message transmission time 2. CPU utilization time 3. Poll size (messages processed at one loop)	1. Urgent messages deliver faster than normal messages
[24]	Messages are grouped into three priority groups based on their characteristics	Intel i7 Processor Mosquitto broker Paho MQTT clients Mininet simulator	1. Scheduling time under different message sizes	1. Better performance than MQL scheduling algorithm 2. Schedules more messages for a given time
[25]	Use reserved message type 0 to denote priority messages	Mosquitto broker Paho MQTT clients VirtualBox to create Ubuntu Linux virtual machine (VM)	1. Latency 2. Message loss rate	1. 35.3% lower latencies for emergency messages

handling procedure. This work will be helpful in many application areas, such as healthcare management and industrial environment, to name but a few.

5.5 CONCLUSION

MQTT is the most widely used protocol for IoT communications due to its peculiar features such as lightweight nature, suitability for constrained applications, and small message header. In many IoT applications, timely processing of critical messages from input sensors are crucial. Standard MQTT protocol does not prioritize incoming messages. In this work, we have surveyed the attempts in the literature to assign priority to incoming messages in the MQTT protocol. We could locate very few contributions related to the focused research area, and found that many of the existing works are proposals only. The actual implementation details are missing in most of the work. Hence our survey opens up a new research area in the Internet-of-Things and its communication protocols: prioritizing critical messages. The future work is to implement a method to forward critical messages on a priority basis without affecting client node performance.

REFERENCES

1. Daissaoui, Abdellah, et al. "IoT and Big Data Analytics for Smart Buildings: A Survey." Procedia Computer Science 170 (2020): 161–168.
2. Al-Fuqaha, Ala, Mohsen Guizani, Mehdi Mohammadi, Mohammed Aledhari, and Moussa Ayyash. "Internet of Things: A Survey on Enabling Technologies, Protocols, and Applications." IEEE Communications Surveys & Tutorials 17.4 (2015): 2347–2376.
3. Mohammed, A. J, Adhami H., Alchalabi A. E., Hoda M., and El Saddik A. "Toward Integrating Software Defined Networks with the Internet of Things: A Review." Cluster Computing (2021): 1–18.
4. Sundari V., Kamatchi, et al. "Comparison Analysis of IoT Based Industrial Automation and Improvement of Different Processes—Review." Materials Today: Proceedings 45 (2021): 2595–2598.
5. Lova Raju, K., and Veeramani Vijayaraghavan. "IoT Technologies in Agricultural Environment: A Survey." Wireless Personal Communications 113 (2020): 2415–2446.
6. Yokotani, T., and Y. Sasaki. "Transfer Protocols of Tiny Data Blocks in IoT and Their Performance Evaluation." 2016 IEEE 3rd World Forum on Internet of Things (WF-IoT) (2016): 54–57. doi: 10.1109/WF-IoT.2016.7845442.
7. Nikolov, Neven. "Research of MQTT, CoAP, HTTP and XMPP IoT Communication Protocols for Embedded Systems." 2020 XXIX International Scientific Conference Electronics (ET). IEEE, 2020.
8. Bansal, Sharu, and Dilip Kumar. "Enhancing Constrained Application Protocol Using Message Options for Internet of Things." Cluster Computing (2022): 1–18.
9. Soni, Dipa, and Ashwin Makwana. "A Survey on Mqtt: A Protocol of Internet of Things (IoT)." International Conference on Telecommunication, Power Analysis and Computing Techniques (ICTPACT-2017) 20 (2017).

10. Basavaraju, Nandeesh, Naveen Alexander, and Jochen Seitz. "Performance Evaluation of Advanced Message Queuing Protocol (AMQP): An Empirical Analysis of AMQP Online Message Brokers." In *2021 International Symposium on Networks, Computers and Communications (ISNCC)*, pp. 1–8. IEEE, 2021.

11. www.dds-foundation.org/(online): Accessed on 18th July 2022.

12. Saint-Andre, Peter, et al. I©The Definitive Guide." O'Reilly Media, Inc., 2009.

13. Bayılmış, C., Ebleme M. A., Çavuşoğlu Ü., Kücük K., and Sevin A. A Survey on Communication Protocols and Performance Evaluations for Internet of Things. Digital Communications and Networks 8.6 (2022): 1094–1104.

14. Naik, Nitin. "Choice of Effective Messaging Protocols for IoT Systems: MQTT, CoAP, AMQP and HTTP." 2017 IEEE International Systems Engineering Symposium (ISSE). IEEE, 2017.

15. Al Enany, Marwa O., Hany M. Harb, and Gamal Attiya. "A Comparative Analysis of MQTT and IoT Application Protocols." 2021 International Conference on Electronic Engineering (ICEEM). IEEE, 2021.

16. Mishra, Biswajeeban. "Performance Evaluation of MQTT Broker Servers." International Conference on Computational Science and Its Applications. Springer, 2018.

17. Al Enany, Marwa O., Hany M. Harb, and Gamal Attiya. "A New Back-off Algorithm with Priority Scheduling for MQTT Protocol and IoT Protocols." International Journal of Advanced Computer Science and Applications 12.11 (2021).

18. Kim, Sung-jin, and Chang-heon Oh. "Method for Message Processing According to Priority in MQTT Broker." Journal of the Korea Institute of Information and Communication Engineering 21.7 (2017): 1320–1326.

19. Oh, Se-Chun, and Young-Gon Kim. "A Study on MQTT based on Priority topic for IIoT." The Journal of the Institute of Internet, Broadcasting and Communication 19.5 (2019): 63–71.

20. Jung, Changsu. "Prioritized Data Transmission Mechanism for IoT." KSII Transactions on Internet and Information Systems (TIIS) 14.6 (2020): 2333–2353.

21. Kim, Yong-Seong, et al. "Message Queue Telemetry Transport Broker with Priority Support for Emergency Events in Internet of Things." Sensors and Materials 30.8 (2018): 1715–1721.

22. Kim, Geonwoo, Jiwoo Park, and Kwangsue Chung. "Priority-Based Multi-Level MQTT System to Provide Differentiated IoT Services." Journal of KIISE 45.9 (2018): 969–974.

23. Hwang, Kitae, et al. "Modification of Mosquitto Broker for Delivery of Urgent MQTT Message." 2019 IEEE Eurasia Conference on IoT, Communication and Engineering (ECICE). IEEE, 2019.

24. Park, Kee Hyun, Insung Kim, and Joonsuu Park. "An Efficient Multi-Class Message Scheduling Scheme for Healthcare IoT Systems." International Journal of Grid and Distributed Computing 11.5 (2018): 67–77.

25. Wilfredo Tovar, H.A., and Marwan Ghalib. "Examination of Vulnerabilities in Message Queuing Telemetry Transport (MQTT) in IoT Systems and Implementation of Countermeasures." 2020. https://www.researchgate.net/publication/338335323_Examination_of_vulnerabilities_in_Message_Queuing_Telemetry_Transport_MQTT_in_IoT_Systems_and_implementation_of_countermeasures: Accessed on 14th September 2022.

Chapter 6

Three-dimensional User Authentication Comprising Graphical Pattern, Iris Recognition, and One-time Password for ATM Transactions

Md. Ariful Islam, Jahir Ibna Rafiq, Aloke Kumar Saha, and Muhammad Firoz Mridha

6.1 INTRODUCTION

The authorized individual visits the neighboring ATMs to transact money conveniently. In the past, customers could only withdraw or deposit money into their accounts by visiting banks. Because of technological advancements, we now use Automated Teller Machines (ATMs) to transfer money. Historically, ATMs' primary role was to disburse cash in banknotes associated with a bank account. ATMs play a significant role in providing customers with convenient access to cash and other financial services. To easily transact the money, customers can use the ATM system 24/7. ATMs are becoming increasingly popular, making them a high-priority target for fraudulent assaults by robbers and hackers at the same rate [1]. Physical security can be in threat because any candidate may transfer money if the ATM card and pin information are known [2]. ATMs typically work with encrypted data, but hackers use hacking devices to decrypt these data. As a result, the balance can be stolen by anybody despite the account holder's awareness. Thus, the secure ATM is a major concern.

Several techniques are proposed to secure user authentication in ATMs, including fingerprint reader [3,4], facial recognition [5,6], and one-time password [7,8]. Sangeetha et al. [9] suggested an ATM system with fingerprint verification to increase protection and safety. Atiqul et al. [10] proposed an ATM transaction system with facial recognition with a convolutional neural network which will read the smile of the consumer to proceed to the next step. Abiew et al. [8] combined PIN and OTP to achieve a secure transaction. However, these techniques are unsatisfactory due to their drawbacks. When a client's hands are sweaty, fingerprint readers may not operate properly, and facial recognition may be problematic if the client has been in an accident. Thus, we propose a hybrid approach with three-factor authentication for more secure ATM transactions. As a result, if one strategy is vulnerable to hackers, the other two are advantageous for security. Our proposed framework adds two extra layers of security to the typical PIN number-based ATM machine to improve

DOI: 10.1201/9781003474111-6

the authentication process for standard and dependable ATM transactions. The overall contribution of the chapter is as follows:

We introduce a three-factor authentication mechanism for secure ATM transactions.
We replaced existing PIN code authentication with iris recognition, one-time password (OTP), and graphical pattern password based on Google's Android pattern unlocking mechanism [11].
We propose an encryption method to maintain the pattern password's security.

The remaining of the chapter is organized in the following order: Sections 6.2 and 6.3 highlight the related work and preliminaries in this domain. Section 6.4 narrates the proposed methodology. Section 6.5 narrates the performance evaluation of our proposed methodology. Section 6.6 illustrates the benefits of using our proposed methodology. Section 6.7 finally brings the chapter to a conclusion.

6.2 RELATED WORK

Many studies are conducted due to the expansion of the usage of ATMs to make transactions safer.

A study by Oruh and Ngozi [12] covers authentication (three-factor) for the Teller System Automated Machine, highlighting security flaws in the two-factor authentication technique of the ATM system, which presently uses the password and smartcard for banking transaction authentication. According to the findings of this study, authentication (two-factor) does not offer proper privacy of ATM system. A system proposal for incorporating biometric security as a third verification in the scheme was created, leading inside a three-identification ATM system that incorporates client smartcard, owner PIN, and user biometric data.

Nti et al. [13] stated that various systems require reliable personal recognition systems to approve or confirm the characteristics of an individual requesting a service. The goal of this system is to make sure that the services provided are accessible only to the intended users and no one else. These systems are prone to impostor deception in the lack of powerful individual recognition techniques. Due to its conventional authentication technique, ATMs have been hit hard throughout the years from PIN thievery and alternative ATM thefts. The authors present a multifactor authentication security setup to increase the safety and security of ATMs and its users. The suggested system has a three-tiered design structure. The verification module is the first layer, and it focuses on the enrollment phase, enhancement phase, feature extraction, and fingerprint matching. The second tier is the database end, which serves as a repository for all ATM customers' preregistered fingerprints as templates and PINs as text. The last tier provides a system platform for linking financial transactions such as balance inquiries, mini statements, and withdrawals. For the implementation phase, Microsoft Windows 8 was utilized as the operating system platform, with C# programming language serving as the front-end development and SQL server 2010 serving as the backend. The application was evaluated using the false acceptance rate, false rejection rate, average matching time, and total error rate, which demonstrate the protection and dependability of the projected system to identify and verify ATM users.

Ghodke et al. [14] stated that biometrics authentication has various benefits over conventional authentication systems, and its use for user authentication has increased significantly in recent years. The existing security of the ATM system was enhanced in this project by incorporating the user's palm print into the bank's database to further authenticate the user. This was accomplished through the design and development of an ATM simulator which simulates a conventional ATM system. The final outcome is a more secure biometrically validated ATM system that boosts client confidence in the banking sector.

Alzamel et al. [15] explained that because of the continual development in electronic transactions, the Automated Teller Machine has become the primary transaction route to conduct monetary transactions. Traditional forms of identification, such as ID cards, or exclusive information, such as a social security number or a password, don't seem to be entirely reliable. Nevertheless, this has multiplied the quantity of dishonest actions administered on Automated Teller Machines, necessitating the implementation of effective security systems as well as the necessity for rapid and precise specific person's identity and verification in ATMs. An integrated fingerprint biometric identification solution for POS networks is proposed in this study as an additional security option for ATM cards. A fingerprint biometric technology with personal identifying numbers was utilized for authentication to boost security. The proposed solution would handle customer concerns like theft, counterfeiting, card loss, and oblivion. As a result, the client will be recognized by placing on the reader of ATM machine of his target finger (based on finger scanning), and the system will identify the consumer without the need for keys or support cards. Author circulated a questionnaire to 586 respondents, and the findings demonstrate the necessity of fingerprint biometric identification for POS networks as an additional security feature for the ATM card.

Although the proposed solution would alleviate consumers' difficulties, like theft, counterfeiting, forgetfulness, or card loss, it is quite expensive.

Another study by Sudharsan et al. [16] suggested an approach for user authentication in ATM with One-Time PIN (OTP) generated for a registered mobile number linked to a bank account. Voting is very important in electing the appropriate person to lead the country. The major goal of authors is to execute two activities, namely, money transaction and ATM voting applications, by providing authentication such as biometric—fingerprint and facial recognition—by comparison with the National ID card for better security and privacy. This voting system through ATMs makes it easier and faster for consumers to improve their vote percentages.

Taralekar et al. [7] stated that each individual has multiple bank accounts at different banks, many people need various ATM cards for transactions, and each account can have its own PIN. In the traditional system, the ATM's customer identification system relies only on bank cards, secure PIN numbers, and other methods of identity verification, measures are imperfect and functions too limited, and sometimes people forget the security PIN or it gets stolen, the card gets lost or stolen. A modern ATM terminal customer identification system, "One touch Multi-banking

Transaction system utilizing Biometric and GSM Authentication," is being offered to overcome shortcomings in older ATM systems. One of the most secure solutions is biometric-based fingerprint verification; illegal access is limited since each fingerprint is unique. This solution also guarantees a protected GSM (OTP: one-time password) transaction. When compared to a standard ATM system, which has minimal risk overhead in managing numerous account transactions and achieves excellent security. However, if the phone is stolen along with the card, the amount can be stolen, rendering the proposed systems unreliable [16].

Karovaliya et al. [17] also proposed a framework combining OTP and face recognition for improving ATM's security. Moreover, the authors stated that there are some minor faults in the face recognition approach. It fails to recognize a face when aged, or beards, hats, and spectacles are used. The goal of their study is to strengthen the security of the traditional ATM mechanism. Authors have proposed a new approach that improves the entire experience, usefulness, and convenience of ATM transactions. Face recognition and one-time password are tools that help to secure accounts and protect user confidentiality. Face recognition technology allows the system to recognize each user individually, so making the face a key. This completely eliminates the potential of fraud caused by ATM card theft and duplication. Furthermore, the OTP is randomly generated which saves the user from having to remember the PIN as it works like a PIN.

A study by Abiew et al. [18] proposed a low-cost authentication mechanism for ATMs. In their system, they offered an OTP-based authentication method for ATMs that uses keyboard dynamics. Financial institutions like banks all around the globe have utilized and continue to employ Automated Teller Machine technology to extend banking hours 7-24 and provide convenience to their customers. Modern ATM systems are fully network-based computerized systems, and as is the case with these systems, their security must be prioritized. Authentication is one of the most significant ways for guaranteeing safe networked systems. Authentication is the process of confirming a user's or a process's identity while attempting to access system information resources. One of the most effective traditional methods of securing digital systems is through good authentication techniques and schemes. The most essential choice in designing secure systems is likely to be selecting an authentication technique that is appropriate for the environment. Authentication protocols can only authenticate the connected party or both the connecting party and the connected party. Typically, the verification procedure is established on authenticating elements such as facts, qualities, actions, or information that are only known to the claimant and the verifier. There are three methods of authentication depending on these factors: knowledge-based, token-based, and biometrics-based. Focusing on the strengths of the three primary authentication classes, authors devised and implemented a safe and hybrid cost-effective authentication framework for ATM systems in this study.

This approach is based on the user's typing speed of his password. Although this approach does not require any additional hardware, it is unreliable when the user suffers from hand discomfort, and his typing speed varies. Thus, we propose an approach combining iris recognition, OTP, and graphical pattern passwords to authenticate the user.

6.3   PRELIMINARIES

This section represents all the necessary technology related to this study.

6.3.1   Automated Teller Machine

An ATM [19] is a specialized computer device that allows bank account users to easily manage their money. It may be used to generate account activity or transaction reports, check account balances, retrieve or deposit cash, and even purchase stamps. After 50 years, ATMs are still in operation countrywide. The first one was utilized in London in 1967. ATMs may be located on-site or off-site. ATMs placed on-site are found in financial institutions. Customers benefit from more availability, variety, and convenience, while banks increase transaction income, save operating expenses, and make the most of staff resources. Off-premise ATMs are often located where there is a straightforward demand for cash, such as airports, food and convenience stores, and shopping complexes. ATMs are straightforward data terminals that include two input and four output devices. They must establish a connection with and communicate with a host processor. The host processor acts as an ISP, which act as a gateway through which card holder's bank account can access all the different ATM networks with a bank card. Figure 6.1 shows an example of ATM.

Figure 6.1 Example of an ATM.

6.3.2   Personal Identification Number

A lot of computerized banking transactions uses a personal identification number (PIN) [20], which is a numerical code. A PIN is employed to extend the amount of security for electronic transactions. Personal identification number, which enhance account security, is typically used with a debit card linked to one's bank account.

At the time a debit card is issued, the cardholder must choose a special PIN that he or she must enter each time he wants to withdraw money from an ATM and often when he wants to make purchases at different merchant establishments. PINs are utilized in a range of additional applications, including home and mobile security, just like passwords. A PIN is essentially a digital tool for confirming one's identification. Figure 6.2 shows an example of PIN for an ATM boot.

Typically, PINs are four to six digits in length and are either supplied by the issuing bank using a coding technique that makes each PIN unique, or they are chosen by the account user. The PIN is usually sent to the cardholder in addition to the associated card or entered at the local branch when creating an account in person through email. When selecting a PIN, it should be simple for the account owner to recall yet tough to break for the intruder. A short and simple PIN, such as "123" or easy-to-guess numbers in case of fraud, common information, such as the account holder's date of birth, wedding anniversary, or social security number, are discouraged. Account holders must use caution in the time of providing

Figure 6.2 Application of PIN for ATM.

or disclosing their personal identification number in order to avoid unauthorized access to banks.

6.3.3   Internet Service Provider

An authority that provides Internet connectivity to both commercial and personal users is known as an Internet service provider (ISP) [13]. ISPs charge their customers for surfing the web, shopping online, doing business, and interacting with family and friends. Initially, only federal agencies and a few academic departments had access to the Internet. In the late 1980s, the technology for giving extensive public access via the World Wide Web was established. Consumers originally had limited access through numerous ISPs, with America Online (AOL) being one of the most successful at the time, which employed dial-up connectivity through a phone line. Figure 6.3 shows an example of ISP.

Even during the mid-1990s, the quantity of ISPs surged to many thousand, and the surge was on. The Internet economy was formed as connectivity options expanded and speeds moved away from slower dial-up connections. More sophisticated technology was created by providers, providing aspect of every business access via bandwidth via cable and digital subscriber line (DSL) modems.

A multilayered network of links lurked beneath it all. Clients were sold access by local ISPs, while bigger ISPs paid for it. In turn, these larger ISPs paid even

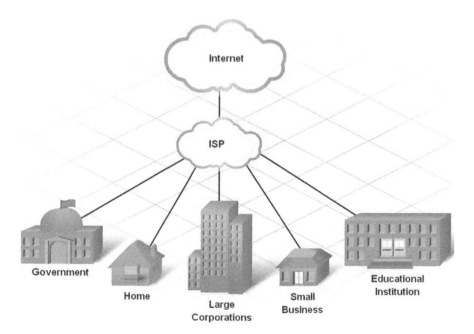

Figure 6.3 Working process of ISP.

larger ISPs for access. The path is taken by operators, who can access all network hotspots for free. These firms control the infrastructure in their respective regions.

Internet companies link their customers to the Internet, whereas simple access providers simply manage communication between individuals and the Internet at large. Other services, however, may be included based on the customer's location and availability. These services include email, web hosting, domain name registration, and browser and software packages.

Households and companies have come to expect the ability to access to the Internet from any place, whether at home or at a nearby coffee shop. To provide high-speed connectivity, businesses must invest in high costs such as fiber optics.

ISPs sometimes appear to have a monopoly in their regions due to the high cost of investment. Thus, a given company can dominate almost all or all of the market in a particular region. Enterprises in the United States may appear to function under an oligopoly compared to monopoly, in which two or more companies work together for market advantage. This notion is supported by the fact that certain large American ISPs grew up on infrastructure left over from the original telecom monopoly, Ma Bell.

Existing ISPs are financing infrastructures and will be the sole players in this market until new technologies that don't rely on fiber emerge. Consider Starlink, an organization under SpaceX formed by Elon Musk that is constructing a low-latency, broadband Internet system aimed at meeting the demands of customers worldwide, powered by a network of low Earth orbit satellites. Because of the increasing need for faster speeds and a better Internet experience, some of the largest ISPs have begun to invest extensively in 5G wireless technology.

6.3.4   Digital Subscriber Line

The Digital Subscriber Line (DSL) [19] is one of numerous methods that provide Internet access and information to homes and businesses. DSL is differentiated by the fact that it utilizes existing telephone lines/connections with little changes. Our phone provider supplied "dial-up" service in the early days of the "World Wide Web" (the 1990s, not the 1890s), which was unreliable and took up the phone line. DSL was created to meet the growing demand for Internet access, including faster and stronger connections. Figure 6.4 shows an example of DSL.

DSL connects our house to the Internet through phone lines, allowing our family to utilize the Internet while still making phone calls. This works because DSL divides telephone transmissions into three frequency bands. The lowest band is used for calls and the other two bands are used for Internet activities such as uploads and downloads.

Since DSL is delivered over phone lines, it makes sense that the main providers would be the phone companies. AT&T is the biggest telecommunications firm in the world and top supplier of DSL services. Verizon and Century Link both provide DSL service.

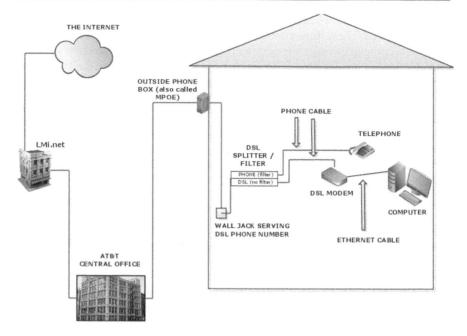

Figure 6.4 Working process of DSL.

DSL isn't as prevalent as it was 20 years ago because providers are transitioning to the future generation of web technology: fiber optics. Additionally, popular cable companies often offer Internet connections that are much faster than DSL.

A better inquiry may be, "How slow is it?" Their top speed is 15 Mbps, which they refer to as "lightning." DSL connections normally have a speed restriction of 6 Mbps, although many cable providers provide peak rates of 100 Mbps. The mid-range cable Internet bundle will most likely give download rates of 25–50 Mbps.

Yes, it is getting better by the day. To begin with, today's DSL is almost probably ADSL, a technological advancement over the original technology. But there is more: ADSL+2, which is billed as "an improvement of ADSL broadband technology" and significantly speeds up downloads. But don't get your hopes up: to find ADSL2+, we'll almost surely need to reside in a major city or heavily populated area, and we'll need to be close to the phone company's "central office."

True, true. People who have a choice, have done their homework, and want a quicker connection will not accept DSL in any form. Speed is everything these days and dial-up is dying out. In actuality, DSL providers, according to new research, would like to replace DSL with fiber optics in the future, the most contemporary technology. The FCC does not appreciate the concept of big firms leaving customers or pressing them to move to better—and more expensive—services, despite the fact that the product is much superior.

Though home broadband use consumes the majority of this time, business Internet use is as important. Internet-related businesses have dominated income development in the twenty-first century, with the Digital Economy estimated to be worth $3 trillion. Modern business is now centered on Internet-related activities. Remember that before we can engage in any Internet-related activity, we must first choose the sort of Internet connection we require. Although there are other possibilities, we'll focus on DSL versus connectors because so many small businesses are unsure of the distinctions.

DSL is an early Internet technology that served as a forerunner to dial-up. It just transport data and link us with the Internet using our phone line. DSL connections are classified into two categories: asymmetric and symmetric. Asymmetric delivers faster downloads and slower uploads, whereas symmetric gives similar upload and download speeds. Unlike cable, DSL gives a dedicated, uninterrupted link to our firm, preventing any potential neighbors from using our connection. Furthermore, DSL provides a continuous Internet connection.

Internet connection differs from DSL in that it forms coaxial cables to transport wire to our office rather than phone lines. Similar to DSL, our Internet provider is able to provide us with the required hardware, such as a cable modem as opposed to a DSL modem. Inside our workplace, the modem is connected to a coaxial wire, which converts the signal into data that our devices can transmit and receive. Furthermore, because cable Internet uses a shared network, it may function poorly and underperform during times of high Internet traffic. This is a significant distinction between DSL and cable.

6.3.5 Near-field Communication

The likelihood of human error is greatly reduced with near-field communications [21], as the receiving device receives your data immediately after you give it. For instance, a pocket dial or going by a location with an NFC chip implanted may ensure that you do not unintentionally buy something (known as "smart poster"). When employing near-field communication, you ought to act consciously. Due to the limited functionality of smartphones with dead batteries, customers may still want a secondary payment system even when NFC technology becomes widely used. However, it has to be seen whether this is a long-term drawback of NFC technology.

NFC is arguably best known as the technology that enables customers to pay for goods and services using their smartphones. NFC technology is utilized in payment systems such as Apple Pay (NASDAQ: AAPL) and Google Wallet (NASDAQ: GOOG). Although NFC is not yet accessible in the Amazon Echo (NASDAQ: AMZN), here is an example of when near-field communications may be useful. Think of using the Echo's tap-to-pay feature to pay for the pizza (or whatever else) you just bought. Figure 6.5 shows an example of NFC.

The first NFC-capable phone was introduced by Nokia in 2007, and by 2010, the telecommunications industry had started more than 100 NFC testing initiatives. The Metropolitan Transit Authority (MTA) in New York City created a

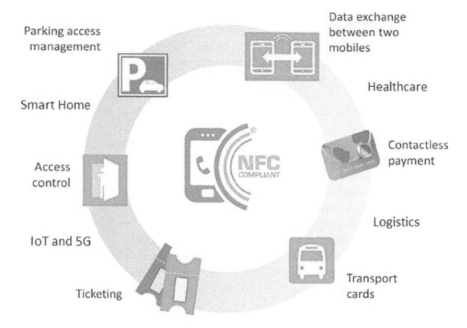

Figure 6.5 Near-field communication.

system in 2017 that enables users to pay subway fees using NFC. What follows is history, as they say.

Beyond streamlining and expediting the payment process, near-field communications offer a wide range of uses due to its constantly growing frontiers. Globally, hundreds of millions of contactless cards and readers are now in use for a variety of purposes, including operating unmanned toll booths, monitoring library books, managing inventories and sales, protecting networks and buildings, and preventing auto theft.

The cards we use to pass through card scanners in subway ticket machines and on buses are powered by NFC technology. Speakers, household appliances, and other electrical gadgets that we can monitor and manage with our cell phones potentially include it. With just a tap, NFC can also be utilized to turn on Wi-Fi and Bluetooth devices in our houses.

6.4 METHODOLOGY

Our research proposes a mixed breed methodology for clients verification strategy dissimilar to the only PIN code-based information sources or bio-measurements input. The framework of our proposed methodology is depicted in Figure 6.6. The

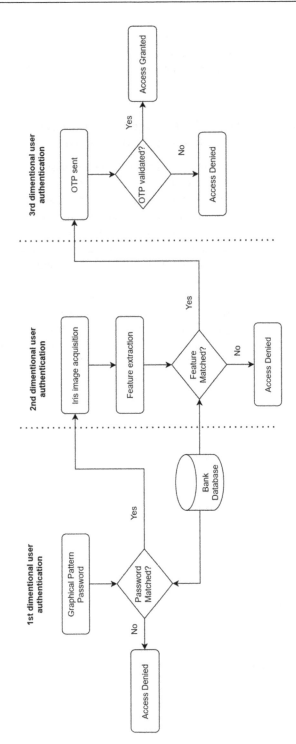

Figure 6.6 Proposed framework.

first part of our procedure is the graphical pattern password which is elaborated in Section 6.4.1. The second part is iris recognition elaborated in Section 6.4.2 and the last part one-time password is described in Section 6.4.3. And lastly, we added details of functional paces in Section 6.4.4 which gives an overall description of the transaction process.

6.4.1   Graphical Pattern Password with Lightweight On-premise Data Encryption System

In our preferred verification system, these graphical pattern password input frameworks are obtained from the unlock system of Google's Android Pattern [22]. The idea is to create lines on the touch interface by connecting the dots, which can identify with some proper pixel coordinates acting about as a state of the tap (resembles dots image to address) which will be correlated against the stocked one. In Figure 6.7(a), a grid containing explicit dots is portrayed. On the touchscreen, a dot includes fixed pixels, laid with a circle-shaped sign, and addressed with two-dimensional directions (X, Y).

In Figure 6.7(b), we simulate a client's input that joins the dots to make a pattern. Here, dots demonstrate where the client starts and how he is moving to make the stocked pattern. From beginning to end, clients need to draw the pattern without lifting up the contacting finger/pointer. A lift-up event is granted as the end of the pattern path. Presently, ATM metamorphoses the pattern into something significant that seems to be a traditional password. For this, we are appraising a Grid function that changes over the way into pre-characterized number arrangements. A two-digit decimal number for every cell which contains a dot is relegated by the Grid function. In Figure 6.7(b), the speck which is in arrange (4,3) dole out number 34 just like Figure 6.7(c). So, we can recalculate the subsequent pathway that the client has drawn before. Path = (4,3) then (3,3) then (2,2) then (1,2) then (1,3) then (2,2) then (3,2) then (4,1) then (3,1) and then (2,1).

We offered an encryption strategy that has been inferred just after the making pattern to keep the secrecy of the pattern password. As we are just taking care of a series of numbers for information encryption, we have enacted an asymmetric encryption strategy that is insubstantial with remembering that ATMs have restricted handling limits. To accomplish this, we evaluated PRESENT as an encryption algorithm [23]. The PRESENT algorithm is 2.5 occasions less compact than the AES algorithm [24]. The very same key is required for both encrypting and decrypting in the symmetric encryption algorithm. Despite that, there is an issue about how the encryption key is conveyed through the system as it is undependable if somebody can take the key during dispatch. Utilizing the pattern password of the particular client will go about as an origin of the prime key, which will reuse with PRESENT algorithm to produce 80 secret bits key. This recently determined mystery key digit stream that was procured before will be encoded. As a similar code is pre-stocked with the specific client's account, the server could recover the prime key for decrypting the note sent from the ATM with that specific account.

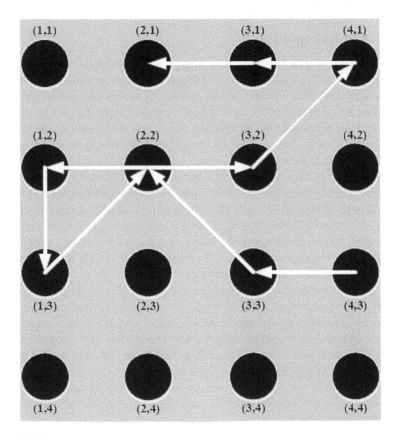

Figure 6.7 The graphical pattern password system.

	1	2	3	4
1	11	22	33	44
2	09	18	29	38
3	05	14	25	34
4	03	12	23	32

Figure 6.7 (Continued).

6.4.2   Iris Recognition

We incorporated iris recognition, often known as iris scanning, which is a technique of generating a high-contrast iris image of a person utilizing visible and near-infrared light. This is the process of employing visible and near-infrared light to generate a high image of iris. It is a biometric technique that works similarly to fingerprint readers and face recognition. Iris scans can determine the people's irises' unique patterns. Iris recognition operate by illuminating the iris with invisible infrared light to detect distinctive patterns that is invisible to the human eye. Our system utilizes iris scanning as it is faster and more accurate than fingerprint or face-recognition scans because it is easier to disguise or change one's face or fingers than to change one's eyes. The iris scan is done with a scanner installed at an ATM. Around 240 biometric features are captured by iris scanners, and they are unique in each eye. After that, the scanners convert the data into a digital representation. The information extracted from the image of the iris is compared with the saved information in the bank database.

The different patterns in the irises, or colored circles in people's eyes, are detected via iris scanning. Infrared light is used by biometric iris recognition scanners to illuminate the iris and identify distinctive patterns that are invisible to the eye of a human. Iris scanners locate and remove iris-obscuring objects like eyelids, eyelashes, and specular reflections. Then, we get the finished product which is a group of pixels that only include the iris. After that, a bit sequence that encrypts the data in the iris is obtained by looking at the pattern of shades and shapes in the eye. One-to-one template matching is applied for digitizing this bit pattern and comparing it to templates that are kept in a database for identification or verification. Iris scanning cameras can be wall-mounted or portable, or they can be handed and portable. Iris scanners capture approximately 240 biometric characteristics, the combination of which is unique to each eye. Then, the scanners convert the data into a digital format. A computer database stores the quantitative representation of information collected from the picture of the iris. Iris scanning is sometimes combined with other biometrics, including fingerprints and facial recognition.

6.4.3 One-time Password

For implementing a one-time password system, we used a text message service. If the user is identified by iris scanning, an OTP is delivered to the user's phone via text messages. Citizens of rural areas have old phones without Internet connections, so text messages are preferred. The user receives OTP instantly after passing the iris recognition test. The user has to enter the 6-digit OTP within 2 minutes of receiving it. If the code is entered incorrectly, the account will be disabled temporarily, and a notification will be sent to the registered cellphone number. This feature is added to limit the use of fraudulent ways of ATM transactions. We have now arrived at the point where we can scan and print actual irises by 3D printing [25]. The implementation of OTP helps to prevent 3D-printed iris attacks.

6.4.4 Details of Functional Paces

The client puts their card into card spaces, and ATM takes the card inside and peruses and gathers fundamental client information from the card. Card provider merchants get all the data accumulated from the card to recognize the real beneficiary bank server. Beneficiary bank server then permits to acknowledge further inputs and informs the specific ATM about the further client inputs. Then the ATM allows for inputting the graphical pattern password, which conveys a 4 × 4 grid interfacing with dots by contacting, starting with one-by-one dots to make a pattern. The grid translation function converts the pattern to digits, with each grid cell being designed by a specified two-digit number. Currently, when using the PRESENT symmetric cryptography method, an encryption key creation function generates an 80-bit key. The same algorithm encrypts the stream utilizing the secret key produced from the inputs of the clients prior to transmitting a particular bank server. PRESENT algorithm assesses a 64-bits block serially to employ encryption and begins transmitting the coded note across the ATM network foundation toward the server. Afterwards, the bank server begin decoding the encrypted bits with the similar secret key produced by a similar PRESENT algorithm from the put-away pattern code of that particular client account and reformate the digits from the previously sent, encrypted memo from the ATM to analyze it with a pre-stocked pattern password on that specific record. Here, our consideration is the pattern password, which was enrolled during the account opening time by the actual clients who had to embed their own graphical pattern password with client interfacing gadgets from appointed branches. At that point, the graphical pattern password was changed into digit stream to stock in particular client represent forthcoming validation.

From that point onward, second-dimensional client info will be grasped, which is iris recognition. The iris scan will be done with a camera, excluding eyelids, eyelashes, as well as specular reflections that frequently cover some iris areas. The final result is a group of pixels that only include the iris. The information from the iris is then encoded into a bit pattern using the contours and coloring of the eye. One-to-one template matching will be performed with the stored template in a database for verification. When the verification is performed and the user is identified as an authenticated user, the user will receive an OTP. The user has to provide the OTP through ATM to the bank. The bank server will allow the client validation by permission notice to the ATM for additional procedures or deny access if the OTP does not coordinate with one another.

6.5   EVALUATION

We evaluated our proposed system with a set of experiments. Man-in-the-middle attack, shoulder-surfing, and brute-force attack are considered for evaluating our proposed system. These attacks are possible in previous systems that utilize only pin code. Our proposed system is not vulnerable to shoulder-surfing and man-in-the-middle attack because our proposed architecture comprises iris scan along with pattern password and OTP. Shoulder-surfing is only achievable in a situation where the perpetrator can see the user's finger movements as he inputs his pin code. Shoulder-surfing is utterly unfeasible because the participant is verified by his iris. Our authentication system requires more time, but it is not vulnerable to man-in-the-middle and brute force attacks. By using trial and error, a brute force assault attempts to guess passwords and encryption keys. Hackers experiment with every possible combination with the intention of obtaining it right in a PIN-based authentication system. The proposed authentication system's performance comparison with the previous system is given in Table 6.1.

Table 6.1 Result Analysis of the Existing and Proposed System

Authentication System	Vulnerable to Man-in-the-middle Attack	Vulnerable to Shoulder-surfing	Vulnerable to Brute Force Attack
[?]	✓	✗	✓
[?]	✓	✓	✓
[?]	✓	✗	✓
Our proposed system	✓	✗	✗

6.6   ESTIMATED RESULTS AND BENEFITS

In our recommended technique, some underlying welfare can be checked. The following are some remarkable focuses that show the given technique's welfare as far as adaptability and viability:

- Effectively re-programmable to change any function, which can give an advantage to the banks to update the planning unique/exceptional starting with one bank then onto the next.
- Utilizing an on-premises encryption strategy can keep up with the honesty of the client's information.
- Iris recognition system avoids the danger of stolen graphical pattern passwords or hacking.
- By using the OTP, we have mitigated the risks associated with biometric authentication.

6.7   CONCLUSION

ATMs are a convenient method for clients to meet their financial needs. ATMs are located all over the world and are used by a significant majority of the world's population. As a result, ATM transactions must be both safe and efficient. A graphical pattern password was fused with iris recognition and OTP for user authentication to improve the level of security. To make it more secure against hackers, we proposed an encryption mechanism. We are confident that our suggested combination of three authentication methods improves the trustworthiness and security of ATM transactions. This method may be combined with the Internet/mobile banking system and other emerging types of authentication systems such as NFC-based gadgets or IoT-based gadgets, which can eliminate the requirement for a conventional ATM card. We intend to enhance our authentication system for physically disabled people, as it is currently incompatible with their circumstances.

Chapter 7

Cybersecurity Risk Management Framework for Cyber-physical Systems

Edyta Karolina Szczepaniuk and
Hubert Szczepaniuk

7.1 INTRODUCTION

The term cyber-physical system (CPS) was proposed by H. Gill in 2006 and is currently one of the priority innovations for the "Industry 4.0" concept. Key technology trends underlying CPSs include Internet-of-Things (IoT), big data, Smart Technologies, and cloud computing [1].
   As defined by H. Gill:

> Cyber-Physical Systems are physical, biological, and engineered systems whose operations are integrated, monitored, and/or controlled by a computational core. Components are networked at every scale. Computing is "deeply embedded" into every physical component, possibly even into materials. The computational core is an embedded system, usually demands a real-time response, and is most often distributed. The behavior of a cyber-physical system is a fully integrated hybridization of computational (logical) and physical action [2].

In other words, CPSs are "smart systems that include engineered interacting networks of physical and computational components" [3]. In such systems, physical objects and computing resources are tightly integrated and show some degree of continuous coordination with each other [4]. An essential feature of CPS is the tight integration of the computing layer and physical processes. CPSs often take the form of embedded systems and networks to monitor and control physical processes that operate in a feedback loop. In this architecture, physical processes are the data source for computing the objects' control signal [5]. In this context, the scope of the application of CPSs makes cybersecurity one of the critical conditions for their further development. Moreover, these systems have specific cybersecurity problems that are different from traditional information systems.
   Attacks on CPSs may destabilize critical infrastructure, including violating the attributes of information security and disrupting the continuity of the organization's operation and the availability of the service. The complexity and interdependence of different elements of CPSs can also increase the risk of a cascading effect caused by

    DOI: 10.1201/9781003474111-7

a cyberattack. In this context, cyberattacks on CPSs pose a serious threat to international security and many national security sectors, including human life and health. Duo et al. presented an overview of selected cyberattacks on CPSs [6]:

- An attack on an Iranian nuclear power plant using the Stuxnet worm (2010)
- Ransomware attacks on companies and institutions in many countries using WannaCry software (2017)
- Attacks on healthcare facilities during the COVID-19 pandemic, for example, on a Czech hospital (2020)
- A ransomware attack on a US fuel pipeline that resulted in the shutdown of a critical fuel network (2021)

The above-mentioned attacks on CPSs illustrate the possible scale of the effects of cybersecurity threats. It can be assumed that the development of new services and the increase in the amount of processed data may lead to problems with the security of CPSs, such as the intensification of cyberattacks and the need to use protection methods [7]. The outlined context shows the need for research on the security of CPSs. The literature emphasizes that risk management is an important element of implementing cybersecurity solutions for CPSs (see, e.g., [8,9]). This process makes it possible to detect vulnerabilities, identify threats, and implement adequate risk minimization strategies. The subject of this chapter also takes into account research directions supported by many countries and international organizations (see, e.g., [10,11]).

The chapter's main objective is to develop a risk management framework for the cybersecurity of CPSs. The chapter proposes a model of the risk management process, which includes theoretical issues related to risk management, the architecture of CPSs, security requirements, threats, vulnerabilities, and elements of risk management. The research results can be a reference point for implementing solutions for the cybersecurity of CPSs.

The chapter structure results from the adopted research objectives and includes an introduction, research methodology, four substantive sections, conclusions, and references. The first section discusses the systemic aspects of cybersecurity risk management in CPSs. The next section concerns the analysis of the CPS architecture and the formulation of cybersecurity requirements. The third part describes the threats and vulnerabilities of CPSs and proposes their classification for risk management purposes. The last section presents the proposed model of the risk management process in the cybersecurity of CPSs. The chapter ends with a summary of the research results and references.

7.2 RESEARCH METHODOLOGY

The chapter deals with the complex issues of risk management in the cybersecurity of CPSs. This subject matter is an interdisciplinary issue, as it finds its basis in technical sciences, security sciences, and management sciences. Moreover, in practice, there are many norms, standards, and methodologies relating to the issues of IT systems risk management in organizations. Therefore, the research methodology is based on a systemic approach that enables the analysis of research issues based on various scientific fields.

The chapter's main objective is to develop a risk management framework for the cybersecurity of CPSs. This goal was concretized with the following specific objectives:

- Characterization of a systemic approach to risk management for the cybersecurity of systems
- Analysis of CPS architecture and definition of cybersecurity requirements
- Identification of threats and vulnerabilities for CPSs
- Developing a risk management process model in the cybersecurity of CPSs

In order to implement the above assumptions, a research approach based on a system analysis was adopted. In addition, the chapter uses research methods such as analysis, synthesis, abstraction, generalization, and modeling.

7.3   SYSTEMIC ASPECTS OF RISK MANAGEMENT IN THE CYBERSECURITY OF CPSS

Risk is a complex and ambiguous concept. Risk definitions emphasize its various aspects depending on the scientific discipline and the area of activity of the entity, e.g., a person, an organization, or a state. The Information Systems Audit and Control Association (ISACA) presented one of the universal definitions of this category. ISACA defines risk as "the combination of the probability of an event and its consequence" [12]. This approach treats risk as a relation between the probability of an event and its consequences. This interpretation allows for the assumption that risk management may be an essential element of decision-making, also in hazardous conditions. Regardless of the definition adopted, many risk typologies in the literature allow distinguishing its various types (see, e.g., [13]).

For further analysis, the definition of Kaplan and Garrick was adopted, who developed a mathematical definition of risk presented by the following set of triples [14]:

$$R = \left\{ \left\langle s_i, l_i, x_i, \right\rangle \right\} \tag{7.1}$$

where
s_i is the identification or description of the scenario;
l_i is the scenario probability; and
x_i is the consequence or measure of the scenario assessment, i.e., the measure of harm.

In this chapter, the above interpretation of risk is limited to the issues of CPS cybersecurity. Therefore, the discussed category will be treated as a relation determining the probability of a threat to CPS and its consequences. Moreover, one of the research assumptions is adopting a systemic approach that considers the system's vulnerability and resilience to threats in the risk assessment (see, e.g., [15]). The following elements and relationships in risk management can be distinguished:

- *Threat:* It is any undesirable phenomenon (process, event) from the point of view of an undisturbed operation of the system [16]. The ISO/IEC 27000 standard defines this term as "a potential cause of an unwanted incident" [17]. Threats exploit system vulnerabilities and increase the risk of a security incident.
- *Vulnerability:* It is a system weakness that can be exposed to a threat or can be used to negatively affect the system [15]. In other words, vulnerability is a security flaw that increases risk and exposes assets to impairment.
- *Risk:* It is expressed by the relationship between the threat and vulnerability and the size of the effects caused by the materialization of threats [18]. The elements that increase the risk are the vulnerabilities, threats, and value of acts.
- *Security measures:* These are mechanisms that protect against threats and minimize the risk of their occurrence. Implementing security measures depends, among other things, on the system's security requirements.
- *Assets (resources):* According to the ISO/IEC 27001 standard, it is "anything that has value to the organization" [19]. Moreover, ISACA indicates that they may have tangible and intangible values [12]. This approach distinguishes the following: human, information, financial resources, and infrastructure. Vulnerabilities are a factor that exposes resources to impairment.
- *Asset value:* Assets have values that depend on the type of resources and the specifics of the organization. In cybersecurity, the value of assets is often assessed in terms of the loss of information security attributes (see, e.g., [20]) as well as image and financial losses for the organization (see, e.g., [21]).
- *Security requirements:* These are a set of features, capabilities, or conditions that should be met to ensure safety. The protection requirements are determined based on the risk analysis results and implemented using security measures that minimize the risk.

The above elements and relationships are crucial in the risk management process. ISO/IEC 31000 defines risk management as "coordinated activities to direct and control an organization with regard to risk" [22]. In the presented approach, risk management supports making rational decisions in the organization. As mentioned before, there are many classifications and types of risk. One of the determinants of their distinction is the specificity of the business activity of a given organization.

Referring the above considerations to the research issues, CPS cybersecurity management can be reduced to optimizing security measures in relation to possible threat scenarios. The implementation of these solutions should be preceded by a risk assessment, including vulnerability analysis and identification of threats and their effects. Therefore, ensuring CPS cybersecurity requires a systemic approach that considers the system's elements and relationships and is based on risk management. The process involves several steps, but the terminology of the topic discussed varies according to standards and methodology. Table 7.1 presents an overview of selected risk management solutions.

According to Table 7.1 and despite existing differences in nomenclature, the main objective of risk management is to minimize the risk of threats. The heterogeneous nature of CPS devices, operating in different IoT domains and communicating using multiple technologies and protocols, make CPSs vulnerable to threats and have multiple security challenges [26]. In addition, risk management for cybersecurity is critical to achieving the organization's strategic goals and

Table 7.1 Selected Risk Management Standards and Methodologies

Standard or Methodology	Risk Management Stages

ISO/IEC 31000	• Establishing the context
	• Risk assessment:
	  • Risk identification
	  • Risk analysis
	  • Risk evaluation
	• Risk treatment
	• Communication and consultation
	• Monitoring and inspection [22]

NIST SP 800–39	• Frame risk • Assess risk • Respond to risk • Monitor risk [23]

BSI Standard 200–3	• Prepare a threat overview
	• Risk classification:
	  • Risk assessment
	  • Risk evaluation
	• Risk treatment:
	  • Risk avoidance
	  • Risk reduction
	  • Risk transfer
	  • Risk acceptance
	• Consolidating of the security concept:
	  • Integration of the additional safeguards identified based on the risk analysis in the security concept [24]

European Union Agency for Cybersecurity (ENISA)	• Identification of threats • Evaluation of threats • Evaluation of risk • Mitigation of risk • Evaluation and assessment of risk controls [25]

Source: Own work based on Refs [22–25].

delivering the services offered by CPSs. Therefore, effective risk management requires a systemic approach that involves the entire organization and considers the specificity of CPSs. Therefore, the risk management issue justifies the need to analyze the CPS architecture and define cybersecurity requirements.

7.4 ARCHITECTURE OF CYBER-PHYSICAL SYSTEMS AND CYBERSECURITY REQUIREMENTS

CPSs are based on the paradigm of integrating calculations and physical processes. A specific feature of CPS is its high level of complexity, which can generate security problems. The analyses assume that effective risk management requires considering the architecture of CPSs and formulating cybersecurity requirements. These elements will be the basis for identifying threats and vulnerabilities in the CPS architecture.

In the literature, the CPS structure is presented using models with different architectures (see, e.g., [26,27,28]). One concept is a three-layer architecture model that includes the perception, transmission, and application layers. The perception layer recognizes signals from the surrounding environment and registers them. End devices are equipped with sensors capable of capturing data from the environment in which they operate (e.g., RFID, GPS, cameras). The transmission layer provides communication between the perception and application layers and is responsible for transmitting information collected by the end devices. This layer uses wired and wireless transmission media, network protocols, and data transmission technologies. The application layer includes software and services enabling integral data exchange between individual network nodes and their processing and storage [29]. The SCADA (Supervisory Control and Data Acquisition) system is an example of a solution used within this layer.

The literature review also found other solutions for CPSs. Lee et al. developed a five-level CPS structure model for industrial systems that includes the following layers [30]:

- *Smart connection:* It realizes the acquisition of accurate and reliable data from machines that can be measured by sensors or obtained from the controller or corporate systems.
- *Data-to-information conversion:* It is responsible for converting data into information.
- *Cyber:* It acts as a central information node and collects information from machines to manage and analyze information.
- *Cognition:* It provides users with information necessary to make decisions.
- *Configuration:* It shares feedback to CPS and performs machine control and configuration functions.

It is worth noting that the authors of the analyzed 5C model also provided practical guidelines for implementing the proposed solutions in the field of quality improvement. The literature on the subject also includes architectures that consider the human factor. One solution is an anthropocentric cyber-physical reference model that assimilates physical, computational, and human components. This model is an extension of the classic CPS architecture that embeds the human–machine interface in the device [31]. Based on this solution, a 3C architecture model for CPS was proposed, which consists of three components, i.e., the human, cybernetic, and physical levels. Compared to the previous model, the 3C architecture within the main levels includes additional interface elements and parameters such as connectors and protocols [32]. The authors of the analyzed models postulate that there is a need to consider the human factor in the architecture of CPSs.

Referring to the research issues, the three-layer architecture can be the basis for further analysis in terms of CPS security (see, e.g., [26,27,28]). This model enables the assessment, inter alia, in the context of computer network security and physical security. Other models referenced in this chapter describe the components of the CPS architecture with particular emphasis on system functionality and usability. Nevertheless, they make little reference to the security aspects. However, it is worth noting that the authors of the developed models adopted research assumptions focused on the design, implementation, and improvement of CPSs. The results of these studies can also be continued in the area of security and risk management.

For further analysis of risk management and cybersecurity, a CPS architecture model was developed for this purpose (Figure 7.1).

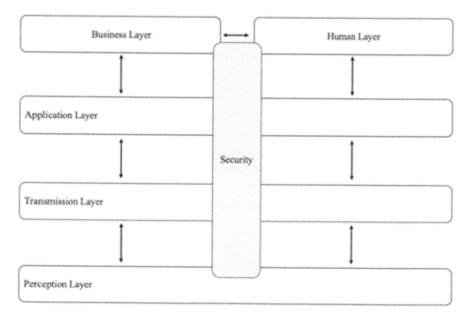

Figure 7.1 The architecture of cyber-physical systems.

Source: Own work.

The model presented in Figure 7.1 takes into account the key elements of CPSs, i.e., the physical and digital domains. In addition, the architecture includes the business layer and the human factor layer. The business layer includes the management system and business logic, which is determined by the specificity of the organization's functioning. This layer and the human factors layer cooperate through the digital domain with the physical layer regarding decision-making, control, and cognition. The application layer is responsible for the software and services that create a platform for exchanging data collected by all devices. Another element is the transmission layer, which implements communication between the application layer and the perception layer and transmits data collected by end devices. The perception layer collects and records data from the physical world using end-device sensors. In addition, the model considers security aspects for each layer. This solution was adopted due to the research results presented in the previous section. The analysis of the theoretical aspects of risk management showed that ensuring the cybersecurity of CPSs requires a systemic approach.

For the model shown in Figure 7.1, the following cybersecurity requirements for CPSs were formulated:

- The security of information and services is implemented, maintained, and improved at the assumed level of information security attributes (see, e.g., [33]).
- The system ensures confidentiality, which means access to data and services only for authorized users (see, e.g., [9,33]).
- The system ensures the availability of data and services at any time at the request of an authorized entity. The availability of CPSs is one of the most important requirements and has a high priority for security (see, e.g., [9,34]).
- The system guarantees data integrity and prevents unauthorized changes (see, e.g., [33,34]).
- The system guarantees the authenticity and responsibility of the users (see, e.g., [33]).
- The system ensures privacy, which guarantees the user the right to access data collected by CPS, including information on how data is processed, secured, and transferred to other entities (see, e.g., [26,34]).
- The reliable system guarantees the ability to adapt to changing security conditions to ensure business continuity and recovery after a security incident and failure. Reliability is a critical requirement for CPSs (see, e.g., [26,34,35]).
- The system components are resistant to failures and disruptions in the functioning of CPSs. Ensuring the resilience of CPSs requires determining possible paths of system penetration and selecting appropriate security measures (see, e.g., [26,33]).
- Operational security is ensured in terms of interaction and coordination between the various layers and elements of CPSs (see, e.g., [26]).

- The human factor is aware of the threats and is not vulnerable to them (see, e.g., [18]).
- The organization of CPS security takes into account legal requirements, norms, and standards. The internal documents developed also take into account the organization's mission and business processes, as well as the results of the risk assessment (see, e.g., [34]).

In conclusion, ensuring the cybersecurity of CPSs requires the implementation of the above security requirements and comprehensive risk management taking into account all layers of the CPS architecture. The model presented in Figure 7.1 and the formulated requirements will form the basis for further considerations on threats and vulnerabilities for CPSs.

7.5   IDENTIFICATION OF THREATS AND VULNERABILITIES FOR RISK MANAGEMENT PURPOSES

Risk management aims to minimize the risk of threats that may affect the organization and functions performed by CPSs. This process includes logically structured activities that ensure the cybersecurity of CPSs. As already mentioned, there are many risk management standards and methodologies that differ, among others, in the naming of individual stages. Regardless of the terminology adopted, the key element of the process is risk identification. This stage includes, in particular, the identification of threats and vulnerabilities, which are then subject to risk analysis. The risk analysis and assessment results support rational decision-making in selecting a risk management strategy. In other words, correctly identifying threats to CPSs enables the organization to prepare for likely threat scenarios. There are different approaches to threat identification in the literature. One approach is identification based on the effects of losing the information security attributes. This solution is used, for example, in BSI Standard 200–3, where the effects of threats are described in terms of confidentiality, integrity, and availability [24]. This method can be beneficial when the organization processes classified information or estimates the risk using quantitative or qualitative–quantitative methods.

Another option is to identify threats to specific assets. This is usually preceded by an inventory of assets and information classification, identifying groups with different levels of availability. Each asset is valued according to this procedure. Threat and vulnerability levels are then determined for each asset. This solution was recommended in ISO/IEC TR 13335-3 (see, e.g., [36]).

In the practice of risk management, other solutions in the field of threat identification and risk analysis are also used. One of the solutions used is Hazard and Operability Studies (HAZOP), which enables hazard analysis and the examination of the effects of deviations from the design conditions of the system (see, e.g., [9,37,38]). An example of a graphic technique used in threat identification and risk assessment for CPSs is Fault Tree Analysis (FTA). The method aims to develop possible events that may disrupt the system's functioning. The fault tree consists of nodes (undesirable events in the system), gates (relationships between nodes), and edges (path of undesirable events in the system) [9]. Attack trees are a similar solution and have a graphical structure. The method was described by Schneier and enables the modeling of attack scenarios and system security assessment [39]. It is also possible to formally describe the attack tree in conjunction with fault tree analysis. For this purpose, Boolean logic Driven Markov Processes (BDMP) is used (see, e.g., [40,41]). The analyzed examples illustrate only selected methods of threat identification, which at a later stage are used to analyze and assess the risk. The following risk assessment methods can be distinguished: quantitative, qualitative, and qualitative–quantitative.

The research issues justify the need to identify threats to the cybersecurity of CPSs for risk management. CPSs are exposed to threats with various specific characteristics. Table 7.2 presents the general classification of threats to the cybersecurity of CPSs, considering various classification criteria.

Table 7.2 General Classification of Threats to the Cybersecurity of CPSs

Classification Criterion	Characteristics and Examples
Source	The classification based on the source criterion takes into account, inter alia, the following threats: technical, natural, and related to human activity. Technical risks are related to unforeseen damage, destruction, or disruption of systems and technical devices. Natural threats include the effects of natural forces, such as a lightning strike. The threats related to the human factor include, among others, cyberattacks on CPS elements
Location	The location criterion makes it possible to distinguish internal threats from external threats. The first group of threats comes from inside the organization, e.g., disclosure of data by an employee, human errors, and failures. External threats come from outside the organization, such as dDoS attacks and man-in-the-middle attacks
Randomness	Due to the randomness criterion, threats can be divided into intentional (deliberate) and unintentional (accidental, random). Deliberate threats are carried out to compromise the security of the system, e.g., a ransomware attack. The second group includes threats that arise unintentionally as a result of an accident or natural disaster, e.g., human errors, power failures, and floods
Information security attributes	Classification of threats according to information security attributes allows for distinguishing threats that cause loss of confidentiality, availability, and integrity. Threats violating confidentiality are related to unauthorized access to resources, e.g., a hacker attack. Another group relates to threats that result in losing access to the resource, e.g., dDoS attacks. Integrity threats result in unauthorized information modification, deletion, or damage, such as computer sabotage

(Continued)

Table 7.2 (Continued)

Classification Criterion	Characteristics and Examples
Attack target and motive	Based on the attack target and motive, it is possible to determine the effects of threats to the system, which may also affect critical infrastructure. According to this criterion, the general classification includes the following types of threats in cyberspace: computer crime, cyberespionage, cyberterrorism, and cyberwarfare. These threats have specific characteristics that classify a specific cyberattack to a given phenomenon. The purpose of computer crime is primarily for material or personal gain. On the other hand, other threats are aimed at obtaining classified information (cyber espionage) and critical infrastructure objects (cyberterrorism and cyberwar)
CPS application area	Classification by application area is based on threats specific to individual sectors of the economy and the implementation of CPSs. This classification includes, inter alia, the following threats: attacks on intelligent vehicles, attacks on the intelligent network (Smart Grid CPS Attack), attacks on industrial control systems, and attacks on medical devices

Source: Own work.

Table 7.2 shows a general classification of threats that can be used for risk management in CPSs. The choice of a specific taxonomy depends on the business goals of the organization and the specifics of its functioning. The criterion of source, location, and randomness allows identifying a broad spectrum of threats to CPSs. This solution can also be used in the risk management process. This enables the implementation of security measures and internal procedures regarding localized vulnerabilities, e.g., human resources security. In addition, the classification enables the development and implementation of contingency plans and business continuity management for specific threat scenarios, including those related to natural hazards. The information security attributes criterion is particularly useful when an organization assesses the impact of threats in terms of loss of confidentiality, integrity, and availability. As mentioned earlier, there are risk management standards and methods in practice that assess risk based on information security attributes. These characteristics can also be used in the process of selecting information protection methods and security measures. The criterion of the attack target and motive is used to analyze threats to national security or international security. This makes it possible to see certain trends in the security environment of entities. In addition, this criterion is necessary to identify the perpetrators of threats and to determine the services competent to detect them. The last of the classification criteria listed in Table 7.2 makes it possible to identify threats according to specific areas of CPS application. The literature review indicates studies on the detailed characteristics of threats and vulnerabilities of CPSs, e.g., for medical systems (see, e.g., [28,42]), industrial control systems (see, e.g., [43,44]), and Smart Grid (see, e.g., [45,46]).

In addition to the general classification, threats and vulnerabilities can also be identified in the context of the architecture of CPSs. Table 7.3 shows examples of threats and vulnerabilities for the architecture model proposed in Figure 7.1.

The considerations made lead to the assumption that identifying threats and vulnerabilities is an essential stage of risk management. The complex nature of CPSs makes them vulnerable to various threats. The classifications of threats and vulnerabilities presented in this section do not fully exhaust the broad research issues. One of the adopted research assumptions was to develop a general classification of threats and vulnerabilities. Research can be continued to develop a comprehensive inventory of threats and vulnerabilities for risk management in a specific organization or a selected classification criterion.

Table 7.3 Examples of Threats and Vulnerabilities for Each Layer of the CPS Architecture

CPS Layer	Threats	Vulnerabilities
Business layer	• Wrong business logic • Incorrect logic implementation • Failure to adjust business logic to legal requirements and security standards [30]	• Insufficient or missing software testing • Inadequate organization and management • No updating of internal procedures
Human layer	• Social engineering • User errors • Unauthorized use of devices and software	• Insufficient staff training • Non-compliance with the safety rules • Incorrect use of hardware and software
Application layer	• Malicious software (Malware) • SQL injection • Cross-site scripting (XSS) • Ransomware attack • Buffer overflow • Attacks on login systems	• Known vulnerabilities of applications and operating systems • Improper management of access rights • Lack of identification and authentication mechanisms
Transmission layer	• Spoofing attack • Sybil attack • Distributed denial of service attack (DDoS) • Man-in-the-middle (MiTM) • Natural hazards	• Known vulnerabilities of communication protocols • Improper management of a computer network • Unsecured connection to the public network
Perception layer	• Fault attack • Sensors failure • Resonance attack • Electromagnetic interference • Wiretapping of signals registered by sensors and end devices	• Lack of physical security • Unstable mains, disruptions, and outages • Sensitivity to voltage and temperature fluctuations

Source: Own work.

7.6   RISK MANAGEMENT PROCESS IN THE CYBERSECURITY OF CYBER-PHYSICAL SYSTEMS

Research findings from the previous sections have shown that ensuring CPS cybersecurity requires a systemic approach. The foundation of the implemented solutions should be risk management. It should be emphasized that this process consists of several stages and requires taking into account the organization's mission and business processes.

Figure 7.2 shows the proposed model of the risk management process in the cybersecurity of cyber-physical systems.

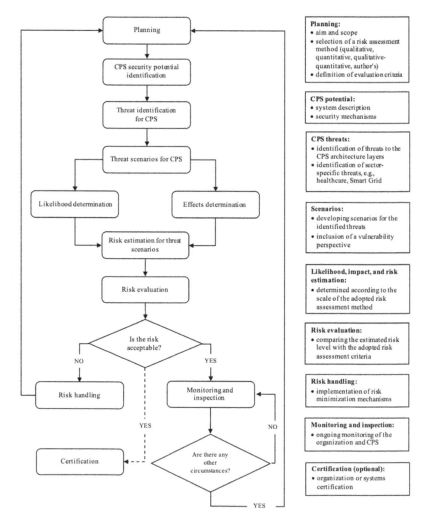

Figure 7.2 Model of the risk management process in the cybersecurity of CPSs.

Source: Own work.

The model presented in Figure 7.2 covers the general risk management process in the cybersecurity of CPSs. It can be a reference point when implementing risk analysis and assessment mechanisms in an organization belonging to any sector of the economy. Moreover, it ensures compliance with recognized standards and unifies their terminology (Table 7.1).

According to the proposed model, planning is the first stage of the process. Planning consists in formally defining a plan to implement risk management in the cybersecurity of the system. This stage requires the development of internal documents of the organization that define the goals, scope, and responsibilities in the risk management process. An essential element is also the determination of security requirements that will affect the assessment of the tested system and the implementation of security measures. Section 7.4 proposes cybersecurity model requirements for CPSs. The selection of the risk assessment method and the adoption of the criteria for its assessment is the basis for the implementation of further stages. As already indicated, many methods and techniques have been developed that an organization can choose to achieve the above assumptions.

Identifying the CPS security potential requires a detailed characterization and analysis of the existing security mechanisms. The risk management elements and relationships described in Section 7.3 are helpful in this regard. In this context, it is also essential to identify the vulnerabilities that can be analyzed in relation to the CPS architecture. Table 7.3 presents examples of vulnerabilities for individual architectural layers. It should be noted that CPSs have specific vulnerabilities. Therefore, they should be analyzed in relation to the system implementation area.

The key stage of the analyzed process is the identification of threats to CPSs. This stage's implementation contributes to preparing the organization for probable threats that may cause security incidents. The organization should select a threat classification for this step. This will enable a holistic view of the issue of threats, which covers a broad spectrum of their sources. Section 7.5 proposes model taxonomies that can be used to develop a comprehensive list dedicated to a particular organization. In particular, we recommend risk analysis for individual layers of the CPS architecture in conjunction with identifying sectoral threats. Another aspect of this stage is the selection of a specific method or technique for identifying threats. Section 7.5 provides examples of solutions such as HAZOP, FTA, or BDMP.

The next step is developing scenarios for the threats identified in the previous stage. This step follows from Kaplan and Garrick's definition of risk adopted in this chapter [14] and presented in Equation 7.1. According to NIST, the threat scenario is "Set of discrete threat events, associated with a specific threat source or multiple threat sources, partially ordered in time" [47]. This stage makes it possible to determine the causes of incidents, identify vulnerabilities, and describe the possible consequences of threats.

Based on the above, the following steps are implemented. This requires determining the likelihood, impact, and risk estimation for the developed threat scenarios. The procedure to be followed within the above-mentioned activities is determined by choice of the risk assessment method specified at the planning stage. In other words, for each scenario, the likelihood and impact are determined according to an adopted scale (qualitative, quantitative, and qualitative–quantitative). Estimating the risk for hazard scenarios involves determining the value of the risk based on predetermined likelihood and impact.

The risk assessment results are compared with the risk assessment criteria adopted at the planning stage. Risk assessment requires a decision on risk acceptance or implementation of a risk management procedure.

If the risk is accepted, the system is approved for further operation. Moreover, ongoing monitoring and regular inspections are essential. In practice, the circumstances may justify the need to improve the implemented solutions as well as the risk analysis and assessment. Such a situation may occur, in particular, as a result of a security incident, the recognition of new vulnerabilities in CPS, and the development of methods and techniques of cyberattacks. Changing legal conditions may also oblige organizations to implement changes that require risk analysis and assessment.

Failure to accept the risk requires launching a risk-handling procedure. The main strategies include the following:

- *Risk control:* Prevention through the use of security measures and minimization by implementing business continuity management plans
- *Risk avoidance:* Limiting activities causing risk of unacceptable level
- *Risk transfer:* Transferring the risk to another entity, e.g., an insurance company (see, e.g., [24,48])

According to the systemic approach, risk control should cover all elements of CPS, considering the identified threats and safety requirements. Table 7.4 shows examples of security measures in relation to the CPS architecture.

Implementing security measures in relation to the layered CPS architecture can provide an effective cybersecurity solution. Another solution may also be to implement security measures with regard to the information security attributes.

The risk management process model shown in Figure 7.2 also includes certification. According to NIST, certification means a comprehensive assessment of security measures in an IT system to support security accreditation. This process also includes the assessment of the correctness of the implemented security measures, their functioning, and results in relation to security requirements [49]. This process may end with a certificate confirming that the system meets certain criteria. The literature emphasizes the need for standardization initiatives for CPSs and related technologies such as the Internet-of-Things (see, e.g., [50]).

The model proposed in this section takes into account the multifactor risk management issues in the cybersecurity of CPSs. The model can be the basis for developing specific procedures to minimize the risk of threats in CPSs.

Table 7.4 Examples of Security Measures for CPSs

CPS Layers	Security Measures
Business layer	• Development of internal documents • Security audits • Business continuity management • Vulnerability management
Human layer	• Access control • Multifactor authentication • Training • Definition of responsibilities
Application layer	• Privacy protection • Backups • Redundancy of service • Application isolation and sandboxing
Transmission layer	• Transport encryption (cryptographic protocols, certificates, identity verification) [29] • Identity management • Firewall • IDS/IPS systems
Perception layer	• Physical protection of CPS devices • Authorization • Access control • End-to-end encryption

Source: Owns work.

7.7 CONCLUSIONS AND FUTURE RESEARCH DIRECTIONS

Risk management is a significant challenge for the cybersecurity of CPSs. With regard to the adopted research objectives, the following conclusions were formulated:

- Risk is a complex and multifaceted concept. A review of the scientific literature shows many risk management methods and techniques. Regardless of the solutions adopted, risk management requires, inter alia, threat identification, vulnerability analysis, risk assessment, and security measures implementation.
- Risk management should be implemented in the context of the architecture of CPSs and security requirements. There are various models of CPS architecture in the literature. In this chapter, the authors proposed a model that takes into account the physical and cybernetic parts, as well as the business layer and the human factor layer. The main requirements of CPS cybersecurity include confidentiality, integrity, availability, authenticity, privacy, reliability, resistance to failures and disruptions, operational security, security of human resources, and compliance with legal requirements.

- Threats to the cybersecurity of CPSs can be classified in various ways. We proposed a taxonomy based on the following criteria: source, location, randomness, information security attributes, target and motive of the attack, and application area of the system. In addition, we developed a list of threats and vulnerabilities referring to the architecture of CPSs, which can be developed according to the needs of the organization.
- The result of the conducted research is a model of the risk management process for the cybersecurity of CPSs. The model can be a reference point for implementing risk analysis and assessment mechanisms in organizations, ensuring compliance with recognized standards, and unifying their terminology.

Research results show that risk management is a complex and multifaceted issue. However, this issue has many open challenges in the cybersecurity of CPSs that may define future research directions. The following are the areas that require further research in particular:

- *Legal aspects, standardization, and certification of CPS in the aspect of cybersecurity:* Adaptation of legal requirements and cybersecurity standards to the areas of CPS application as well as certification taking into account security requirements
- *CPS architecture in the context of cybersecurity:* Analysis of vulnerabilities occurring in individual layers of the system, designing a reliable communication infrastructure to ensure collection, analysis, and decision-making in real time
- *Threats to CPSs:* Threat scenarios, attack detection, and testing the resistance of the system and its components
- *Risk management:* Building awareness in risk management at all levels of the organization, analysis of risk assessment methods, including identifying threats, vulnerabilities, and damage assessment
- *Security:* Security implementation based on risk analysis results and development of security effectiveness assessment methods
- *CPS cybersecurity in relation to the area of deployment:* Analysis of legal aspects, architecture, vulnerabilities, threats, and security measures specific to a given area of CPS application, e.g., healthcare, the energy sector

CPSs are nowadays recognized as an innovative technology with potential applications in many sectors of the economy. The specificity of this environment makes ensuring cybersecurity a significant challenge in the further development of CPSs. Therefore, risk management is a critical element in ensuring the resilience of CPSs to existing and future threats.

REFERENCES

1. Alguliyev, R., Imamverdiyev, Y., Sukhostat, L. (2018). Cyber-Physical Systems and Their Security Issues. *Computers in Industry*. Volume 100, pp. 212–223. Elsevier. https://doi.org/10.1016/j.compind.2018.04.017.

2. Gill, H. (2008). From Vision to Reality: Cyber-Physical Systems. *HCSS National Workshop on New Research Directions for High Confidence Transportation CPS: Automotive, Aviation, and Rail.* Available online: https://labs.ece.uw.edu/nsl/aar-cps/Gill_HCSS_Transportation_Cyber-Physical_Systems_2008.pdf (Accessed 1 July 2022).

3. NIST Special Publication 1500–201. (2017). Framework for Cyber-Physical Systems. Volume 1, Overview. https://doi.org/10.6028/NIST.SP.1500-201.

4. Kramer, B. J. (2014). Evolution of Cyber-Physical Systems: A Brief Review. In: Suh, S., Tanik, U., Carbone, J., Eroglu, A. (Eds.), Applied Cyber-Physical Systems. Springer, New York, NY. https://doi.org/10.1007/978-1-4614-7336-7_1.

5. Lee. E. A. (2008). Cyber Physical Systems: Design Challenges. In: 11th IEEE International Symposium on Object and Component-Oriented Real-Time Distributed Computing (ISORC), pp. 363–369. https://doi.org/10.1109/ISORC.2008.25.

6. Duo, W., Zhou, M., Abusorrah A. (2022). A Survey of Cyber Attacks on Cyber Physical Systems: Recent Advances and Challenges. *IEEE/CAA Journal of Automatica Sinica.* Volume 9, pp. 784–800, IEEE. https://doi.org/10.1109/JAS.2022.105548.

7. Rathi, R., Sharma, N., Manchanda, C., Bhushan B. Grover M. (2020). Security Challenges & Controls in Cyber Physical System. In: IEEE 9th International Conference on Communication Systems and Network Technologies (CSNT), pp. 242–247. https://doi.org/10.1109/CSNT48778.2020.9115778.

8. Peng Y., Lu, T., Liu, J., Gao, Y., Guo, X., Xie F. (2013). Cyber-Physical System Risk Assessment. In: Ninth International Conference on Intelligent Information Hiding and Multimedia Signal Processing, pp. 442–447. https://doi.org/10.1109/IIH-MSP.2013.116.

9. Lyu, X., Ding, Y., Yang, S. H. (2019). Safety and Security Risk Assessment in Cyber-Physical Systems. *IET Cyber-Physical Systems: Theory & Applications.* Volume 4, Issue 3, pp. 221–232. https://doi.org/10.1049/iet-cps.2018.5068.

10. World Economic Forum. (2018). Fourth Industrial Revolution Beacons of Technology and Innovation in Manufacturing. Available online: https://www3.weforum.org/docs/WEF_4IR_Beacons_of_Technology_and_Innovation_in_Manufacturing_report_2019.pdf (Accessed 1 July 2022).

11. European Parliament. (2016). Industry 4.0. *Study for the ITRE Committee.* Available online: www.europarl.europa.eu/RegData/etudes/STUD/2016/570007/IPOL_STU(2016)570007_EN.pdf (Accessed 1 July 2022).

12. ISACA Glossary. (n.d.). Available online: www.isaca.org/resources/glossary (Accessed 4 July 2022).

13. Wiesche, M., Keskinov, H., Schermann, M., Krcmar, H. (2013). Classifying Information Systems Risks: What Have We Learned So Far? In: 46th Hawaii International Conference on System Sciences, pp. 5013–5022. https://doi.org/10.1109/HICSS.2013.130.

14. Kaplan, S., Garrick, B. J. (1981). On The Quantitative Definition of Risk. *Risk Analysis.* Volume 1, Issue 1, pp. 11–27. https://doi.org/10.1111/j.1539-6924.1981.tb01350.x.

15. Haimes, Y. Y. (2009). On the Complex Definition of Risk: A Systems-Based Approach. *Risk Analysis.* Volume 29, Issue 12, pp. 1647–1654. https://doi.org/10.1111/j.1539-6924.2009.01310.x.

16. Sienkiewicz, P. (2013). *25 wykładów.* AON, Warsaw.

17. ISO/IEC 27000. (2020). Information Technology—Security Techniques—Information Security Management Systems—Overview and Vocabulary.

18. Szczepaniuk, E. K., Szczepaniuk, H. (2022). Analysis of Cybersecurity Competencies: Recommendations for Telecommunications Policy. *Telecommunications Policy*. Volume 46, Issue 3, Elsevier. https://doi.org/10.1016/j.telpol.2021.102282.
19. ISO/IEC 27001. (2017). Information Technology—Security Techniques—Information Security Management Systems—Requirements.
20. Kassa S. G. (2017). IT Asset Valuation, Risk Assessment and Control Implementation Model. *ISACA Journal*. Volume 3, pp. 1–9. Available online: www.isaca.org/-/media/files/isacadp/project/isaca/articles/journal/2017/volume-3/it-asset-valuation-risk-assessment-and-control-implementation-model_joa_eng_0118.pdf (Accessed 4 July 2022).
21. Karabacak, B., Tatar, U. (2012). An Hierarchical Asset Valuation Method for Information Security Risk Analysis. In: International Conference on Information Society. Available online: https://fuse.franklin.edu/facstaff-pub/42 (Accessed 6 July 2022).
22. ISO/IEC 31000. (2018). Risk Management—Guidelines.
23. NIST Special Publication 800–39. (2011). Managing Information Security Risk: Organization, Mission, and Information System View. Available online: https://csrc.nist.gov/publications/detail/sp/800-39/final (Accessed 6 July 2022).
24. BSI-Standard 200–3. (2017). Risk Analysis Based on IT-Grundschutz. Available online: www.bsi.bund.de/SharedDocs/Downloads/EN/BSI/Grundschutz/International/bsi-standard-2003_en_pdf.html?nn=128620 (Accessed 6 July 2022).
25. ENISA. (2022). Risk Management Standards. *Analysis of Standardisation Requirements in Support of Cybersecurity Policy*. https://doi.org/10.2824/001991.
26. Yaacoub, J. A., Salman, O., Noura, H. N., Kaaniche, N., Chehab, A., Malli, M. (2020). Cyber-Physical Systems Security: Limitations, Issues and Future Trends. *Microprocessors and Microsystems*. Volume 77, Elsevier. https://doi.org/10.1016/j.micpro.2020.103201.
27. Kim, N. Y., Rathore, S., Ryu, J. H., Park, J. H., Park, J. H. (2018). A Survey on Cyber Physical System Security for IoT: Issues, Challenges, Threats, Solutions. *Journal of Information Processing Systems*. Volume 14, Issue 6, pp. 1361–1384. https://doi.org/10.3745/JIPS.03.0105.
28. Raju, M. H., Ahmed, M. U., Atiqur Rahman Ahad, M. (2020). Security Analysis and a Potential Layer to Layer Security Solution of Medical Cyber-Physical Systems. In: Balas, V., Solanki, V., Kumar, R., Ahad, M. (Eds.), A Handbook of Internet of Things in Biomedical and Cyber Physical System: Intelligent Systems Reference Library. Volume 165. Springer, Cham. https://doi.org/10.1007/978-3-030-23983-1_3.
29. Szczepaniuk, H., Szczepaniuk, E. K. (2021). Cybersecurity Management within the Internet of Things In: Sharma, S. K., Bhushan, B., Debnath, N. (Eds.), IoT Security Paradigms and Applications Research and Practices. CRC Press, Taylor & Francis Group, Boca Raton.
30. Lee, J., Bagheri, B., Kao, H. A. (2015). A Cyber-Physical Systems Architecture for Industry 4.0-Based Manufacturing Systems. *Manufacturing Letters*. Volume 3, pp. 18–23. https://doi.org/10.1016/j.mfglet.2014.12.001.
31. Pirvu, B. C., Zamfirescu, C. B., Gorecky, D. (2016). Engineering Insights from an Anthropocentric Cyber-Physical System: A Case Study for an Assembly Station. *Mechatronics*. Volume 34, pp. 147–159. https://doi.org/10.1016/j.mechatronics.2015.08.010.
32. Ahmadi, A., Sodhro, A. H., Cherifi, C., Cheutet, V., Ouzrout, Y. (2018). Evolution of 3C Cyber-Physical Systems Architecture for Industry 4.0. In: Borangiu, T., Trentesaux, D., Thomas, A., Cavalieri, S. (Eds.), International Workshop on Service Orientation in Holonic and Multi-Agent Manufacturing. Springer, Cham.

33. Szczepaniuk, E., Szczepaniuk, H., Rokicki, T., Klepacki, B. (2020). Information Security Assessment in Public Administration. *Computers & Security*. Volume 90, Elsevier. https://doi.org/10.1016/j.cose.2019.101709.
34. NIST Special Publication 800–53. (2020). Security and Privacy Controls for Information Systems and Organizations. https://doi.org/10.6028/NIST.SP.800-53r5.
35. Ali, N., Hussain, M., Kim, Y., Hong, J. E. (2020). A Generic Framework For Capturing Reliability in Cyber-Physical Systems. In: *Proceedings of the 2020 European Symposium on Software Engineering*. https://doi.org/10.1145/3393822.3432331.
36. Łuczak, J., Tyburski, M. (2010). Systemowe zarządzanie bezpieczeństwem informacji ISO/IEC 27001. Wydawnictwo Uniwersytetu Ekonomicznego w Poznaniu, Poznań.
37. Cook, A., Smith, R., Maglaras, L., Janicke, H. (2016). Measuring the Risk of Cyber Attack in Industrial Control Systems. *BCS eWiC*. https://doi.org/10.14236/ewic/ICS2016.12.
38. Tariq, U., Aseeri, A. O., Alkatheiri M. S., Zhuang Y. (2020). Context-Aware Autonomous Security Assertion for Industrial IoT. *IEEE Access*. Volume 8, pp. 191785–191794. https://doi.org/10.1109/ACCESS.2020.3032436.
39. Schneier, B. (1999). Attack Trees. *Dr. Dobb's Journal*. Volume 24, Issue 12, pp. 21–29.
40. Bouissou, M. (2009). BDMP (Boolean Logic Driven Markov Processes) as an Alternative to Event Trees. In: Martorell, S., Soares, C. G., Barnett, J. (Eds.), Safety, Reliability and Risk Analysis: Theory, Methods and Application. CRC Press, Taylor & Francis Group, London.
41. Alanen, J., Linnosmaa, J., Pärssinen, J., Kotelba, A., & Heikkilä, E. (2022). Review of Cybersecurity Risk Analysis Methods and Tools for Safety Critical Industrial Control Systems. *VTT Technical Research Centre of Finland*. VTT Research Report No. VTT-R-00298–22. Available online: https://cris.vtt.fi/ws/portalfiles/portal/58013041/D1.4.1_cybersecurity_methods_and_tools_VTT_research_report_signed.pdf (Accessed 15 July 2022).
42. Tyagi, A. K., Sreenath, N. (2021). Cyber Physical Systems: Analyses, Challenges and Possible Solutions. *Internet of Things and Cyber-Physical Systems*. pp. 22–33, Elsevier. https://doi.org/10.1016/j.iotcps.2021.12.002.
43. Yeboah-ofori, A., Abdulai, J. D., Katsriku, F. (2018). Cybercrime and Risks for Cyber Physical Systems: A Review. *Preprints*. https://doi.org/10.20944/preprints201804.0066.v1.
44. Vávra, J., Hromada, M. (2015). An Evaluation of Cyber Threats to Industrial Control Systems. In: *International Conference on Military Technologies (ICMT) 2015*, pp. 1–5, IEEE. https://doi.org/10.1109/MILTECHS.2015.7153700.
45. Ding, W., Xu, M., Huang, Y., Zhao, P., Song, F. (2021). Cyber Attacks on PMU Placement in a Smart Grid: Characterization and Optimization. *Reliability Engineering & System Safety*. Volume 212, Elsevier. https://doi.org/10.1016/j.ress.2021.107586.
46. Pandey, R. K., Misra, M. (2016). Cyber Security Threats—Smart Grid Infrastructure. In: *National Power Systems Conference (NPSC)*, pp. 1–6, IEEE. https://doi.org/10.1109/NPSC.2016.7858950.
47. NIST Special Publication 800–160. (2021). Developing Cyber-Resilient Systems: A Systems Security Engineering Approach. Volume 2. https://doi.org/10.6028/NIST.SP.800-160v2r1.
48. Lidermann, K. (2017). Bezpieczeństwo informacyjne. Wydawnictwo Naukowe PWN, Warsaw.

49. FIPS 200. (2006). Minimum Security Requirements for Federal Information and Information Systems. Available online: https://csrc.nist.gov/publications/detail/fips/200/final (Accessed 15 July 2022).
50. Szczepaniuk, H., Szczepaniuk, E. K. (2022). Standardization of IoT Ecosystems: Open Challenges, Current Solutions, and Future Directions. In: Bhushan, B., Sharma, S. K, Unhelkar, B., Fazal Ijaz, M., Karim, L (Eds.), Frameworks for Enabling and Emerging Technologie. CRC Press, Taylor & Francis Group, Boca Raton.

Chapter 8

Benefits of Developing Blockchain for Monetary Standards Based on Cyber-physical Systems

Characteristics, Application, and Challenges

Sanand Mishra and Ayasha Malik

8.1 INTRODUCTION

The concept of Bitcoin was conceptualized by Satoshi Nakamoto, a mysterious symbol. They published a state paper estimating the value of Bitcoin in May 2008. He stayed quiet and did not reveal who he was. He sketched out how the money would perform. The primary dominant blockchain advancement was Bitcoin, or advanced cash exploration [1]. The current advancement was called blockchain, and it was created to separate the technology that worked Bitcoin from the money and utilize it for various interconnected organizational participation. Nearly every major money-related academy in the entire world is doing blockchain inquiries at this point, and 16% of funds are anticipated to be utilizing blockchain in 2016 [2]. The "smart contract" was the third innovation, epitomized in a newer block-chain technology framework known as Ethereum, which created small software programs specifically into the blockchain that permitted budgetary gadgets, such as advances or bonds, to be spoken to instead of being treated as the cash—the same with tokens of Bitcoin. The fourth biggest development, "Proof of Stake," is the current cutting-edge blockchain technology. Modern-era blockchains are backed up by "Proof of Work," in which choices are made by the collective group with the most processing power [3]. These bunches are called "miners" and work tremendously at information centres to supply this security in trade for crypto cash instalments. These data centres lack unused frameworks, changing them with intricate monetary disobedient for a comparable if a not higher level of concern. The last crucial advancement of blockchain scaling is something that's happening. A flexible blockchain quickens the method without relinquishing security by finding out how many computers are essential to approve each exchange and isolating the work effectively [4]. To oversee this without compromising the legendary security and vigour of blockchain may be a troublesome issue, but not a recalcitrant one. A scaled blockchain is anticipated to be quick and sufficient to

DOI: 10.1201/9781003474111-8

exert control over the network of things and compete with the major instalment brokers (VISA and Quick) managing accounts worldwide. Bitcoin may be a sort of computerized cash that can be traded on the blockchain, the shared record innovation [5]. Bitcoins are, in substance, power changed over into lengthy strings of cyphers that have cash value. Bitcoin may be a form of digital currency, made and held electronically [6]. Nobody is in charge of it. There are no printed Bitcoins, such as typical cash, they're created by individuals, businesses running computers and utilizing software that tackles scientific issues. Bitcoins are, in substance, power transformed into lengthy strings of cyphers that have cash prices. Bitcoin may be a mode of advanced cash, produced and adhered to by electronic cash. Blockchain is a distributed ledger automation that is worn to exchange Bitcoins. It is additionally finding its function in different alternative spaces, such as the e-polling framework, administration, well-being, and so on. The insurance of exchanges has gotten to be like the main concern nowadays.

Along with preservation, uncommon properties of blockchain have to be considered in our task. It is well-familiar to us that any development must suffer a portion of the challenge; the same is true for blockchains. Bitcoins are extremely valuable in terms of cash despite their lack of physical presence, and their value in terms of physical cash fluctuates daily [7]. Because of these basic functionalities of blockchain, we can say that blockchain is the most secure technology.

- *Records:* All included data of the individual block is known as the record in blocks, including entire details of the sender, receiver, and the different types of coins [8].
- *Hash:* A hash is an exclusive key such as a finger pattern and a mixture of numbers or characters. For each block, the hash is generated through the assistance of the use of a particular cryptologic hash collection of rules such as SHA256.
- *Previous hash:* A block containing a distinctive hash key and containing the hash of the preceding block additionally. That property supports creating an associated sequence in the blockchain structural design and the main objective behind this is its protection [9].
- *Proof of Work (PoW):* Hashes are the smart approaches to avoid obstruction but then in the current era computers are extremely high-level and can enumerate plenty of hashes in sequence through 2-WA. Based on minutes, the hackers may have interacted through the block; later they recompute all the hashes of various blocks to make the blockchain legitimate once more. To avoid and prevent this problem, blockchain makes the idea of proof of execution, which is to recommend the construction of more current blocks.
- *Proof of Stake (PoS):* There is plenty of power and computers are exhausted due to verification of the operating system [10]. It does not need costly computer capacity, an individual who owns 1% of Bitcoin can generate 1% of "stakes stock proof". Confirmation of the pole could also give additional security from brutal raids on the public, getting a strike and decreasing the premiums for strikes can be extra costly.
- *Proof of Authority (PoA):* The PoA is an identification-based consent method that suggests a minor and detailed type of blockchain web which has the

power to authenticate the transactions or communications with the webs that are distributed and disseminated to appraise its disseminated records. It presents practical and effective responses for blockchain webs [11].

Although the blockchain period is generating a hierarchy to guarantee sensitive elasticity, blocking systems are not resilient to cyber strikes and scams. Serious needs can handle the supposed weakness of blockchain structure, and the quality has been effective in numerous cheats or frauds throughout centuries [12]. The blockchain is not a specific structure, except that it includes cryptology, mathematics, algorithms, and commercial interpretation, combining peer-to-peer groups and employing an enhanced protocol structure that supports and fixes the conventional allocation. Additionally, the following are the main categories of blockchain:

- *Public blockchain networks:* Anyone may join and participate in a public blockchain, like Bitcoin, which is accessible to all. Significant processing power requirements, little to no transaction privacy, and lax security are possible drawbacks. These are significant factors for blockchain application cases in businesses.
- *Private blockchain networks:* A private blockchain network is similar to a public blockchain network in that it is a decentralized peer-to-peer network. However, a single entity controls the network's governance, conducting a consensus mechanism and administering the shared ledger. Depending on the use case, this can significantly boost participant trust and faith [13]. There are solutions for running a private blockchain behind a corporate firewall and even hosting it.
- *Consortium blockchains:* The duties of maintaining a blockchain might be split among several groups. Who may submit transactions or access the data is decided upon by these previously chosen entities. When all parties must have permission and share ownership of the blockchain, a consortium blockchain is the best option for business. Furthermore, the difference between the three categories of blockchain is stated in Table 8.1.

This chapter is organized as follows: Section 8.2 introduces the special characteristics of blockchain security such as strength and resilience, pristine and

Table 8.1 Blockchain Comparisons between the Public, Consortium, and Private [14]

Property	Public	Consortium	Private
Consensus determination	All miners	The selected set of nodes	One organization
Read permission	Public	Could be public or restricted	Could be public or restricted
Immutability	Nearly impossible to tamper	Could be tempered	Could be tempered
Efficiency	Low	High	High
Centralized	No	Partial	Yes
Consensus process	Permissionless	Permissioned	Permissioned

untainted, security, increased capacity, easier settlement, and decentralized organization. The benefits of blockchain, including healthcare, innovation, reduced costs, and cybersecurity, are discussed in Section 8.3. Section 8.4 discusses the areas and uses of blockchain like monetary, e-voting systems, network operations, operational monitoring, and logical contracts. Section 8.5 explains the challenges to blockchain such as reconciliations, guidelines, the need for additional support, tradition, price and effectiveness, confidentiality, and protection. The CPS is discussed in Section 8.6. Furthermore, Section 8.7 summarizes the technical challenges in CPS and Section 8.8 concludes this work.

8.2   SPECIAL CHARACTERISTICS OF BLOCKCHAIN SECURITY

The engineering of the framework demonstrates the primary choice made as the foundation of a blockchain. Blockchains have an agreement on their record that all hubs have data [15], and if any hub changes it, it is educated to all other hubs.

- *Strength and resilience:* Blockchain innovation is completely solid. Squares of data are saved on the blockchain, which is indistinguishable from the blockchain arrangement. No single expert can take control of the blockchain and thus doesn't have a single source of failure [16]. In 2008, Bitcoin was created. And since then, there have been no instances of disappointment on the Bitcoin blockchain.
- *Pristine and untainted:* This condition of the agreement is fulfilled by the blockchain. The principle of agreement is founded on the notion that to make any changes to the blockchain exchange, we must receive the approval of each unique hub; otherwise, we will be unable to do so. Because of this quality, our blockchain arrangement accomplishes the function of straightforwardness. Simplicity is a feature of the entire blockchain organization. Moreover, the blockchain organization virtually eliminates the chances of undermining information.
- *Security:* We have seen the highlights of the agreement. Now, the same idea may be implemented for network security. This could be described as "In case somebody would like to access all the data around a bank." At that point, a gifted individual may complete it easily because the number of frameworks to be hacked is, as it were, "one." However, the blockchain case is diverse, so if one desires to compromise this node network, at that point he'll have to break into all the systems, hacking as if one specific framework were enough won't be effective for him. Subsequently, blockchain innovation includes comprehensive verification and assent to security [17].
- *Increased capacity:* In ordinary exchanges, including banks, normally, all the actions are controlled by a small number of data centres, but with blockchain, hundreds of frameworks are cooperating. This occurs when dealing with transactions at a high rate and in a short period.

- *Easier settlement:* Within the conventional strategy of payments, including banks, due to the presence of several centralized frameworks, the payment process can take anywhere between a few days and a week [18]. Because the number of frameworks included in blockchain technology is much higher than in traditional frameworks, transactions can be settled in significantly less time, or even immediately. This saves the budgetary industry some time and money.
- *Decentralized organization:* The blockchain could be a decentralized innovation. Decentralization implies that no single substance has control over the entire preparation. Blockchain technology is used by a global network of computers to collectively manage the database that keeps track of Bitcoin exchanges. In other words, rather than being controlled by a single central expert, Bitcoin is governed by its overall system [19].

8.3 BENEFITS OF BLOCKCHAIN TO THE SOCIETY

- If somebody listens for the first time using blockchain, at that point, it could look difficult or complex, yet, the thought after the blockchain is very straightforward. It is a database with infiltration conveyance that is used by millions of devices all over the world. Currently, the database, or data, can be about anything from logical disclosures to actual needs such as cash or votes. It ensures that outsiders believe and judge each other [20], and it also eliminates the possibility of deception or selling out. In our technological age, belief and faith are set up through mass relationship, or participation, which is the foremost imperative of all "shrewd code," outnumbering effective institutions like banks and administration, or the undertakings of innovation.
- The basis for all of this interest and mindfulness or perhaps interest was created by blockchain innovation in that everyone is aware of the disloyalty and conscious of the ills that banks can cause them [21]. As a result, they anticipate that blockchain innovation will have a significant impact on the budgetary benefit businesses by reducing the volume of transactions and their complexity, allowing banks to move forward with their controls and openness.
- Currently, it is well acknowledged that blockchains are straightforward, providing a decentralized platform and a means for capturing the exchanges that happen every day, or rather, every second. Bitcoin is the most popular example of this innovation [22]. Since Bitcoin facilitates faster, less expensive open records on blockchain-based exchanges of money, other methods must produce unused cash that can be used for non-financial exchanges like voting which comes with a package of benefits and advantages.
- Because of the transparency of crypto-currencies, an individual has a chance to acquire the accounts of all transactions, which means every individual can see its code. Suppose a hacker tries to make any alterations to the documents of any specific blocks, then it will affect the entire data that exists in their previous blocks because each block is interlinked with their addresses.

When a block is designed, a hash is designed immediately. If any changes are made to the blocks, they will be identified and corrected to their hash in the meantime [23]. Work verification has a computational problem that requires significant attempts to remove the issue, although the time required to validate the outcomes of computer trouble may be extremely short in comparison to the effort required to correct a computational issue through this mechanism. Through the strike, the striker should get as much stock as individuals in Bitcoin. So the striker was hurt by his strike.

- PoA blockchains are attached to verifying nodes, and they depend on a restricted count of block verifiers, which creates a fairly ascendable gadget. Nodes and operations are recognized with the assistance of pre-certified applicants, who play a role as facilitators of the gadget. The PoA method enables numerous businesses to maintain their security and confidentiality while reaping the benefits of blockchain production [24]. Microsoft Azure is a high-level appropriate standard in which PoA is used, and it's a stage that provides the solution for non-communal webs and systems, which aren't required for any regional currency like Ether and Ethereum. Blockchain skills can support agreement administration and examine the source of a commodity. It can be applied in polling programs or dealing with headings and actions.

- It is particularly advantageous for financial transactions; by applying block-chain knowledge, banks and corporations can improve their financial operations. In a short time, an individual can obtain or deliver economic records, and there is no responsibility for the delay. As a result, any scams that occur in this open-source blockchain resource cannot be hidden, and businesses are protected from fraud. A consortium blockchain is employed by large corporations [25]. It's simply controlled by ways of pre-establishing blocks. Cryptocurrency is a simulated currency structure that does not depend on banks to ensure operations. It is a homogeneous approach that can permit the entire system to deliver and accept costs everywhere. In place of a simulated currency [26], there is a demand to trade inside the actual globe, a cryptocurrency disbursement alternative that occurs like a digital contribution to the online data file, which explains a unique operation. While transmitting digital money, the operation of the transaction is documented in the shared record, and the information can be kept in a digital folder.

- When ownership histories and foundation information are required or expected, blockchains are ideal for these occupations because they can oversee supply chains and deliver the truth and rightness that a specific product has been morally and legally sourced or a product has been manufactured where it should be manufactured [27]. Additionally, it can easily resolve the issue of audio or picture robbery. Blockchain opens doors in the field of open administrations, for example, payments for health and welfare or autonomous contracts for companies that operate without human supervision. Additionally, the various benefits of blockchain are shown in Figure 8.1.

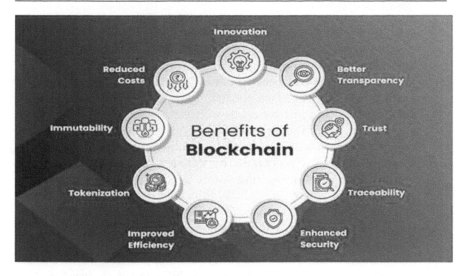

Figure 8.1 Benefits of blockchain.

8.4 AREAS AND USES OF BLOCKCHAIN

- *Monetary:* Cash is one of the principal uses of the blockchain. It was outlined for Bitcoins, i.e., online money [28]. This implies that it can be treated as worldwide money. Until now, numerous inquiries have been made to expand the use of blockchain, but few applications of it do not include Bitcoins. Bitcoins play a significant role in the advancement of blockchain innovation. However, there are currently a few open guidance and conversation materials on this subject, with an emphasis on how the blockchain industry takeover by Bitcoin may influence more extensive advancement of the innovation and other applications of distributed records [29]. Currently, community participation is necessary to extract Bitcoin and engage in financial transactions. Individuals' bank accounts can work together through a smart contract by submitting payments that carry out a characteristic described in the smart contract. Similar to a standard contract, smart contracts can describe processes and repeatedly insert them into the code [30]. Development businesses, results companies, management companies, company representatives, and consumers are all invited to contribute to the extension and promotion of these transformational entertainment talents, which were developed under the administration of experts and public corporations. At the beginning of programs, this security mechanism requires an additional crypto exchange [31]. Still, there is a challenge, as the consumer can also overlook this earlier on distributed data if the consumer immediately declines to sign in for the software.

- *E-voting system:* Indeed, after this breakthrough, innovation races were held offline. This innovation has resulted in extremely likely outcomes in this election framework because none of them change the outcome [32] and it is less expensive than conducting surveys offline. Several methods for increasing participation, as well as re-establishing links between citizens and political education, have been proposed, allegations that should be viewed with caution [33]. Electronic voting can be done in a variety of ways, for example, by utilizing the web or a dedicated, separate arrangement; requiring voters to go to a polling place; allowing unattended voting; or both; additionally, it can be done regularly utilizing any contraptions tools, for example, utilizing the blockchain is straightforward and disseminated among clients who can be utilized for forestry and confirmation.

- *Network operations:* With a straightforward user interface, the Blockchain Platform from IBM gives the framer the ability to launch, insist, and set up a connection. When a network is launched, three arranging peers and two certificate providers are generated [34, 35]. A founder can use this as a ready-made base to build their business network. The network's founders can then extend invitations to more users by employing any number of peers. To make it simple for them to join the network, participants will receive email reminders of their invitations [36]. Using the Network Operations user interface, a founder can also set up essential network features like identity confirmation and channel creation. This makes it possible for channels to be used for confidential transactions and for only authorized users to access the network.

- *Operational monitoring:* As a network expands in terms of transactions and users, users must be able to keep an eye on its activity. Both a network traffic dashboard and a network health monitor are offered by the IBM Blockchain Platform. These dashboards make it possible to adjust network operations proactively and define how resources are used within the network.

- *Logical contracts:* In contrast to the conventional record, the blockchain records unquestionably show a few curious and novel highlights. It is not fair to record beyond that; however, it also plays a more dynamic and possibly independent role in the usage and management of exchanges. Blockchains also provide the standout feature of exchanges that are set to execute when particular criteria are satisfied, providing an "assurance of implementation." Auto-executing clever contracts are being developed quickly as a result. A "digitalized exchange convention that executes the provisions of a contract" is how shrewd contracts are defined [37]. Moreover, the numerous applications of blockchain are shown in Figure 8.2.

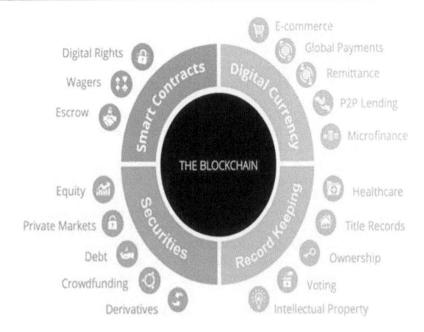

Figure 8.2 Application of blockchain.

8.5 CHALLENGES TO BLOCKCHAIN

- *Reconciliations:* Researchers are all cognizant of the reality that in terms of creativity and advancement, the administrative specialist frequently slacks. Each day, unused items and new transactions based on blockchain exchanges are emerging, yet tragically; exchanges are out of our hands and ought to be composed. Straightforwardness is the foremost vital blockchain feature, but heavily regulated businesses may require creating new controls for blockchain [38,39]. Essentially, numerous uncommon properties could be modified due to different circumstances. Consequently, we require legitimate directions for administering the blockchain.
- *Guidelines:* Similar to controls, we now require a single set of standards for structuring exchanges on a blockchain. There are three fully accessible consortium companies, and each has its claim metrics and markup language [40]. The wide range of blockchain applications complicates this advancement, and in handling various use cases, the most suitable form requirements must be used. The strategies that emerge to manage this environment will provide support, influence the choice of actions, and perhaps even bring such conglomerates closer.
- *Need additional support:* Executives worry that the idea hasn't been tested enough in trials and that Custom software is another barrier to appropriation.

What limitations does blockchain ultimately face? What are its drawbacks in handling a big number of project exchanges and information, notwithstanding the early POCs' plaudits for its adaptability? As appropriation increases, various programs will run across challenges with adaptability [41]. And how much processing power and time will be required to manage such a huge volume of exchanges?

- *Tradition:* We have had a particular manner, or should I suggest convention, of working exchanges for ages. Blockchain innovation moves us away from unique methods to accomplish goals [42]. It could be a significant shift from a centralized to a decentralized system, but not all educators understand the concept of decentralization. Blockchain is more of a commerce handler and less of an innovator.

- *Price and effectiveness:* There are different sorts of blockchains, and every one of them has a different range of exchange viability and speeds. The types that donate the most speed and viability out of all the varieties cost a lot of money [43]. Hence, to provide the greatest benefits to individuals while assisting the most extreme benefits from blockchain innovation, one must choose the most expensive blockchain.

- **Confidentiality and protection:** The "wallets" rather than the "people" are what the Bitcoin exchanges are connected to. The exchanges and contracts used in blockchain applications must be linked to well-known people. This creates a real address for almost all of the information stored and accessible on the blockchain's security [44]. The architecture of the blockchain has not yet been compromised. The instruction that "technology has its claim advantages and disadvantages" is difficult to instil, nevertheless. This is frequently the cause of some educators' struggles to implement this innovation [45].

8.6 CYBER-PHYSICAL SYSTEM

The world's economy has undergone revolutionary upheaval as a result of the steam engine, electricity, and digital economy [46]. Today, the industrial, transportation, energy, and health sectors may all benefit from using sensor data from machines. Efficiency may be increased by the use of big data analysis, preventative maintenance, and service-oriented production; even a 1% decrease in costs across key economic sectors might have a significant impact. CPSs are systems that combine physical components with built-in computational power and data storage [47]. These CPSs can be linked to one another in networks, where they can communicate and exchange data and information with other systems and objects. For example, a CPS like the Industrial Internet-of-Things (IoT) combines the developments of two revolutionary movements. The Industrial Revolution gave rise to a vast array of tools, infrastructure, fleets, and networks; on the other hand, the Internet Revolution has more recently made significant strides in computer, information, and communication technologies [48]. Credence Research estimates that the global CPS market was worth US$60.50 billion in 2018 and would increase at a compound annual growth rate of 9.3% over the following ten years.

8.7   CHALLENGES IN CPS

New needs are formed in emerging applications as a result of their popularity, which is more unique to the new CPSs like the IoT. High security, improved scalability, better network resource use, effective energy management, and reduced operating costs are a few of these. The capacity needs for CPSs will specifically increase as a result of an increase in the number of heterogeneous [49], connected devices, and a significant number of innovative services. Future CPSs will thus urgently need to provide the secure connection needed for this anticipated traffic surge. The current secure communication architectures are capable of offering a suitable level of security, but they have drawbacks, including restricted scalability, excessive network resource use, and high operational costs, mostly because of the complicated, rigid security management processes that are set up in a centralized approach [50].

Additionally, because of the centralized design of the IoT and CPSs, data are frequently housed in separate data silos, which complicates data analysis and drags down data research. Furthermore, since the user has limited control over how the data is shared and gathered, full faith in cloud and application providers is required [51]. This is a serious privacy concern, particularly for IoT devices gathering highly sensitive data like health-related metrics.

Furthermore, the CPS/IoT also has a huge ecosystem. IoT devices' capabilities are generally diverse. Additionally, it supports a broad range of various operating systems, software stacks, topologies, and communication technologies. Additionally, because IoT devices have sleep modes, CPS/IoT networks are quite dynamic. It is difficult to keep up a consistent service platform as a result [52]. To ensure the network operates properly, several parties must cooperate.

8.7.1   Blockchain to Solve These Challenges

- Decentralization, immutability, distributed trust, enhanced security, speedier settlements, smart contracts, digital currency, and minting are just a few of the properties that blockchain will offer that may be used to address these problems. Blockchain technology will enable IoT devices and CPSs to transmit data to private blockchain ledgers so that it may be incorporated into shared transactions with tamper-proof records [53]. Thanks to the distributed replication of blockchain, vertical industries, and various CPS data, users may access and deliver IoT data without the need for centralized management and administration. All parties engaged in the CPS ecosystem may verify each transaction, preventing disputes and ensuring that each user is held accountable for their contributions to the transaction as a whole. As a result, creating such a reliable and secure model for each component of the CPS ecosystem might offer an attractive alternative to the conventional client–server transaction paradigm [54].

- Smart contacts powered by blockchain can automate a variety of CPS-related processes, including IoT data exchange, device ownership transfer, new user registration, security certificate deployment and revocation, and more (for instance, a piece of auto-executable code upon meeting the predefined conditions). It is feasible to use digital currency in place of fiat money, thanks to a minting process. It is advantageous for transactions to settle quickly without the requirement for a third-party moderator [55]. A digital currency also makes it possible to build a digital market where resources from multiple CPSs, including smart grids, transportation networks, logistical systems, and others, may be traded.

- For certain application fields, the pairing of blockchain with CPSs has already been proven to provide advantages and prospects [56]. First, a transparent, decentralized, and reliable traceability scheme is needed in supply chain management to track the source of raw materials, the quality of the products measured by device sensors, the handover actions between different players, and other issues like the detection of the source of infection, food fraud, illegal production, and food recall. The device is a very significant application space where a CPS is already well embedded and blockchain technology may provide significant added value. In this situation, blockchain will make it possible to address the issue of reliability and provide opportunities to include automation and accountability through a reputation- and trust-based architecture. In several other application sectors, such as e-health, vehicular networks, smart grids, and others, there are numerous further instances.

- It is not simple and has inherent complexities to deploy distributed ledger technology for a CPS/IoT. First, conventional consensus techniques, such as proof of work, are frequently excessively complicated in CPS/IoT-based systems and result in inadequate throughput and latency levels for many applications. Additionally, mining incentives are needed by traditional blockchain applications, which are not immediately present in a CPS-based use case [57]. As a result, specialized distributed ledger systems and architectures that provide enough scalability while taking into account the real-time nature of many CPS applications and the restricted nature of IoT devices are essential research fields.

- Mathematical modelling may be used to demonstrate that distributed ledger systems provide extremely high security; however, experience has demonstrated that this claim is not at all accurate in practice. More than US$2 billion in cryptocurrencies have been stolen between the beginning of 2017 and the beginning of 2019 by hackers (both lone, opportunistic, and skilled cybercrime groups), according to data that has just been made public; the actual amount is likely far greater. Few attacks are the result of platform implementation defects; these systems have extremely complicated code and are therefore easily vulnerable to modest, subtle leaks. As a result, while creating specialized blockchain CPS-specific devoted apps, extra attention should be paid to that. Although most systems now rely on the proof-of-work consensus for transaction verification, the majority of hacks target transactions, taking advantage of the 51% rule attack that causes multiple spends.

- On well-known blockchains like Bitcoin, this assault is incredibly expensive, but on the more than 1,500 other smaller digital currencies available today, it becomes considerably more appealing. In addition, a potential specialized distributed ledger technology called Tangle, which specifically addresses scaling problems in IoT applications, is much more prone to assault and only needs 34% control. Exploiting flaws in smart contracts is another recent and extremely popular sort of attack. For blockchain CPSs in particular, several specialized smart contracts must be created to provide users with functionality tailored to their needs. Due to the difficulty of readily reversing already completed transactions, these issues are particularly difficult to address [58]. To prevent all of these blockchain hacking scenarios, several businesses have begun to provide auditing services that use AI to spot fraudulent activity and questionable transactions. Formal verification proofs have also been produced to find faults or possible weaknesses in both platforms and smart contracts.
- Last but not least, a significant obstacle to the future widespread use of blockchain-based technology is to raise the acceptability rate among developers as customers as well as a large audience [59]. Despite the well-known benefits that technology may provide in terms of automation, the openness of procedures, personal privacy, and the autonomy of banks or other intermediaries, just a small percentage of people and businesses are now using it. This is mostly due to a lack of faith in the underlying technology brought on by repeated instances of criminality against blockchain-based systems, which is not just a result of ignorance and underappreciation of the fundamental concepts. Issuing certifications for blockchain solutions or platforms that have passed a comprehensive audit based on certain public criteria is one possible way to get over this obstacle [60]. Additionally, insurance providers might specify certain insurances to assist in cases of fraud.

8.8 CONCLUSIONS

Learning about the working instruments and features of blockchains allows us to conclude that this innovation will undoubtedly benefit society. Their top qualities to recommend include agreement, trust, frankness, and so on. Because of their nature, blockchains are exceptionally protected. These days, security should be everyone's top concern, and blockchain fully provides it. To compromise a blockchain, one should always compromise many connected machines, and it is inconceivable to do it. The highlight of blockchain is that it has numerous benefits for society. Because blockchain is straightforward, it could help people in ridding themselves of numerous curses, like debasement. Because of the area of straightforwardness, the exchange record cannot be changed by a single party; if it endeavours to do so, at that point, it will appear on all of the blockchain's frameworks. It can also be used in situations where it is necessary to determine possession histories, etc., with surprising accuracy. The art of the progress of CPSs, or future engineering systems, is receiving increased attention from several nations in the form of funding possibilities. The authors will attempt to develop a framework to guarantee the dependability property of these systems by their behaviour evaluation, starting with this study, which highlights the need to develop CPSs in various application domains, the research challenges, and the early achievements in this field.

REFERENCES

[1] Abraham, I., & Mahlkhi, D. (2017). The blockchain consensus layer and BFT. Bull. EATCS, 123, 1–22. Available online at: https://dahliamalkhi.files.wordpress. com/2016/08/blockchainbft-beatcs2017.pdf
[2] Al-Jaroodi, J., & Mohamed, N. (2019). Blockchain in industries: A survey. IEEE Access, 7, 36500–36515.
[3] Slimov, K. ERP and digital transformation. Available online at: https://erpnews.com/ erp-and-digital-transformation (Accessed 05 December 2022).
[4] Buterin, V. (2015). On Public and Private Blockchains. Available online at: https:// blog.ethereum.org/2015/08/07/on-public-and-private-blockchains/
[5] King, S. (2013, July 7). Primecoin: Cryptocurrency with prime number proof-of-work.
[6] Janowicz, K., Regalia, B., Hitzler, P., Mai, G., Delbecque, S., Fröhlich, M., et al. (2018). On the prospects of blockchain and distributed ledger technologies: For open science and academic publishing. Semantic Web, 9, 545–555.doi: 10.3233/SW-180322
[7] Treiblmaier, H. (2018). The impact of the blockchain on the supply chain: A theory-based research framework and a call for action. Supply Chain Management: An International Journal, 23(6), 545–559.
[8] King, S., & Nadal, S. (2012, August). Ppcoin: Peer-to-peer crypto-currency with proof of stake. Self-Published Paper, 19.
[9] Scott, B. (2016). How can cryptocurrency and blockchain technology play a role in building social and solidarity finance?. UNRISD Working Paper, No.2016–1. United Nations Research Institute for Social Development (UNRISD), Geneva. Available online at: www.econstor.eu/bitstream/10419/148750/1/861287290.pdf
[10] Szabo, N. (1997). The idea of smart contracts.
[11] Barcelo, J. (2014). User privacy in the public bitcoin blockchain.
[12] Iris.ai. Democratize Science Through Blockchain-Enabled Disintermediation. Available online at: https://projectaiur.com/wp-content/uploads/2018/05/Project-Aiur-whitepaper-summary-v.1.1.pdf
[13] Malik, A., Gautam, S., Abidin, S., and Bhushan, B. (2019). Blockchain technology-future of IoT: Including structure, limitations and various possible attacks. 2nd International Conference on Intelligent Computing, Instrumentation and Control Technologies (ICICICT). Kannur, pp. 1100–1104. doi:10.1109/ICICICT46008.2019.8993144

[14] Nakamoto, N. (2017). Centralized bitcoin: A secure and high-performance electronic cash system. SSRN Electronic Journal. doi:10.2139/ssrn.3065723

[15] Christidis, K., & Devetsikiotis, M. (2016). Blockchains and smart contracts for the Internet of things. IEEE Access, 4, 2292–2303. doi:10.1109/access.2016.2566339

[16] Perboli, G., Musso, S., & Rosano, M. (2018). Blockchain in logistics and supply chain: A lean approach for designing real-world use cases. IEEE Access, 6, 62018–62028. doi:10.1109/access.2018.2875782

[17] Kumar, N. M., & Mallick, P. K. (2018). Blockchain technology for security issues and challenges in IoT. Procedia Computer Science, 132, 1815–1823. doi:10.1016/j.procs.2018.05.140

[18] Malik, A., Kashyap, R., Arora, K., & Bhushan, B. (2022). Nutri chain: Secure and transparent midday meals using blockchain and IoT. In: Saini, H. S., Singh, R. K., Tariq Beg, M., Mulaveesala, R., & Mahmood, M. R. (eds) Innovations in Electronics and Communication Engineering, vol 355. Springer, Singapore. https://doi.org/10.1007/978-981-16-8512-5_41

[19] Tian. F. (2016). An agri-food supply chain traceability system for China based on RFID & blockchain technology. In: 2016 13th International Conference on Service Systems and Service Management (ICSSSM). doi:10.1109/icsssm.2016.7538424

[20] Hofmann, E., Strewe, U. M., & Bosia, N. (2017). Concept—Where are the opportunities of blockchain-driven supply chain finance? In: Supply Chain Finance and Blockchain Technology, 51–75. doi:10.1007/978-3-319-62371-9_5

[21] Malik, A., Yadav, N., Srivastava, J., Obaid, A. J., & Saracevic, M. (2022). Blockchain in the pharmaceutical industry for better tracking of drugs with architectures and open challenges. In: Blockchain Technology in Healthcare Applications: Social, Economic, and Technological Implications (1st ed.). CRC Press. https://doi.org/10.1201/9781003224075

[22] Mohanty, D. (2018). Ethereum architecture. In: Ethereum for Architects and Developers, 37–54. doi:10.1007/978-1-4842-4075-5_2

[23] Malik, A., Kumar, A., Srivastava, J., & Bhushan, B. (2022). Blockchain technology with supply chain management: Components, opportunities, and possible challenges. In: Sharma, D. K., Peng, S. L., Sharma, R., & Zaitsev, D. A. (eds) Micro-Electronics and Telecommunication Engineering, vol 373. Springer, Singapore. https://doi.org/10.1007/978-981-16-8721-1_11

[24] Haque, A. B., Najmul Islam, A., Hyrynsalmi, S., Naqvi, B., & Smolander, K. (2021). GDPR compliant Blockchains—a systematic literature review. IEEE Access, 1–1. doi:10.1109/access.2021.3069877

[25] Haque, A. B., Shurid, S., Juha, A. T., Sadique, M. S., & Asaduzzaman, A. S. (2020). A novel design of gesture and voice-controlled solar-powered smart wheelchair with obstacle detection. In: 2020 IEEE International Conference on Informatics, IoT, and Enabling Technologies (ICIoT). doi:10.1109/iciot48696.2020.9089652

[26] Pranto, T. H., Noman, A. A., Mahmud, A., & Haque, A. B. (2021). Blockchain and smart contract for IoT-enabled smart agriculture. PeerJ Computer Science, 7. doi:10.7717/peerj-cs.407

[27] Indumathi, J., Shankar, A., Ghalib, M. R., Gitanjali, J., Hua, Q., Wen, Z., & Qi, X. (2020). Blockchain-based Internet of medical things for uninterrupted, ubiquitous, user-friendly, unflappable, unblemished, unlimited health care services (BC Iomt U6 HCS). IEEE Access, 8, 216856–216872. doi:10.1109/access.2020.3040240

[28] Bhardwaj, A., Shah, S. B., Shankar, A., Alazab, M., Kumar, M., & Gadekallu, T. R. (2020). Penetration testing framework for smart contract blockchain. Peer-to-Peer Networking and Applications. doi:10.1007/s12083-020-00991-6

[29] Kumar, A., Abhishek, K., Nerurkar, P., Ghalib, M. R., Shankar, A., & Cheng, X. (2020). Secure smart contracts for Cloud-based manufacturing using the Ethereum blockchain. Transactions on Emerging Telecommunications Technologies. doi:10.1002/ett.4129

[30] Bhushan, B., Khamparia, A., Sagayam, K. M., Sharma, S. K., Ahad, M. A., & Debnath, N. C. (2020). Blockchain for smart cities: A review of architectures, integration trends, and future research directions. Sustainable Cities and Society, 61, 102360. doi:10.1016/j.scs.2020.102360

[31] Lee, J., Azamfar, M., & Singh, J. (2019). A blockchain-enabled cyber-physical system architecture for industry 4.0 manufacturing systems. Manufacturing Letters, 20, 34–39.

[32] Rathore, S., & Park, J. H. (2020). A blockchain-based deep learning approach for cyber security in next-generation industrial cyber-physical systems. IEEE Transactions on Industrial Informatics, 17(8), 5522–5532.

[33] Rathore, H., Mohamed, A., & Guizani, M. (2020). A survey of blockchain-enabled cyber-physical systems. Sensors, 20(1), 282.

[34] Saxena, S., Bhushan, B., & Ahad, M. A. (2021). Blockchain-based solutions to secure IoT: Background, integration trends and a way forward. Journal of Network and Computer Applications, 103050. doi:10.1016/j.jnca.2021.103050

[35] Machado, C., & Fröhlich, A. A. M. (2018, May). IoT data integrity verification for cyber-physical systems using blockchain. In: 2018 IEEE 21st International Symposium on Real-Time Distributed Computing (ISORC) (pp. 83–90). IEEE.

[36] Wang, J., Chen, W., Ren, Y., Alfarraj, O., & Wang, L. (2020). Blockchain-based data storage mechanism in a cyber-physical system. Journal of Internet Technology, 21(6), 1681–1689.

[37] Latif, S. A., Wen, F. B. X., Iwendi, C., Li-li, F. W., Mohsin, S. M., Han, Z., & Band, S. S. (2022). AI-empowered, blockchain and SDN integrated security architecture for IoT network of cyber-physical systems. Computer Communications, 181, 274–283.

[38] Shu, H., Qi, P., Huang, Y., Chen, F., Xie, D., & Sun, L. (2020). An efficient certificate-less aggregate signature scheme for blockchain-based medical cyber-physical systems. Sensors, 20(5), 1521.

[39] Ho, N., Wong, P. M., Soon, R. J., Chng, C. B., & Chui, C. K. (2019, December). Blockchain for cyber-physical systems in manufacturing. In: Proceedings of the Tenth International Symposium on Information and Communication Technology Association for Computing Machinery, New York, NY, USA, (pp. 385–392).

[40] Goyal, S., Sharma, N., Kaushik, I., & Bhushan, B. (2021). Blockchain as a solution for security attacks in named data networking of things. In: Security and Privacy Issues in IoT Devices and Sensor Networks, 211–243. doi:10.1016/b978-0-12-821255-4.00010-9

[41] Goyal, S., Sharma, N., Bhushan, B., Shankar, A., & Sagayam, M. (2020). It enabled technology in secured healthcare: Applications, challenges, and future directions. In: Cognitive Internet of Medical Things for Smart Healthcare, 25–48. doi:10.1007/978-3-030-55833-8_2

[42] Farouk, A., Alahmadi, A., Ghose, S., & Mashatan, A. (2020). Blockchain platform for industrial healthcare: Vision and future opportunities. Computer Communications, 154, 223–235. https://doi.org/10.1016/j.comcom.2020.02.058

[43] Zhao, W., Jiang, C., Gao, H., Yang, S., & Luo, X. (2020). Blockchain-enabled cyber—physical systems: A review. IEEE Internet of Things Journal, 8(6), 4023–4034.

[44] Vatankhah Barenji, A., Li, Z., Wang, W. M., Huang, G. Q., & Guerra-Zubiaga, D. A. (2020). Blockchain-based ubiquitous manufacturing: A secure and reliable cyber-physical system. International Journal of Production Research, 58(7), 2200–2221.

[45] Khalil, A. A., Franco, J., Parvez, I., Uluagac, S., & Rahman, M. A. (2021). A literature review on blockchain-enabled security and operation of cyber-physical systems. arXiv preprint arXiv:2107.07916.

[46] Yu, C., Jiang, X., Yu, S., & Yang, C. (2020). Blockchain-based shared manufacturing in support of cyber-physical systems: Concept, framework, and operation. Robotics and Computer-Integrated Manufacturing, 64, 101931.

[47] Bhushan, B., Sahoo, C., Sinha, P., & Khamparia, A. (2020). Unification of Blockchain and Internet of Things (BIoT): Requirements, working model, challenges and future directions. Wireless Networks. doi:10.1007/s11276-020-02445-6

[48] Jiang, L., Chen, L., Giannetsos, T., Luo, B., Liang, K., & Han, J. (2019). Toward practical privacy-preserving processing over encrypted data in IoT: An assistive healthcare use case. IEEE Internet of Things Journal, 6(6), 10177–10190. https://doi.org/10.1109/jiot.2019.2936532

[49] Xu, Q., Su, Z., & Yang, Q. (2019). Blockchain-based trustworthy edge caching scheme for the mobile cyber-physical system. IEEE Internet of Things Journal, 7(2), 1098–1110.

[50] Dedeoglu, V., Dorri, A., Jurdak, R., Michelin, R. A., Lunardi, R. C., Kanhere, S. S., & Zorzo, A. F. (2020, January). A journey in applying blockchain for cyber-physical systems. In: 2020 International Conference on Communication Systems & Networks (COMSNETS) (pp. 383–390). IEEE.

[51] Nguyen, G. N., Le Viet, N. H., Elhoseny, M., Shankar, K., Gupta, B. B., & Abd El-Latif, A. A. (2021). Secure blockchain enabled cyber—Physical healthcare systems using a deep belief network with the ResNet model. Journal of Parallel and Distributed Computing, 153, 150–160.

[52] Tyagi, A. K., Aswathy, S. U., Aghila, G., & Sreenath, N. (2021). AARIN: Affordable, accurate, reliable, and innovative mechanism to protect a medical cyber-physical system using blockchain technology. International Journal of Intelligent Networks, 2, 175–183.

[53] Tanha, F. E., Hasani, A., Hakak, S., & Gadekallu, T. R. (2022). Blockchain-based cyber-physical systems: Comprehensive model for challenge assessment. Computers and Electrical Engineering, 103, 108347.

[54] Braeken, A., Liyanage, M., Kanhere, S. S., & Dixit, S. (2020). Blockchain and cyber-physical systems. Computer, 53(9), 31–35.

[55] Skowroński, R. (2019). The open blockchain-aided multi-agent symbiotic cyber—Physical systems. Future Generation Computer Systems, 94, 430–443.

[56] Zhou, Z., Wang, B., Dong, M., & Ota, K. (2019). Secure and efficient vehicle-to-grid energy trading in cyber-physical systems: Integration of blockchain and edge computing. IEEE Transactions on Systems, Man, and Cybernetics: Systems, 50(1), 43–57.

[57] Gupta, B. B., Li, K. C., Leung, V. C., Psannis, K. E., & Yamaguchi, S. (2021). Blockchain-assisted secure fine-grained searchable encryption for a cloud-based healthcare cyber-physical system. IEEE/CAA Journal of Automatica Sinica, 8(12), 1877–1890.

[58] Boucher, O., Aloqaily, M., Tseng, L., & Boukerche, A. (2020). Blockchain and fog computing for cyber-physical systems: The case of smart industry. Computer, 53(9), 36–45.

[59] Eyal, I. (2017). Blockchain technology: Transforming libertarian cryptocurrency dreams to finance and banking realities. Computer (Long. Beach. Calif), 50(9), 38–49.

[60] van Lier, B. (2017). Can cyber-physical systems reliably collaborate within a blockchain? Metaphilosophy, 48(5), 698–711.

Chapter 9

Fuzzy Logic Modeling for Cyber Aircraft Autopilot System

A Case Study on Automated Driving

Qasem Abu Al-Haija

Department of Cybersecurity, Faculty of Computer & Information Technology, Jordan University of Science and Technology, PO Box 3030, Irbid 22110, Jordan, qsabuhaija@just.edu.jo

9.1 INTRODUCTION

An aircraft is a flying machine supported for flight by the dynamic action of air on its surfaces, such as airplanes, gliders, and helicopters. A normal aircraft flight would include several stages in its flight mission profile, including taxi, take-off, ascend, cruise, descent, approach, and landing [1]. The complete flight profile for aircraft is illustrated in Figure 9.1.

As depicted in Figure 9.1, the final landing of the aircraft flight is initiated when the pilot starts to descend toward the ground at a prescribed altitude and downward velocity. Therefore, aircraft system designers usually prefer to develop a dedicated autopilot unit to perform the *descent–approach–land* phase of an aircraft that ensures that the aircraft will touch down very gently and avoid damage. Indeed, several techniques were used to design the autopilot controller for the aircraft landing process, such as the classical control systems [2] and the fuzzy control systems [3]. However, several recent control studies have reported the desirability of using fuzzy controllers for implementing several dynamic control systems, especially those with an observable and controllable plant, such as the auto-aircraft controller for the landing approach.

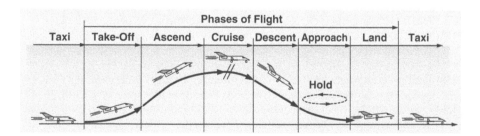

Figure 9.1 Aircraft mission profile.

DOI: 10.1201/9781003474111-9

This is due to the ability of fuzzy logic controllers to adapt themselves to the changes during the control operation, which provide more fixable to shape their surface of control. Figure 9.2 shows a simplified view of the aircraft system architecture adopting the fuzzy controller with two inputs (altitude and velocity) and one output (Force). Indeed, like any cyber-physical system [4], an aircraft controller should provide a robust defense system against the vulnerability of several cyberattacks, such as the attack models presented in Refs. [5–9]. Examples of well-known cyberattacks that exploit the vulnerability of cyber-physical aviation controller of the aircraft system include (but are not limited to) False Data Injection (FDI) attacks, Sensor Spoofing (SSP) attacks, and Distributed Denial of Service (DDoS) attacks [10].

Fuzzy logic (as introduced in 1965 by Lofti Zadeh) [3] resembles the human decision-making methodology and deals with vague and imprecise information [5,9]. Unlike the two-valued logic variables (i.e., Crisp), fuzzy logic is a more fixable system that involves the use of an infinite number of logic variables where each of which can be characterized by linguistic variable(s), domain set(s), the universe of discourse, membership function(s), and many other attributes. Such flexibility makes the large adoption of fuzzy logic great in various control applications such as temperature control for air conditioners, an anti-braking system for vehicles, control of traffic lights and washing machines, large economic systems, and autopilot landing control for aircraft systems.

Figure 9.3 illustrates the block diagram of the fuzzy logic controller (FLC).

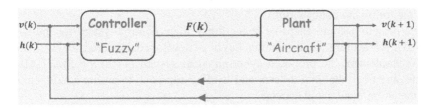

Figure 9.2 The simplified architecture for the aircraft system with fuzzy controller.

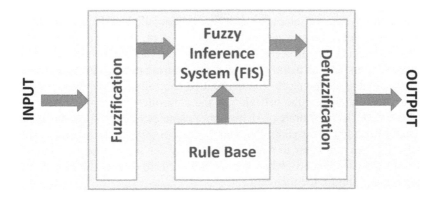

Figure 9.3 Block diagram of fuzzy logic controller.

The fuzzy logic controller encompasses four major components, as shown in Figure 9.3:

Fuzzifier: To convert the crisp input values into fuzzy values

Rule-base (knowledge-base): To store all the input–output fuzzy relationships (rules), including the membership functions and domains

Fuzzy inference system (inference engine): To simulate human decisions by performing approximate reasoning such as the Mamadani inference model

Defuzzifier: To convert the fuzzy values into crisp values from fuzzy inference engines such as the centroid of area method [5,8]

Fuzzy logic has been extensively used to develop an intelligent controller for aircraft systems [11–16]. In this chapter, we will employ the Mamdani fuzzy control model [3] to design a fuzzy logic control system to monitor and control the final descent and landing approach for auto-aircraft for a safe landing. Dynamically, the proposed controller encompasses two state variables, namely, the downward velocity $v(t)$ and the aircraft altitude $h(t)$, in which they need to be tracked to generate the control variable, i.e., the force $f(t)$, that is to be fed to the plant (aircraft system) to act accordingly. We are taking advantage of the graphical user interface (GUI) provided with the fuzzy logic toolbox of the MATLAB computing platform to develop the model for the proposed auto-aircraft controller for a safe landing. Finally, the fuzzy controller modeling, coding, results, and analysis are reported in this report. Specifically, this chapter has the following contributions:

We present a comprehensive cyber fuzzy logic control system for the automated driving aircraft controller that has been developed, explored, and validated.

We implement the proposed cyber-physical system (CPS) via MATLAB to model and track the final descent and landing approach to ensure a safe landing for the aircraft and avoid damage.

We employ two states in the proposed CPS system, including the landing velocity v(t) and aircraft altitude h(t), both modeled as inputs to the controller to generate the proper aircraft's engine force f(t), which is modeled as the control variable for the auto-aircraft controller.

We fuzzify system variables using different linguistic variables and their corresponding memberships to model the fuzzy system. Also, the internal fuzzy inference system (FIS) has been modeled using the Mamdani control model. The fuzzy control output was deffuzified using the centroid of area (CoA) to generate the corresponding crisp values. The deffuzified controller signals were plotted to analyze the continuous-time behavior of the controller dynamics to gain more insights into the landing strategy. Hence, both parameters [v(t), h(t)] contribute to the output force f(t) of the controller, which starts to spike at the initial time units fuzzily and then continues to decrease uniformly for the rest of the simulation time toward the landing area where the aircraft needs to stop its engine (i.e., f(t) = 0lb: sec) preparing for the final descent.

We provided extensive simulation results, which revealed that our fuzzy controller has a smooth rate of change of the downward velocity from initializing the aircraft descent at –50 ft/s to the landing position at 0 ft/s. Eventually, the developed fuzzy controller was successfully and efficiently designed to ensure that the aircraft would touch down very gently and avoid damage.

Finally, the rest of this chapter is organized as follows: the main problem statement of the autopilot controller is stated in Section 9.2. Section 9.3 presents the proposed system model for the fuzzy controller design. In Section 9.4, we provide and discuss the results and findings of our system implementation. Finally, Section 9.5 concludes the work.

9.2 PROBLEM STATEMENT

It is desired to design an autopilot for an aircraft's final descent and landing approach using a fuzzy logic control system [10]. It is assumed that the desired downward velocity $v(t)$ is proportional to the aircraft altitude $h(t)$ square. Thus, at high altitudes, a large downward velocity is desired. As the altitude diminishes, the desired downward velocity gets smaller and smaller. This ensures that the aircraft will touch down very gently and avoid damage. This is a two states system, i.e., $v(t)$ and $h(t)$, with one control input, $f(t)$. Indifference equations, the plant to be controlled, are described by the following simplified two-state equations (Equation 9.1):

$$v(k + 1) = v(k) + 0.75 * f(k) \quad \text{and} \quad h(k + 1) = h(k) + 1.5 * v(k) \quad (9.1)$$

Here $v(k + 1)$ is the new velocity and, $v(k)$ is the old velocity, $h(k + 1)$ is the new altitude, and $h(k)$ is the old altitude, and $f(k)$ is the control forces generated by the fuzzy controller.

9.2.1 Task Statement I

Let the range for the aircraft altitude $h(k) = 0$ to 2000 ft, the aircraft velocity $v(k)$ = −50 to +50 ft/s, and for the force $f(k) = -75$ to +75 lb·s.

1. Fuzzify the altitude input variable $h(k)$ into four fuzzy sets using the following linguistics variables: *Near–Zero (NZ)*, *Small (S)*, *Medium (M)*, and *Large (L)* altitude. Select the appropriate type of fuzzy membership functions for each set and plot these membership functions.
2. Repeat step 1 for the downward velocity $v(k)$ using the following fuzzy variables: *Down–Large (DL)*, *Down–Small (DS–*, *Zero [Z]*, *Up–Small (US)*, and *Up–Large (UL)* velocity.
3. Repeat step 1 for the control force $f(k)$ using the following fuzzy variables: *Down–Large (DL)*, *Down–Small (DS–*, *Zero [Z]*, *Up–Small (US)*, and *Up–large (UL)* force.

4. Use common sense and engineering judgment to determine the fuzzy rules. Finally, use the discrete fuzzy centroid strategy to defuzzify the fuzzy output $f(k)$.

9.2.2   Task Statement II

Perform the following tasks using the following initial conditions: h(0) = 1950 ft/s and v(0) = −45 ft/s.

1. Calculate the control force that must be applied on the aircraft for the first four cycles.
2. Using MATLAB, design and simulate the performance of the fuzzy controller from the initial conditions to landing. Plot the controller output force $f(k)$, the aircraft altitude $h(k)$, the downward velocity $v(k)$, and the relationship between the aircraft altitude $h(k)$ and the downward velocity $v(k)$. Use simulation interval $\triangle T = 0.25$ s.

9.3   FUZZY CONTROLLER DESIGN

This section discusses the comprehensive phases for the proposed design and implementation of the fuzzy logic controller for an aircraft's final descent and landing approach. We have used the Fuzzy toolbox of MATLAB [17], which provides complete steps to develop the fuzzy controllers. Thus, the FLC design process composes the following phases.

9.3.1   Phase 1: Preparing the Overall Controller Schematic

The top view of the proposed fuzzy control system design of the aircraft's autopilot for the final descent and landing approach is illustrated in Figure 9.4. At this stage, we have prepared the controller inputs (velocity and altitude) and outputs (Force), selected Mamadani as an inference method, configured the AND OR methods as "MIN" and "MAX" operations, as well as the defuzzifier as "Centroid" operation.

9.3.2   Phase 2: Configuring the Controller I/O

We have prepared the controller parameter as fuzzy functions by fuzzifying system dynamics ranges to end up with the membership functions illustrated in Figure 9.5. As can be seen from the figure, since both velocity (input parameter) and force (controller output) have five linguistic variables (i.e., five fuzzy sets), each can be implemented using five overlapped membership functions. However, the case for the aircraft altitude was different since it was fuzzified into four fuzzy sets and, thus, four membership functions that can split the horizon range of this input parameter.

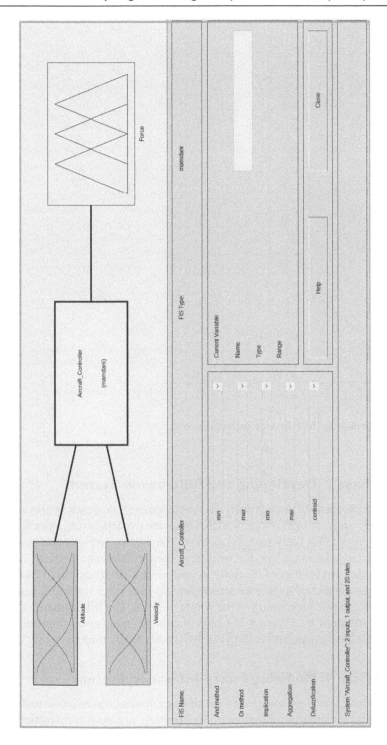

Figure 9.4 Top view of the proposed fuzzy controller.

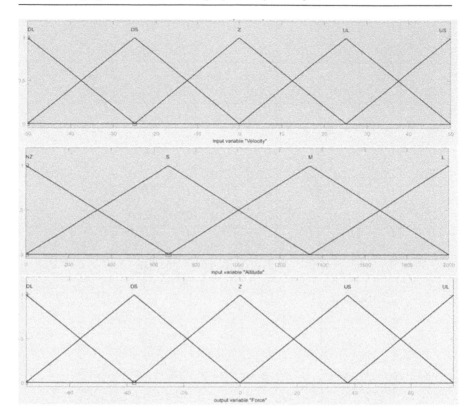

Figure 9.5 Membership functions for each parameter.

9.3.3 Phase 3: Developing the Rule-based System

To design the proper Fuzzy controller, we developed our rule-based system using the following matrix of rules (Figure 9.6) that maps the two inputs (i.e., velocity and altitude) to the possible fuzzy output (i.e., Force) linguistics. Using common sense and engineering judgment, a map has been developed to determine the fuzzy rules.

The complete list of rules of the fuzzy aircraft controller accumulated 20 rules base since the number of linguistics accompanying each input is 4 and 5, respectively, forming a rule base matrix of the length of 4 × 5. The list of rules is given below and followed by Figure 9.7, which shows the same rules implemented using the rule base engine provided by the MATLAB Fuzzy toolbox.

9.3.4 Phase 4: Modeling Fuzzy Inference System

As all rules have been configured to cover all possible relations of inputs and outputs, the inference process can be started by applying any input combinations of

		Velocity $v(k)$				
		DL	DS	Z	US	UL
Altitude $h(k)$	NZ	UL	UL	Z	DS	DS
	S	UL	US	Z	DS	DL
	M	US	Z	DS	DL	DL
	L	Z	DS	DL	DL	DL

Figure 9.6 Rule-based matrix for the fuzzy controller.

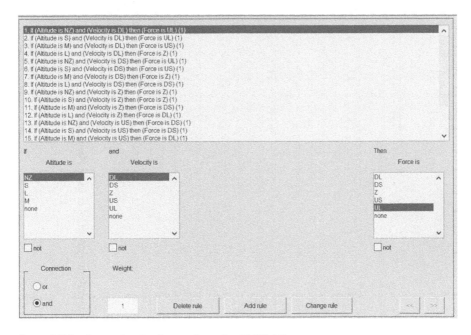

Figure 9.7 Implementing the fuzzy rules using MATLAB.

$v(k)$ and $h(k)$ to find out the response of the controller, which determine the proper force accordingly. The rule inference system is illustrated in Figure 9.8. This FIS uses the Mamadani method, which applies the min–min–max composition and centroid defuzzification. Also, the figure provides an example of applying the input combination: $[h(k), v(k)] = [1000, 0]$, which shows the controller output force of -18.5 lb·s.

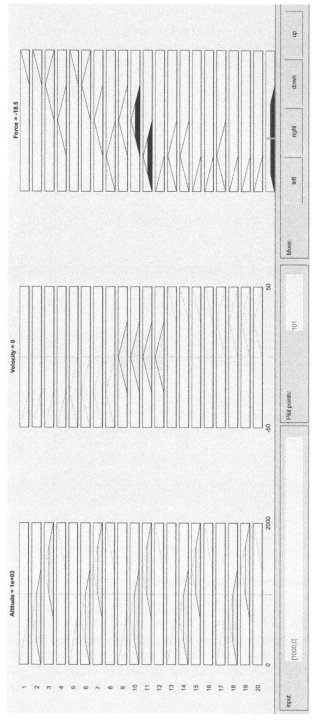

Figure 9.8 Rule-based viewer for aircraft fuzzy controller using Mamadani FIS.

9.3.5   Phase 5: Visualizing Overall I/O Relationships

To better understand the controller functionality, we provide the relationships of the *Defuzzified Input Output* using the Mamadani fuzzy model (i.e., *min–min–max* composition) and *Centroid of Area (COA)* as defuzzification process of extracting crisp value from a fuzzy set. Such relationships are provided in Figure 9.9, which illustrates the two possible relations (since we have two inputs and one output): the *force versus velocity* relationship and the *force versus altitude* relationship.

Finally, the overall combined relationship between all inputs $v(k)$ and $h(k)$ with all corresponding outputs $f(k)$ is presented in Figure 9.10.

9.4   RESULTS AND DISCUSSIONS

The auto-aircraft control has always been a subject of interest as it can be related closely to many dynamical models involving adaptive control. In this chapter, we have implemented the fuzzy controller for a two-state auto-aircraft landing

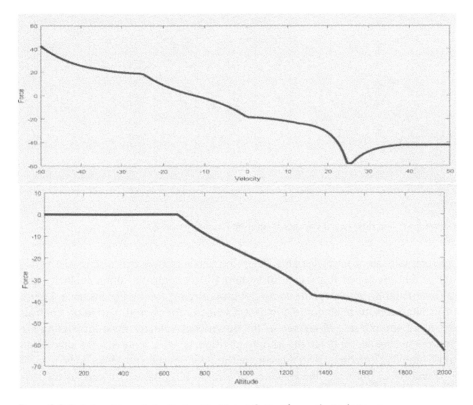

Figure 9.9 Relationships of the *Defuzzified Input Output* for each single input.

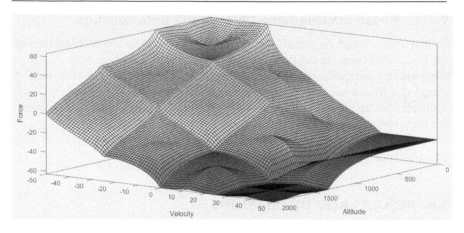

Figure 9.10 Surface plot for the overall relationships of the *Defuzzified Input Output.*

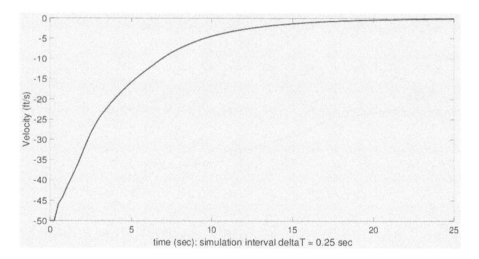

Figure 9.11 The downward velocity of aircraft *v(t)* versus time *t*.

system with one control variable. Therefore, this section will discuss the validity of the developed fuzzy control system for its controller input (velocity and altitude) and its impact on the control output (aircraft force). For instance, Figure 9.11 illustrates the behavior of downward velocity for aircraft. Our fuzzy controller has a smooth rate of change of the downward velocity from initializing the aircraft decent at –50 ft/s to the landing position at 0 ft/s. Note that the simulation time here is 25 seconds, with the sample time configured at 0.25 seconds.

Figure 9.12 illustrates the tendency of aircraft altitude, which verifies the efficiency of the developed fuzzy controller since it provides a uniform exponential decrease of the altitude toward the landing position, which is strongly proportional

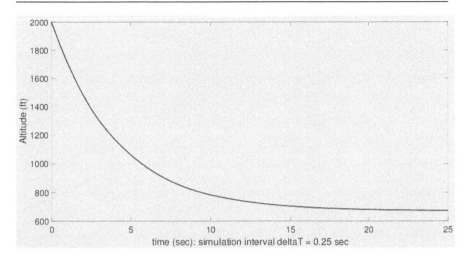

Figure 9.12 The altitude of aircraft *h*(t) versus time *t*.

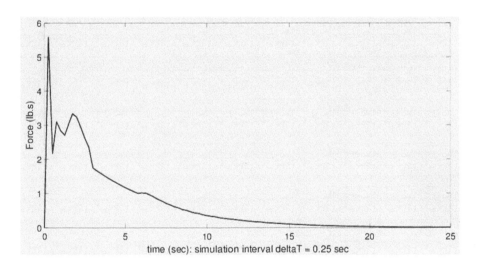

Figure 9.13 The controller force of aircraft *f*(t) versus time *t*.

to the change of downward velocity. Again, the simulation time here is 25 seconds, with the sample time configured at 0.25 seconds.

Figure 9.13 illustrates the behavior of the output force $f(t)$ of the controller, which starts to spike at the first couple of time units fuzzily and then continues to decrease uniformly for the rest of the simulation time (i.e., landing time) toward the landing area where the aircraft needs to stop its engine (i.e., $f(t) = 0$ lb·s) preparing for the final descent.

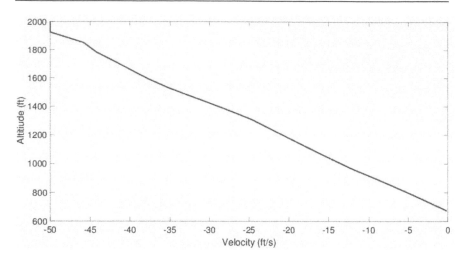

Figure 9.14 The relationship between downward velocity $v(t)$ and aircraft altitude $h(t)$.

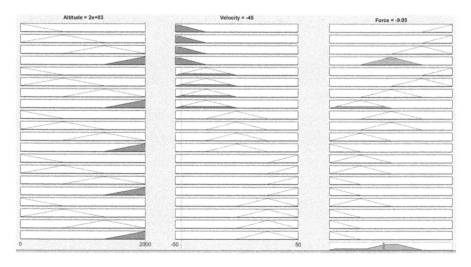

Figure 9.15 Obtaining the initial force $f(0)$ the fuzzy controller's rule base viewer.

Finally, Figure 9.14 illustrates the relationship between downward velocity and the aircraft altitude. From the plot, as the altitude decreases, the velocity decreases too. Both of them almost reach the landing position at the same time (Figure 9.15).

9.5   CONCLUSIONS

A fuzzy logic controller (FLC)-based Mamdani fuzzy technique for modeling and tracking the landing approach and final descent for safe aircraft landing and avoiding damage using MATLAB simulation package has been developed and reported in this chapter. The simulation results showed that the proposed FLC model provided a smooth rate of change in downward velocity $v(t)$ from the initial velocity downward to saturate statically at *zeroft/s* while pushing down the aircraft by decreasing altitude $h(t)$ toward the landing area continuously on time sampled at 0.25 second. As a result, both of the parameters $[v(t), h(t)]$ contribute to the output force $f(t)$ of the controller, which starts to spike at the first couple of time units fuzzily and then continues to decrease uniformly for the rest of simulation time (i.e., landing time) toward the landing area where the aircraft needs to stop its engine (i.e., $f(t) = 0$ lb·s) preparing for the final descent. One last thing, according to the simulation results and appendix plots, the centroid deffuzifier seems to be the best option to model the dynamics for our controller system since it provides the most stable and smooth results when compared with results generated using other deffuzifiers. In the future, we will seek to investigate and discuss the employment of other intelligent schemes to construct the autopilot controller using neural network models, fuzzy-neuro models, heuristic and meta-heuristic models, and machine/deep learning models [18,19].

REFERENCES

1. C. S. Wasson, System Engineering Analysis, Design, and Development: Concepts, Principles, and Practices. John Wiley & Sons, Inc., Hoboken, New Jersey, 2nd edition, ISBN 978-1-118-44226-5, Apr 2016.
2. K. A. Tehrani and A. Mpanda, Introduction to PID Controllers—Theory, Tuning, and Application to Frontier Areas, InTech-Open Press, London, UK, ISBN 978-953-307-927-1, 2012.
3. A. P. Engelbrecht, Computational Intelligence: An Introduction. 2nd edition, ISBN 978-0-470-03561-0, John Wiley & Sons Ltd, Hoboken, NJ, Apr 2007.
4. A. A. Smadi, B. T. Ajao, B. K. Johnson, H. Lei, Y. Chakhchoukh and Q. Abu Al-Haija, *A Comprehensive Survey on Cyber-Physical Smart Grid Testbed Architectures: Requirements and Challenges*, Electronics 2021, 10, 1043. DOI: 10.3390/electronics10091043.
5. Q. A. Al-Haija, *On the Security of Cyber-Physical Systems Against Stochastic Cyber-Attacks Models*, 2021 IEEE International IoT, Electronics and Mechatronics Conference (IEMTRONICS), 2021, pp. 1–6, DOI: 10.1109/IEMTRONICS52119.2021.9422623.
6. A. A. Alsulami and S. Zein-Sabatto, *Resilient Cyber-Security Approach For Aviation Cyber-Physical Systems Protection Against Sensor Spoofing Attacks*, 2021 IEEE 11th Annual Computing and Communication Workshop and Conference (CCWC), 2021, pp. 0565–0571, DOI: 10.1109/CCWC51732.2021.9376158.
7. S. A. P. Kumar and B. Xu, *Vulnerability Assessment for Security in Aviation Cyber-Physical Systems*, 2017 IEEE 4th International Conference on Cyber Security and Cloud Computing (CSCloud), 2017, pp. 145–150, DOI: 10.1109/CSCloud.2017.17.
8. A. A. Alsulami and S. Zein-Sabatto, *Detection and Defense from False Data Injection Attacks in Aviation Cyber-Physical Systems Using Artificial Immune Systems*, 2020 International Conference on Computational Science and Computational Intelligence (CSCI), 2020, pp. 69–75, DOI: 10.1109/CSCI51800.2020.00019.
9. Q. Abu Al-Haija and S. Zein-Sabatto, *An Efficient Deep-Learning-Based Detection and Classification System for Cyber-Attacks in IoT Communication Networks*, Electronics 2020, 9, 2152. DOI: 10.3390/electronics9122152.

10. R. F. Ibrahim, Q. Abu Al-Haija and A. Ahmad, *DDoS Attack Prevention for Internet of Thing Devices Using Ethereum Blockchain Technology*, Sensors 2022, 22, 6806. DOI: 10.3390/s22186806.

11. C. M. Scott and O. Gonzalez, *On the Development of a Fuzzy Logic Model-Less Aircraft Controller*, AIAA 2020–0765. AIAA SciTech 2020 Forum. Jan 2020.

12. A. Rasheed, *Aircraft Dynamics Using Fuzzy-PID Controller Design*, 2018 International Conference on Electrical Engineering (ICEE), 2018, pp. 1–6, DOI: 10.1109/ICEE.2018.8566756.

13. Y. Liu, Q. Zhou, T. Lan and J. Lei, *Adaptive Fuzzy Sliding Mode Controller Design for Saucer-Shaped Aircraft*, 2017 2nd International Conference on Control and Robotics Engineering (ICCRE), 2017, pp. 82–85, DOI: 10.1109/ICCRE.2017.7935047.

14. I. N. Ibrahim and M. A. Al Akkad, *Exploiting an Intelligent Fuzzy-PID System in Nonlinear Aircraft Pitch Control*, 2016 International Siberian Conference on Control and Communications (SIBCON), 2016, pp. 1–7, DOI: 10.1109/SIBCON.2016.7491828.

15. A. Khalid, K. Zeb and A. Haider, *Conventional PID, Adaptive PID, and Sliding Mode Controllers Design for Aircraft Pitch Control*, 2019 International Conference on Engineering and Emerging Technologies (ICEET), 2019, pp. 1–6, DOI: 10.1109/CEET1.2019.8711871.

16. X. Bu, Q. Qi and B. Jiang, *A Simplified Finite-Time Fuzzy Neural Controller with Prescribed Performance Applied to Waverider Aircraft*, IEEE Transactions on Fuzzy Systems, DOI: 10.1109/TFUZZ.2021.3089031.

17. MATLAB Documentation, *Fuzzy Logic Toolbox: User's Guide*. by MathWorks, Inc., 2019. Retrieved online: www.mathworks.com/help/.

18. Q. Abu Al-Haija and A. Al-Badawi, *High-Performance Intrusion Detection System for Networked UAVs Via Deep Learning*, Neural Comput & Applic 2022, 34, 10885–10900. https://doi.org/10.1007/s00521-022-07015-9.

19. Q. Abu Al-Haija, SysML-Based Design of Autonomous Multi-Robot Cyber-Physical System Using Smart IoT Modules: A Case Study, In Hemanth, D. J. (eds) Machine Learning Techniques for Smart City Applications: Trends and Solutions: Advances in Science, Technology & Innovation. Springer, Cham. 2022. https://doi.org/10.1007/978-3-031-08859-916.

Chapter 10

Harnessing the Power of Artificial Intelligence in Software Engineering for the Design and Optimization of Cyber-physical Systems

Shubham Tiwari and Ayasha Malik

10.1 INTRODUCTION

Various practices intersect specific stages of the Software Development Life Cycle (SDLC) in programming tasks. To extract important information from data acquired throughout the SDLC, various information extraction approaches are used. This chapter analyzes numerous artificial reasoning tasks that have applications in the automation of programming plans [1]. To address certain programming-related issues, artificial intelligence techniques such as data mining, artificial neural networks, and fuzzy logic have been utilized. However, the complexity of programming tasks necessitates the automation of all discussed procedures to address the associated instability [2]. A large amount of data from all stages of the SDLC has been evaluated. However, this data contradicts the findings of the prerequisites study, implementation, unit testing, integration, and system testing, as well as the design and maintenance phases. The engineering of the software design and composition is based on the information gathered during the design and planning phase, for the purpose of remodeling. The mining of large amounts of data has been found to be beneficial for the efficient reuse of information and ID disclosure [3,4]. However, for the development of software, as well as for recycling and support automation for authorized standards, artificial intelligence (AI) should be used in cooperation [5]. The main goal of this research is to propose various functions and features related to AI in the field of computer programming for the advancement of the field. The testing of the most advanced AI techniques is carried out in the final phase, which is also relevant for the field of product remodelling and the overall development of the field of programming. Applications are categorized according to their location, type of AI technology, and automation level by AI-SEAL, which stands for AI in software engineering application levels. This illustrates that AI in the field of computer programming is a challenging and rapidly developing domain and that a thorough exploration is necessary to address the issues and problems related to programming in the field [6–8].

AI has both positive and negative implications for different groups of people. It can be beneficial for customers, businesses, and even those with malicious intent.

DOI: 10.1201/9781003474111-10

AI is used for a variety of tasks, such as assisting with online searches through Google Assistant, helping with phone conversations through Siri, and even recognizing faces on Facebook [9]. Additionally, AI is helping credit card companies detect and prevent fraud, saving them billions of dollars annually. However, it raises the question of whether it is a good idea to rely on AI to keep confidential information secure. In today's era, advancements in technology have opened up the possibility of creating new types of computer systems, known as Cyber-Physical Systems (CPS), that can work in coordination with the real world [10]. These systems typically involve a combination of real-world actions and computer systems. Additionally, an overview of this topic is provided herein:

- The framework of AI and its applications is discussed in this work.
- Various artificial techniques are stated in this piece of work, which are relevant in this field.
- Applications of AI in SE along with its types are featured in this work.

The remaining portion of this chapter is summarized as follows: In Section 10.2, the application of AI in the field of software engineering, along with various types of AI, is explained. This section also covers how to extract information from data using AI and the advantages of AI. Section 10.3 discusses the use of AI in computerized software development and covers the concept of data mining through RPA and AI. The section also describes how to reuse software. Section 10.4 covers the evaluation methods of AI. In Section 10.5, the intersection of CPS and AI is discussed. The section provides an overview of CPS, including its definition, characteristics, and applications. It also examines how AI can improve the performance of CPS and the current state of research in this field, highlighting the challenges and opportunities that arise when AI is integrated with CPS. In Section 10.6, potential future developments and implications for both CPS and AI are discussed, including some types of neural networks and distributed AI. Section 10.7 concludes the chapter.

10.2   THE USE OF AI IN SOFTWARE ENGINEERING

To address potential software engineering issues, data mining has been conducted to extract valuable information from various programming repositories [11]. This technique has also been applied in automated reasoning. The use of domain knowledge, along with advancements in the field of programming, remains an important area of research for automating intuitive programming tasks [12]. To support the development process of products, various business concepts are now readily available in the market. In the field of programming, the task of AI is to search for and gather information related to programming and AI and apply it to the field [13]. This study examines the role of AI in programming, combining the three key areas of programming, data mining, and automated reasoning to improve the concept of intuitive programming and, ultimately, automate the entire programming development process [14].

10.2.1   AI's Forms

We can bifurcate AI into various categories, but two potential categories are capacities and functionalities.

- *Narrow AI:* Narrow AI is smart enough to perform a specific task or operation that has been assigned to it. It is currently the most practical type of AI. However, this type of AI is limited in its capabilities as it is designed to perform specific tasks, which is why it is also referred to as weak AI. If we try to push it beyond its intended capabilities, it can malfunction or fail. A prime example of this is SIRI by Apple. SIRI is programmed to perform a fixed set of functions. Another example of Narrow AI is IBM's Watson Supercomputer, which is equipped with machine learning and natural language processing. Other examples of Narrow AI include chess-playing programs, e-commerce sites, and systems for recognizing speech and images [15].
- *General AI:* The goal of General AI is to create a system that can perform logical functions with the same level of effectiveness as a human. The ultimate objective is to build a system that is capable of independent thought. However, to date, no AI has been able to fully replicate the cognitive abilities of the human mind. This is a complex task that will require significant research and development [16].
- *Super AI:* The Super AI model can surpass human capabilities in all areas and perform every task more efficiently. This AI is considered to be an advancement of General AI, as it can solve complex problems, form perceptions, and learn on its own. However, it is currently still in the hypothetical phase. If this system were to be implemented in real life, it would be one of the greatest achievements in human history [17].
- *Reactive machines:* The primary types of AI machines are Reactive machines, which do not store memories of past events for future reference. The main focus is on identifying opportunities and taking action on them quickly. Examples of this type of AI include IBM's Deep Blue system and Google's AlphaGo system [18].
- *Limited machines:* Contrary to reactive machines, limited machines can retain previous experiences for a short period. However, the stored information may only be useful for a limited duration. A self-driving car is a prime example of this. The primary function of a self-driving car is to record the speed of surrounding vehicles, the speed limit, and the distance between itself and other vehicles. Additional data is also recorded for driving purposes [19].
- *Theory of mind:* Isn't it cool that a machine can decipher human emotions, its beliefs, and is also able to socialize with other human beings? This AI's idea and motive are the same as discussed above. It is presently in a progress phase and may require more time before marketing. A group of attempts have been made and are still being made to create and improve this AI [20].
- *Self-awareness:* Taking the world of AI one step ahead, this self-awareness AI is an impending AI. What's special about this AI? Well, this AI will be

so analytical that it will have its plans, understanding, and introspection. Once done, these AIs will be super smart compared to human minds. It is still in the theoretical phase but if it will be developed, then it will have the possibility to transform this globe [21].

10.2.2   Data Mining with the Aid of Information-based Systems

To effectively address various software engineering problems related to the storage and management of information, discovery through experimentation is essential. Data mining and associated software categories, such as user interfaces, lines of code, cyclomatic complexity, and density, play a crucial role in the classification and improvement of software for the efficient application of data mining methods. Software engineering in conjunction with artificial intelligence is beneficial for the sustainable elements of information systems [22].

10.2.3   SE Elicited from Business Intelligence

The upcoming trend of AI in software engineering (SE) [23] involves identifying and organizing objects that exist in the physical world. For example, expert information and research areas such as information-based systems. Automated intelligence, specifically in the field of software engineering, is gaining momentum in both research and award-winning areas. Integrating AI with business intelligence leads to the automation of the software development process [24].

10.3   REUTILIZATION OF COMPUTERIZED SOFTWARE CONSTRUCTION WITH SI

The field of SDLC is a subset of software construction. A significant amount of data is managed at each stage of the process. Clear communication and management of data is crucial at each level of the SDLC, especially when dealing with software-related issues. The examination of specific information related to each phase of the SDLC improves the comprehension and analysis of the process, making it more efficient. To save time and simplify the development process, software is often reused. This approach is beneficial for all parties involved, as it ensures the use of high-quality, well-organized, and adaptable software components. To achieve a successful and structured transition, automated and various software engineering techniques can be employed to attain a well-organized approach. This can be achieved by making changes in the software development process to automate it, thus avoiding the constant selection of software engineering issues. Additionally, it helps to preserve software attributes, making the software more adaptable to technology and improving its overall organization. This ultimately reduces the total time and cost required for the final development of the application [25–27].

10.3.1 Structured Software Development with the Help of AI

The construction of software using computer technology involves a combination of SE and various AI approaches. Data mining is used to select the best candidates and identify useful skills, which helps to reuse and enhance AI strategies and make decisions. This results in the automation of SE tasks, including the re-utilization of software. A thorough examination of Systems Integration (SI) [28] is conducted to reuse current business intelligence concepts, allowing a large franchise to acquire the BI framework. The progression of the application will lead to a combination of AI strategies at every stage of software development. Reusing the organization, architecture, and processes of a business by the Software Reuse organization is done to recover SE [29]. Combining the three powerful fields of AI, data mining, and SE aids in the development of SI, allowing for the automation and renewal of software construction strategies. Data mining and AI processes are related to SI, as they support all phases of the SDLC. In addition, this text describes various AI strategies that are crucial for the organized development of software in the re-utilization domain [30].

10.4 REUSABILITY ASSESSMENT OF ARTIFICIAL TECHNIQUES

To improve different software development processes, various areas of research have been examined. It was found that neural networks, fuzzy logic, information-based systems, and Machine Learning (ML) are effective AI strategies that can enhance operations. AI is rapidly growing in popularity, and it is being utilized in nearly every field, such as software development and testing, software architecture, and requirement engineering. In this section, we will discuss the three most widely used AI strategies in the software engineering industry. These strategies are outlined systematically and comprehensively [31,32]. A range of techniques can assist in software development. In this chapter, we will explain how data mining, ML, and neural networks can provide specific advantages in the field of SE. The most important procedures are outlined in Table 10.1 [35] and are relevant across the entire field of SE, with a specific focus on the development of business software and the recycling of existing software [33,34]. The numerous data mining approaches utilized in the extraction of SE data for the reutilization of software are listed in Table 10.1.

There is a variety of ML approaches that are employed by the SE platform. Deep learning (DL) enables the engineers to extract the necessary requirements from developing source code and do the computation through multi-layer neural networks [36]. Figure 10.1 shows us the relationship between AI, ML, and DL.

Table 10.1 AI in SE

AI Techniques [35]	Artificial Intelligence in Software Engineering		
	Data Mining in Software Engineering	Software Engineering Area	Applications
1	Knowledge discovery	Software reuse	Software reusability activities
2	Classification	Software reuse	Identifying software components
3	Clustering	Software reuse	Predicting reusability

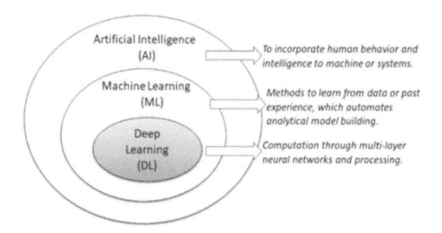

Figure. 10.1 The relationship between DL, ML, and AI.

10.5   CYBER-PHYSICAL SYSTEMS

CPS is a complex setup that has different levels which work together with the real world. According to many researchers, CPS is becoming more important for the industry as well as scientific studies. CPS is being noticed by the government and they also got some plans to use CPS to eradicate current problems. It is expected that by using this trendy technology with the physical world, systems can be made more efficient, safer, better, and more competitive. In this section, we are discussing how the chemical industry can benefit with the help of CPS. We will also discuss how CPS can perform better with the help of AI. As we mentioned earlier, AI is a boon for CPS; it can help CPS understand things better. Further, we will discuss the relationship between many important topics and CPS, and how it connects to important parts of chemical engineering like system control and optimization. Finally, we will discuss the link between other trendy and emerging topics like "digital twins" and how it connects with CPS in chemical industries [37,38].

10.5.1 Exploring the Utilization of Artificial Intelligence in Enabling Cyber-physical Systems

The main purpose of this chapter is to demonstrate how AI can boost CPS performance by making it understand things. Within the CPS, AI can be fruitful for things like a prediction about something and finding problems. It can help the system work better. For this part of the chapter, we will be discussing, in brief, the future outlook of CPS and the chemical industry together. As aforementioned, AI can work as an enabling component that provides important perception to the CPS. Furthermore, we will be discussing the connection of CPS with crucial subjects like system control and optimization, which is a part of chemical engineering. A connection between "digital twins" and CPS is also discussed [39].

10.5.2 Investigating the Intersection of Control, Optimization, Artificial Intelligence, and Cyber-physical System

The important factor in the chemical industry is to make sure that the process is working smoothly and making the most of it. If this is not happening, the process can't operate even if the basic ways for controlling and checking are used. A lot of information and research is present regarding the control issues and making the chemical industry better. Many new ideas and innovations on these topics can be found throughout history. For now, we are not going to dig into a lot about these topics, but they are a crucial part of the chemical industry. So, whenever we discuss innovations in said field, it is necessary to remember these components that help CPS work better [40].

10.5.3 Cyber-physical Systems, Digital Twins, and AI

If the digitalization of CPS is done in such a way that a virtual copy of CPS is made, then it's like a mirror of the real one, i.e., cyber and physical systems. This virtual copy of CPS can be used for various things like making the system better and checking if it is working. It opens up a lot of possibilities if the virtual copy of CPS is made. "Digital twin" is known as the virtual copy of CPS. This can be used to analyze what's happening in the world in real-time, learn from it, and get the required data. It also helps with the virtualization of CPS in a succinct virtual environment, which can be useful for the assessment of the physical environment, continuously learning from it, and in the end providing real, precise, and reliable information about the whole scenario [41].

10.5.4 Exploring the Capabilities of Artificial Intelligence in Cyber-physical Systems

A combination of computer systems, networks, and things happening in the real world makes a CPS. These can watch and control the real-world parts. CPS is built by different machines and tools that can sense things and computer intelligence. It uses these things to analyze the physical world with the help of algorithms that are connected to the Internet [42]. This simply means CPS can perform according to what's happening in real life. As the field of data analysis, AI and communication is growing exponentially, more and more scientists want these kinds of machines to interact with the provided environment. Some examples can be taken as self-driving cars, which use sensors to drive carefully, and also the appliances/products that save energy on their own. CPS is invigorating important switches and changing the way we live. It is acting like a building block for things like smart products and buildings. As this continues to grow and will become common in our daily lives, we will see four areas of CPS more often [43].

10.5.4.1   Swarm Intelligence: All for One and One for All

There is one interesting technology/area of AI known as "swarm intelligence." It is the working of many small "minds" together to make the whole system faster, more efficient, smarter, creative, and better at understanding [44]. One more important and interesting thing about "swarm intelligence" is that they don't have one central control, can be made smaller or bigger, can change easily, work on their own, and can also work together. From this, we can simply conclude that all machines and robots work together to achieve the same goal. One thing that can help swarm systems work better is having good communications networks like 5G because it will allow the seamless interaction and transfer of data easily among the swarm members [45,46]. That is, robots will be able to talk and share info without any disturbance. Maybe soon, swarm systems may help in things that seem impossible for a normal being now. For example, rescue operations in dangerous environments. These systems can also plot untold places in real time while people are still moving and can also warn them about any danger approaching. In layman's terms, this can help people even in extreme situations [47].

10.5.4.2   The Mitigation of Distance as a Factor in Networked Systems

One new way to connect is the "tactile Internet," which will allow us to interact in real-time with things that are far away. It is currently under development, but once it is developed, then the way of our communication will change and we will be able to understand how far we have reached by using this advanced technology. One of the best and most interesting examples is that robots could be used by doctors to perform surgeries even when they are far away. Isn't it interesting and so helpful for mankind? This will help more and more people to get medical help on time. But this is still a hypothetical situation, to make this happen we need to work on technology. Working on technology means having faster and better communication networks like 5G, other technologies like VR and AR, robots, and AI. All these things collectively would make the surgery possible [48].

10.5.4.3 Advancing the Integration of Artificial Intelligence and Machine Learning at the Point of Action

For controlling the flow of data at the borderline between two different networks, hardware called an "Edge Device" is used. Edge Devices are becoming more mighty, smaller, and cheaper. But cheaper and smaller doesn't necessarily mean that it won't perform [49]. We can use these devices in AI and ML which will help us to make real-time decisions closer to the place where the whole data gets stored. This means making models that take into account where the data comes from and adapting the way the system makes decisions based on the situation. These systems are necessary for CPS to perform better, especially when the time is critical and no mistake can be tolerated like in surgeries with the help of robots or what we were talking about earlier, self-driving cars. It provides us with real-time information which directly helps CPS to work and perform better [50].

10.5.4.4 Open, Yet Protected

As technology is increasing and becoming more common, many smart devices and the Internet of Things (IoT) are also becoming more common among people. It is becoming a new normal in our lives as the majority of the population today is connected to the Internet. Researchers found that by the year 2030, more than 125 billion devices will be connected around the world. Eight billion people with 125 billion devices! But as more and more devices are being made and innovated, it is also important to review the old devices, rather than handling the new devices, as it poses too much risk. For instance, if more devices get connected, it will be easier for anyone to hack them. For device safety, we need to make sure that different systems are working together and also learning as time passes by. This will change the safety of our devices, especially when more people are getting connected. Machines and robots can perform many things either good or bad, but it's the responsibility of a company or a person to use them for good purposes. They should work on making new products and services, creating more employment, but with good intentions and keeping the user's data safe [51].

10.5.4.5 Prospects and Future Directions

As the advancement in technology continues to grow and the way of living is changing, it is making people more excited but also worried at some times. But this whole concept is about connecting the real world with the virtual world. Things like swarm intelligence, the tactile Internet, and edge computing are advancing in their fields and making the technology more intelligent, which can understand things better. Humans are going through a phase where everything is changing so rapidly. We should be more aware that the changes we are making are positively impacting our lives. New technologies like Amazon's Alexa and Apple's Siri will always listen to us, and there are dangers online that can put our information at risk. The best and only way to deal with all these changes is to accept and work accordingly [52].

10.6 UTILIZATION OF ARTIFICIAL INTELLIGENCE IN ENABLING CYBER-PHYSICAL SYSTEMS IN INDUSTRIAL APPLICATIONS

The goal of this chapter is to show and evaluate the capability of AI-derived cyber-physical systems, which allows the system to think on its own. On a primary level, AI can prove to be a useful part of CPSs, for example, to detect a fault or to predict system behaviour in real-time. This topic has been discussed previously in the literature. As the advancement in AI systems continues, it increases the complexity as well. There are still different parts that don't work smoothly together. It needs to change. This simply means better tools and technologies are required to control them and make any decision. It is one of the biggest challenges for scaling AI systems. This challenge needs to be addressed as AI plays a big and important role in making big systems work well. It connects all the parts and makes sure they work smoothly and decisions are being taken quickly on their own [53].

What else AI can do is help the system to learn itself and to think itself. This is all possible by teaching the system to do some tasks or letting it do itself. This is called supervised and unsupervised training, which enables systems to perform a particular task. Apart from this, AI models can help systems change and adapt on their own as their learning grows. People want to learn more about how to make big AI systems and how to use them in different things. This is important because AI can be used to do things that people usually do. This is what we are talking about when we talk about using AI in special systems that can do different jobs.

Nowadays businesses are making use of AI models to make things run smoothly without any interference. The best part about this is that it is helping different businesses to communicate with the CPSs structures and make decisions. This process is called "autonomy." The idea of autonomy is becoming more popular as technology is increasing and innovations are being made, like self-driving cars. This helps businesses to use less manpower. The idea is to make sure machines can work on their own and be friendly to people. It needs certain things like being able to work in small parts, being equal, sharing information, knowing what's happening around them, and being able to manage themselves. This idea hasn't been talked about much because we didn't have the technology to make it happen. But now, with the Internet-of-Things, we can start working toward making this idea a reality.

A group of machines that are connected to perform different tasks such as sharing information in real time is known as an industrial IoT network. This proves to be fruitful for AI-enabled systems which are computer programs that can do tasks on their own i.e., think and learn. This network also enables AI-enabled systems to share information and work in a union to manage the whole system. In layman's terms, it simply creates an environment that allows AI to work better [54]. Knowing how to use AI in moving systems is still a problem that needs to be solved. "Dynamic AI" is very important for systems in chemical engineering that change a lot and are hard to predict. These systems usually take a long time to settle and need someone to keep an eye on them to make sure they keep working well in the future. To address this problem, Recurrent Neural Networks (RNNs) are the best approach. One other type of RNN is known as Deep Neural Networks (DNN). It is good at solving problems in various spaces, but not enough research has been done on the correct way to use this in industry. DNNs have not played a major role in chemical engineering as yet. Although AI is advancing every single day, it's still not very good at solving problems about the change of systems [55]. One other type of AI is called distributed AI, which enables big systems to think for themselves, work in unity, adapt, and change how the CPSs work.

10.7   CONCLUSION

A huge area of AI functions for the reutilization of software in the field of SE and its types are covered in this chapter. Merging data mining with AI to allow SE applications is one of the results of SE. It can advance the computerized reutilization of software for the development of software. By assessing the number of frameworks narrated, one can spot important research chances in the field of AI in the context of the reutilization of the software. Hence, this chapter described several things in brief such as automation, AI applications, mechanization of AI to do human-related tasks, voice recognition, own perceptions and decision-making, etc. To identify patterns in digitalized documents, images, and text messages, AI has been used in RPA. The main advantage of RPA is that it releases the physical employees by cleverly automating everything like the collection of data and classification chores, and also neglects most clerical mistakes. This chapter also discussed the power of AI-enabled CPS in various industrial applications. It also tells us how AI can boost the performance of CPSs in different areas and prove to be useful. Areas like control, optimization, and real-time monitoring can benefit. This chapter also highlighted the challenges and problems which need to be acknowledged to fully utilize the abilities of AI-driven CPSs. The future of CPS is very promising and holds great potential for increasing safety and efficiency.

REFERENCES

[1] Bansla, A. et al. (2012). Artificial intelligence. International Journal of Applied Engineering Research, 7(11), 89–92.
[2] Hossain, R. (2022). A short review of the robotics. International Journal of Robotics and Autonomous Systems, 7(2), 52–63.
[3] Singh, G. et al. (2013). An overview of artificial intelligence. SBIT Journal of Sciences and Technology, 2(1), 1–4.
[4] Shehab, M. et al. (2020). Artificial intelligence in software engineering and inverse: Review. International Journal of Computer Integrated Manufacturing, 3(6), 1–10.
[5] Sheth, A. et al. (2016). Robotics-new era. Contemporary Research in India, 4(2), 257–261.
[6] Reddy Nadikattu, R. (2016). The emerging role of artificial intelligence in modern society. International Journal of Creative Research Thoughts (IJCRT), 4(4), 906–911.

[7] Joglekar, S., & Kadam, S. (2021). Artificial intelligence: Roadmap from automation to divinity. International Journal of Scientific Research in Science, Engineering and Technology, 9(8), 458–463.

[8] Saxena, S., Bhushan, B., & Ahad, M. A. (2021). Blockchain-based solutions to secure IoT: Background, integration trends and a way forward. Journal of Network and Computer Applications, 103050. doi: 10.1016/j.jnca.2021.103050

[9] Prasad, P. (2017). The new era of robotics: Devices and systems. International Engineering Journal for Research and Development, 3(2), 1–4.

[10] Ammar, H. H. et al. (2012). Software engineering using artificial intelligence techniques: Current state and open problems. International Conference on Computer and Information Technology (ICCIT), 4(6), 24–29.

[11] Yarlagadda, R. T. (2015). Future of robots, AI and automation in the United States. International Engineering Journal for Research and Development (IEJRD), 1(5), 1–5.

[12] Swamy, G. (2020). The emerging application area and type of artificial intelligence. International Engineering Journal for Research and Development (IEJRD), 5(5), 20–25.

[13] Reddy Nadikattu, R. (2017). The supremacy of artificial intelligence and neural networks. International Journal of Creative Research Thoughts, 5(1), 950–954.

[14] Das, S. et al. (2015). Applications of artificial intelligence in machine learning: Review and prospect. International Journal of Computer Applications, 115(9), 31–39.

[15] Radanliev, P., De Roure, D., Van Kleek, M., Santos, O., & Ani, U. (2021). Artificial intelligence in cyber physical systems. AI & Society, 36(3), 783–796.

[16] Malik, A., Kumar, A., Srivastava, J., Bhushan, B. (2022). Blockchain technology with supply chain management: Components, opportunities, and possible challenges. In: Sharma, D. K., Peng, S. L., Sharma, R., Zaitsev, D. A. (eds) Micro-Electronics and Telecommunication Engineering, vol 373. Springer, Singapore. https://doi.org/10.1007/978-981-16-8721-1_11

[17] Gupta, R., Tanwar, S., Al-Turjman, F., Italiya, P., Nauman, A., & Kim, S. W. (2020). Smart contract privacy protection using AI in cyber-physical systems: Tools, techniques and challenges. IEEE Access, 8, 24746–24772.

[18] Sakhnini, J., & Karimipour, H. (2020). AI and security of cyber physical systems: Opportunities and challenges. Security of Cyber-Physical Systems, 1–4.

[19] Bhushan, B., Khamparia, A., Sagayam, K. M., Sharma, S. K., Ahad, M. A., & Debnath, N. C. (2020). Blockchain for smart cities: A review of architectures, integration trends, and future research directions. Sustainable Cities and Society, 61, 102360. doi: 10.1016/j.scs.2020.102360

[20] Pathak, P., Pal, P. R., Shrivastava, M., & Ora, P. (2019). Fifth revolution: Applied AI & human intelligence with cyber physical systems. International Journal of Engineering and Advanced Technology, 8(3), 23–27.

[21] Oliveira, L. M., Dias, R., Rebello, C. M., Martins, M. A., Rodrigues, A. E., Ribeiro, A. M., & Nogueira, I. B. (2021). Artificial intelligence and cyber-physical systems: A review and perspectives for the future in the chemical industry. AI, 2(3), 27.

[22] Malik, A., Yadav, N., Srivastava, J., Obaid, A. J., & Saracevic, M. (2022). Blockchain in the pharmaceutical industry for better tracking of drugs with architectures and open challenges. B. (eds) Blockchain Technology in Healthcare Applications: Social, Economic, and Technological Implications (1st ed.). CRC Press. https://doi.org/10.1201/9781003224075

[23] Thekkilakattil, A., & Dodig-Crnkovic, G. (2015, July). Ethics aspects of embedded and cyber-physical systems. In 2015 IEEE 39th Annual Computer Software and Applications Conference (Vol. 2, pp. 39–44). IEEE.

[24] Plakhotnikov, D. P., & Kotova, E. E. (2020, May). The use of artificial intelligence in cyber-physical systems. In 2020 XXIII International Conference on Soft Computing and Measurements (SCM) (pp. 238–241). IEEE.

[25] Özdemir, V. (2019). The big picture on the "AI turn" for Ital health: The internet of things and cyber-physical systems. OMICS: A Journal of Integrative Biology, 23(6), 308–311.

[26] Zhou, J., Zhou, Y., Wang, B., & Zang, J. (2019). Human—cyber—physical systems (HCPSs) in the context of new-generation intelligent manufacturing. Engineering, 5(4), 624–636.

[27] Törngren, M., & Grogan, P. T. (2018). How to deal with the complexity of future cyber-physical systems? Designs, 2(4), 40.

[28] Liu, X., Xu, H., Liao, W., & Yu, W. (2019, November). Reinforcement learning for cyber-physical systems. In 2019 IEEE International Conference on Industrial Internet (ICII) (pp. 318–327). IEEE.

[29] Latif, S. A., Wen, F. B. X., Iwendi, C., Li-li, F. W., Mohsin, S. M., Han, Z., & Band, S. S. (2022). AI-empowered, blockchain and SDN integrated security architecture for IoT network of cyber physical systems. Computer Communications, 181, 274–283.

[30] Farivar, F., Haghighi, M. S., Jolfaei, A., & Alazab, M. (2019). Artificial intelligence for detection, estimation, and compensation of malicious attacks in nonlinear cyber-physical systems and industrial IoT. IEEE Transactions on Industrial Informatics, 16(4), 2716–2725.

[31] Battina, D. S. (2016). AI-augmented automation for DevOps, a model-based framework for continuous development in cyber-physical systems. International Journal of Creative Research Thoughts (IJCRT), ISSN, 2320–2882.

[32] Malik, A., Kashyap, R., Arora, K., & Bhushan, B. (2022). NutriChain: Secure and transparent midday meals using Blockchain and IoT. In: Saini, H. S., Singh, R. K., Tariq Beg, M., Mulaveesala, R., Mahmood, M. R. (eds) Innovations in Electronics and Communication Engineering. vol 355. Springer, Singapore. https://doi.org/10.1007/978-981-16-8512-5_41

[33] Broo, D. G., Boman, U., & Törngren, M. (2021). Cyber-physical systems research and education in 2030: Scenarios and strategies. Journal of Industrial Information Integration, 21, 100192.

[34] Veith, E. M., Fischer, L., Tröschel, M., & Nieße, A. (2019, December). Analyzing cyber-physical systems from the perspective of artificial intelligence. In Proceedings of the 2019 International Conference on Artificial Intelligence, Robotics and Control (pp. 85–95).

[35] Radanliev, P., De Roure, D., Nicolescu, R., Huth, M., & Santos, O. (2022). Digital twins: Artificial intelligence and the IoT cyber-physical systems in industry 4.0. International Journal of Intelligent Robotics and Applications, 6(1), 171–185.

[36] Tao, F., Qi, Q., Wang, L., & Nee, A. Y. C. (2019). Digital twins and cyber—physical systems toward smart manufacturing and industry 4.0: Correlation and comparison. Engineering, 5(4), 653–661.

[37] Goyal, S., Sharma, N., Bhushan, B., Shankar, A., & Sagayam, M. (2020). It enabled technology in secured healthcare: Applications, challenges, and future directions. Cognitive Internet of Medical Things for Smart Healthcare, 25–48. doi: 10.1007/978-3-030-55833-8_2

[38] Wan, B., Xu, C., Mahapatra, R. P., & Selvaraj, P. (2022). Understanding the cyber-physical system in international stadiums for security in the network from cyber-attacks and adversaries using AI. Wireless Personal Communications, 127(2), 1207–1224.

[39] Agostinelli, S., Cumo, F., Guidi, G., & Tomazzoli, C. (2021). Cyber-physical systems improving building energy management: Digital twin and artificial intelligence. Energies, 14(8), 2338.

[40] Inderwildi, O., Zhang, C., Wang, X., & Kraft, M. (2020). The impact of intelligent cyber-physical systems on the decarbonization of energy. Energy & Environmental Science, 13(3), 744–771.

[41] Shaw, S., Rowland, Z., & Machova, V. (2021). Internet of Things smart devices, sustainable industrial big data, and artificial intelligence-based decision-making algorithms in cyber-physical system-based manufacturing. Economics, Management and Financial Markets, 16(2), 106–116.

[42] Chen, X., Eder, M. A., Shihavuddin, A., & Zheng, D. (2021). A human-cyber-physical system toward intelligent wind turbine operation and maintenance. Sustainability, 13(2), 561.

[43] Bhushan, B., Sahoo, C., Sinha, P., & Khamparia, A. (2020). Unification of Blockchain and Internet of Things (BIoT): Requirements, working model, challenges and future directions. Wireless Networks. doi: 10.1007/s11276-020-02445-6

[44] Daglarli, E. (2021). Explainable artificial intelligence (xai) approaches and deep meta-learning models for cyber-physical systems. In Artificial Intelligence Paradigms for Smart Cyber-Physical Systems (pp. 42–67). IGI Global.

[45] Ramasamy, L. K., Khan, F., Shah, M., Prasad, B. V. V. S., Iwendi, C., & Biamba, C. (2022). Secure smart wearable computing through artificial intelligence-enabled internet of things and cyber-physical systems for health monitoring. Sensors, 22(3), 1076.

[46] Li, B., Wu, Y., Song, J., Lu, R., Li, T., & Zhao, L. (2020). DeepFed: Federated deep learning for intrusion detection in industrial cyber—physical systems. IEEE Transactions on Industrial Informatics, 17(8), 5615–5624.

[47] Zhong, B., Lavaei, A., Cao, H., Zamani, M., & Caccamo, M. (2021). Safe-visor architecture for sandboxing (AI-based) unverified controllers in stochastic cyber—physical systems. Nonlinear Analysis: Hybrid Systems, 43, 101110.

[48] Clark, A., Zhuravleva, N. A., Siekelova, A., & Michalikova, K. F. (2020). Industrial artificial intelligence, business process optimization, and big data-driven decision-making processes in cyber-physical system-based smart factories. Journal of Self-Governance and Management Economics, 8(2), 28–34.

[49] Adil, M., Khan, M. K., Jadoon, M. M., Attique, M., Song, H., & Farouk, A. (2022). An AI-enabled hybrid lightweight authentication scheme for intelligent IoMT based cyber-physical systems. IEEE Transactions on Network Science and Engineering.

[50] Malik, A., Gautam, S., Abidin, S., & Bhushan, B. (2019). Blockchain technology-future of IoT: Including structure, limitations and various possible attacks. In 2nd International Conference on Intelligent Computing, Instrumentation and Control Technologies (ICICICT) (pp. 1100–1104). Kannur, India. doi: 10.1109/ICICICT46008.2019.8993144

[51] Alohali, M. A., Al-Wesabi, F. N., Hilal, A. M., Goel, S., Gupta, D., & Khanna, A. (2022). Artificial intelligence enabled intrusion detection systems for cognitive cyber-physical systems in industry 4.0 environment. Cognitive Neurodynamics, 1–13.

[52] Zhou, X., Liang, W., Shimizu, S., Ma, J., & Jin, Q. (2020). Siamese neural network based few-shot learning for anomaly detection in industrial cyber-physical systems. IEEE Transactions on Industrial Informatics, 17(8), 5790–5798.

[53] Platzer, A. (2019, September). The logical path to autonomous cyber-physical systems. In International Conference on Quantitative Evaluation of Systems (pp. 25–33). Springer, Cham.

[54] Song, F., Ai, Z., Zhang, H., You, I., & Li, S. (2020). Smart collaborative balancing for dependable network components in cyber-physical systems. IEEE Transactions on Industrial Informatics, 17(10), 6916–6924.

[55] Doghri, W., Saddoud, A., & Chaari Fourati, L. (2022). Cyber-physical systems for structural health monitoring: Sensing technologies and intelligent computing. The Journal of Supercomputing, 78(1), 766–809.

Chapter 11

Blockchain Technology and Artificial Intelligence

Overview, Transformation, and Application

Nandini and Bharat Bhushan

11.1 INTRODUCTION

Artificial intelligence (AI) in the form of decision support system and neural network is used practically in every aspect of day-to-day life. AI is a dominating technology due to its high-level accuracy as well as requires less computational power [1]. In large firms, robots are replacing workshop employment which lead employees to management positions. Chess is one of the most popular games where AI has been applied [2]. Although less intelligent than individuals, these robots deploy using brute force techniques to quickly scan hundreds of locations. Nowadays, neural networks are used to predict atmospheric (weather) conditions. The past records are known as data set used by the neural network to examine the further records for trends, and forecast future weather conditions [3]. AI systems can be used in smart healthcare, but first they must be "trained" using the data set produced by clinical procedures like screening, therapy assignment, and so on. It analyzes data from electrodiagnosis, genetic testing, and diagnostic imaging at the diagnosis stage [4].

Although the benefits of AI technology will largely outweigh the hazards, it is important to consider the obstacles and risks that may arise [5]. Finding every bug in a piece of computer code is impossible, whether using human assistance or only technological techniques. This implies that some types of computer assaults will be capable of exploiting technologies that, in some way or another, fall under the umbrella of AI [6]. It is disconcerting that AI technologies are so frequently used and that the majority of them are sensitive to hostile attacks. Adversarial attacks frequently take the form of input modifications for ML or DL models with the goal of misclassifying the input data. The task category to which the algorithm belongs greatly influences adversarial attacks on AI models [7]. Evasion attacks use adversarial instances to exploit system flaws and cause the intended mistakes without changing a system's behavior. The idea behind evasion attacks is that an adversary may learn a substitute classifier using fake data to successfully avoid the targeted classifier without having previous knowledge of the decision function of a classifier. Although adversarial samples are frequently perceptually identical to "clean" samples, they nonetheless offer a severe security risk to machine learning (ML) applications [8].

DOI: 10.1201/9781003474111-11

Decentralized AI refers to artificial intelligence integrated with blockchain technology [9]. Since storing and managing data is the primary function of blockchain, when it is integrated with AI, the data that are maintained can make decisions on their own and might own their own intelligence. The AI's working data may also be shared to different other networks via a trustworthy and secure blockchain method [10]. Given that the blockchain is a very secure and reliable platform and that AI can process enormous amounts of data, the two technologies can operate better together [11]. Without the need of middlemen, decentralized AI can process data and run analysis on digitally signed and protected data that is kept on the blockchain [12,13].

Despite the fact that blockchain has been popular several times, there aren't many thorough studies that discuss the development and use of blockchain for AI [14,15]. This chapter compares the suggestions in the extant literature that have focused on merging blockchain and AI, and it presents a comprehensive framework for applying blockchain to AI situations. A detailed investigation of blockchain-based AI applications has described the new blockchain platforms, apps, and protocols that are oriented particularly toward the AI sector. This chapter evaluates the available research and also identifies and investigates some of the open research questions that are related to using blockchain technology for AI.

This chapter is divided into different sections as follows: Section 11.2 presents the overview of blockchain, uses of blockchain, types of blockchain, and some consensus protocols for blockchain. Section 11.3 describes prevalent issues in blockchain, operational maintenance, quality assurance, malicious behavior detection, blockchain interoperability, and lack of adoption and trust among users. Section 11.4 elaborates on AI-based secure computing, blockchain that can transform AI, decentralized AI applications, blockchain-based AI applications.

11.2 OVERVIEW OF BLOCKCHAIN

Blockchains are recognized as technical advancements that have the potential to fundamentally transform the way society trades and contracts [16]. Every zone of blockchain has been covered in the following sections.

11.2.1 Blockchain

Blockchain is a chain data structure. Each piece of data is treated as a block, and that block is sequentially connected to every other block in chronological order [17]. Blockchain is a decentralized technology which is cryptographically guaranteed to neither be manipulated nor falsified. The small-world prototype used by blockchain networks can preserve data integrity and consistency as well as network stability in the event of node changes [18]. Despite having a brief history, blockchain has quickly advanced and won the trust of numerous applications. Blockchain has established its functions as a secure and decentralized database independent of financial applications like Bitcoin and comparable apps. Block-chain technology can be integrated with numerous non-financial applications, including networking [19]. Blockchain decentralized storage is used to store large amounts of data that links current blocks to previous blocks via smart contract code. A smart contract is a contract that automatically executes a contained action when conditions are met, without third-party intervention.

11.2.2 Understanding Blockchain

Blockchain is among the most significant advancement in technology in recent days. It has gained popularity mainly for its absolute security and capability of managing the numerous aspects of online authentication challenges.

11.2.2.1   Blockchain as a Platform for Transaction

Blockchain was originally introduced in Bitcoin as a completely public block-chain that, in the absence of reliable central authority, would be accessible to all participants worldwide anytime a transaction was recorded on it [20]. In order to complete a transaction, the prior owner has to sign a hash of the payment wherein they acquired the Bitcoin and the current owner's public key using the ciphertext that confirms the public key. The blockchain is made up of a series of blocks that are placed in order, and each block contains transaction verifications. In order to be included in the next block, transactions are required to be processed and validated by miners. Each block's transactions are hashed to form a Merkle tree, grouped, and hashed once more till either one hash is left, identified as the Merkle root. Merkle roots are appended into the block's header. Every block header contains previously used block header's hash, thus producing a block after block [21]. Figure 11.1 shows the process of transaction when one individual transfers a certain amount of Bitcoin they hold to another.

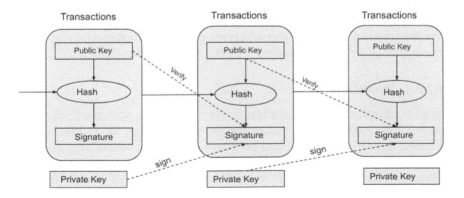

Figure 11.1 Transaction process life cycle.

11.2.2.2 Blockchain as a Platform for Computing

Consider a blockchain serves as a fundamental computing platform at two layers: transactional and systemic [22]. Unlike previous financial cryptosystems that precisely specified transaction semantics, Bitcoin introduced transactions as small programs of scripted computer code that is a variant of the FORTH language. The possibilities for advanced programs like "smart contracts" also seem to be open, but there are limitations. Storage space is very expensive as transactions in blocks are byte by byte. Every transaction must be validated by each node if confronted with the issue of stalling and the inability to know when the arbitrary program is terminated [23]. These constraints propose a minimally efficient language without loops, giving the idea of ubiquitous computing to the test and penalizing users for inefficient computations. The script can be considered Turing complete by using two stacks that form a two-pushdown automaton. With this arrangement, loops in the script are unrolled using extra stacks [24].

11.2.3   Classification of Blockchain Technology

Blockchain is mainly of two types: private and public blockchains. However, there are also some variations like consortiums and hybrid blockchain. Each blockchain consists of clusters of nodes working together in a P2P (peer-to-peer) network system [25]. Every node in the network has an enhanced version of the shared ledger. Each node can validate transactions, initiate or receive transactions, and create blocks.

11.2.3.1   Private Blockchain

Private blockchain is either a restricted or permissioned blockchain whether it works merely in a protected or closed network. These blockchains are mostly used inside an organization or by companies where the only participants in the blockchain network are selected members. Permission, security, authorization, and accessibility levels are in the hands of the governing organization. Therefore, private blockchains are used in a similar way to public blockchains, but with smaller and more limited networks [26]. Private blockchain networks are used for supply chain management, voting, ownership of assets, digit identity, and more. There are some private blockchain examples which are practically implemented—projects using HyperLedger (Fabric, Sawtooth), Corda, and multichain [27].

11.2.3.2   Public Blockchain

Public blockchains are permissionless and non-interfering scattered blockchain systems. Any individual having Internet access may sign up to blockchain, become a node with authority, and become a part of blockchain network. The users of public blockchain have access to both recent and old information, may ensure transactions, can engage in mining, and can give proof of work on incoming blocks. The most significant uses of public blockchain are mining and trading of cryptocurrencies. Therefore, the blockchain like Bitcoin and Litecoin are the most famous and universal blockchains. If security standards and procedures are strictly followed by the user, then blockchains are mostly secure [28]. However, there is only one problematic issue that occurs when users do not follow safety procedures carefully, for example, Bitcoin and Ethereum.

11.2.3.3   Consortium Blockchain

A consortium blockchain is a form of semi-decentralized blockchain that uses a number of different networks handled by many different organizations, as compared to private blockchains controlled by one entity. This particular blockchain enables several businesses to function as a block, communicating information and cooperating in mining. Most banks, governments, and other authorized organizations use consortium blockchains frequently. Energy Web Foundation are examples of consortium blockchain [29].

11.2.3.4   Hybrid Blockchain

A private and a public blockchain are combined to form a hybrid blockchain. It makes use of both types of blockchains' features. In other words, anyone may have both a private and public authorization system. Users of such a hybrid network may manage who has the information accessing rights stored in the blockchain. Users may easily connect private blockchains with several public blockchains using flexible hybrid blockchain technology. The private network of hybrid blockchain is often where transactions are confirmed. On public blockchain, people may share and verify it as well. Public blockchain require additional nodes for verification and higher hashing. As a result, blockchain networks will have more security and transparency. Example of hybrid blockchain is Dragonchain [30].

11.2.4   Consensus Protocol for Blockchain

Due to the autonomy and decentralization of the blockchain network, automated methods are necessary to make sure that all the participating nodes coincide on only authorized transactions. In order to offer a useful service on the blockchain network, these protocols are set up to prevent malicious actions like "double spending" attacks. Simply said, these protocols are algorithms that regulate all activity on a blockchain network. This section explains the various consensus protocols used by the blockchain network, their benefits and drawbacks, and the circumstances in which they are most beneficial [31].

11.2.4.1   Proof of Work

Proof of Work (PoW) was the initial consensus technique implemented on the blockchain network. It is the oldest and most widely used protocol in the modern blockchain system. PoW is the only proof that someone had expended a certain amount of effort. The primary rule is that before that the user should verify their authenticity before sending a mail message. The objective of this proof of work is that arithmetic problems are regularly solved, and the difficulty should also meet the critical listed method [32]. Maintain connections to protect yourself from PoW repeat attacks. It should be simple when checking the recipient to prevent unnecessary processing cost. It should be difficult enough to prevent third parties from cracking it [31].

11.2.4.2   Proof of Stake

To address issues with the PoW approach, such as the unnecessary expense of computer resources and the 51% attack, researchers have suggested a new sort of consensus mechanism called proof of stake (PoS). This protocol confirms blocks based on the stake of the validators (miners) when they stake a portion of their Bitcoin. The PoS protocol was adopted by Ethereum, one of the largest blockchain networks, to improve network scalability and reduce power consumption. It may be used to improve security, validate transactions, and increase productivity. Several cryptocurrencies employ the PoS method, including Gridcoin, Tezos, and Steem [32].

11.2.4.3   Delegated Proof of Stake

Delegated proof of stake (DPoS) was intended by Daniel Larimer on April 2014 to speed up transactions and overcome the confidentiality concerns which in PoS an offline block can also gain cash. Two new functions—identities and delegates—are added to the DPoS system, and each has the deposits that will be taken. The block transaction cost, on the other hand, will be shared by all members if any member takes excellent care of the system. As a result, the payment will motivate the delegate to put more effort into keeping the system secure [31]. Since each user signs the block in turn, if due to any situation any user is unavailable or fails to sign the block, then he faces the risk of having someone else sign the block in his place. The delegate must thus ensure that there will be enough Internet time for the profit. Another name for this particular DPoS protocol is a deposit-based proof of stake [32].

11.2.4.4   PoA

Proof of Authority (PoA) is a type of consensus protocol for permissioned blockchains that have grown in popularity because, relative to fewer message exchanges, they outperform traditional BFT algorithms. The PoA protocol, which was first proposed as a part of the Ethereum ecosystem for private networks, was used to create the client Aura and Clique. The PoA protocol is implemented as follows: the miner able to solve the computational problem is granted the right to develop a new block header; this header includes the hash value of the preceding block as well as the name of N trader who would have taken part in a potential new block. Miner transmits the (possible) new block header after mining the previous block header [32]. Similar to Bitcoin, relevant parties and participants in

N transactions sign the transactions using their private keys, and the final trader prepares the block, broadcasts it, and takes part in the handling competition. The ledger's proceeds are divided among miners and merchants through this process. The signature of each of these N individuals serves as the Proof of Authority. The advantage is that without the guidance and advice of merchants, miners who control the computing power cannot dominate auditing or handling capabilities (as it can't be signed by their private keys) [33].

11.2.4.5 Ripple

The open-source, Internet-based Ripple protocol enables the decentralized currency exchange, payment, and settlement services. The client (application) initiates transactions in the Ripple network, which are subsequently sent through tracking and validating the blocks to the whole network. The tracking node's primary responsibilities are the propagation of transaction records and the handling of client blockchain requests. The validating node can update the blockchain with new information by using the consensus protocols. Between the authenticating nodes in Ripple, consensus is obtained. A predefined UNL (Unique Node List) of reliable nodes is available for each validating node [31]. On the transactions, the list's nodes have a vote. The identities of the nodes taking part in the choice were previously known nodes. Therefore, as it only requires a less period of time to confirm the transaction, it is more efficient than alternative consensus protocols like PoW. Apparently, Ripple is the best option for the private blockchain. It can accept 20% of the network's nodes having complex problems without affecting the correct consensus since it has a BFT capacity of $n = 1$ [32].

Various types of consensus algorithms are compared in Table 11.1.

Table 11.1 Comparison of Consensus Protocols

Properties	PoW [31,32]	PoS [32]	DPoS [31,32]	PoA [32,33]	Ripple [31,32]
Blockchain type	Permission-less	Open	Open	Permissioned	Open
Transaction finality	Probabilistic	Probabilistic	Probabilistic	Immediate	Probabilistic
Transaction rates	Low	Low	High	High	High
Token needed	Yes	Yes	Yes	–	Yes
Cost of participation	Yes	Yes	Yes	–	Yes
Trust model	Untrusted	Untrusted	Untrusted	–	Untrusted
Adversary	≤25%	<51%	<51%	–	<20%
Example	Bitcoin	Peercoin	Bitshares	Rublix	Ripple

11.3   PREVALENT ISSUES IN BLOCKCHAIN

In general terms, the blockchain network is reliable and scalable but the data security is highly linked with the level of hash computing power that supports the blockchain. The next generation is growing ever more fascinated in blockchain technology and the development of its special suitability for the technological environment. The following are some of the common attacks of blockchain technology:

- *51% Attacks:* There are instances where two blocks having conflicting transactions are mined simultaneously. In such a situation, only the block that gets a priority of network authorization is maintained in the chain, likewise the one rots away. The outcomes might be severe if a group of hostile hackers were able to seize 51% or more of the mining power [34]. The hackers can then exploit their dominant position to commit fraud and transaction cancelation. Although theoretically feasible, it would be virtually hard to rewrite the entire blockchain. They might even be able to change part of the blocks. Blockchain security problems, such as 51% or more of the mining power, might be conceivable at a time when there aren't enough miners on the communication network [35].
- *Sybil attacks:* The attacker creates multiple bogus nodes on the network in this attack. This attack was named after the well-known fictional personality. Using the very same nodes, the hacker can obtain majority agreement and impede transactions in chains. Therefore, a massive Sybil attack is nothing more than the 51% attack [34].
- *Double spending attacks:* The term "double spending" refers to using the same funds twice. Everyone is aware that there are only two ways to complete every given transaction. One is not online, while the other is. In order to prevent duplicate spending, Bitcoin uses a confirmation mechanism and a global ledger known as the blockchain [36]. Two new roles known as witness and delegate are introduced by DPoS, each of which has a number of members.
- *Private key security attacks:* Public-key cryptography is the essential building block of blockchain technology. As a result, using public-key cryptography incorrectly might cause security issues for blockchains. An attacker can be able to discover separating the public key's private key if key signing is performed improperly in blockchain (for instance, by utilizing the same key for multiple signatures instead of Merkle tree). Owning the private key is equivalent to controlling all the personal data that is kept on a blockchain [37].
- *Selfish mining attacks:* Selfish mining is the practice of one miner or a group solving a hash, producing a new block, and then removing it from the public blockchain. This causes a split, which is then mined in order to surpass the open blockchain. The group's blockchain may introduce its most recent block to the network if it surpasses the honest blockchain in time.

The group's fork would replace the original blockchain since the network is designed to only acknowledge the most recent block. By changing the blockchain, the miners essentially stole Bitcoin from other users [38].

11.3.1   Operational Maintenance

It is challenging to pinpoint the possible elements influencing the performance of blockchain due to the decentralization and variety of blockchain systems. Since various consensus techniques are used, for instance, Hyperledger Fabric's transaction throughput bottleneck differs from that of Bitcoin and Ethereum. Additionally, smart contracts, like other software systems, are made up of several computer applications that might include errors, malicious code, or run incompatible settings. As a result, it is essential to accomplish the intelligent and reliable operational maintenance of complex blockchain systems [39]. Blockchain maintenance will help in finding errors that slow down the network and highlight structural problems that might leave the entire blockchain vulnerable to attack. These are just a handful of the numerous reasons why a business should carefully consider blockchain upkeep. However, adhering to routine DLT (Distributed Ledger Technology) maintenance procedures may also assist businesses in identifying profitable innovation opportunities. To assume responsibility for the system and prevent leaving it to chance, routine blockchain maintenance is carried out [40]. By doing regular blockchain maintenance someone will be proactive in preserving the security and innovation of nodes and systems. Some basic steps for maintaining a blockchain are discussed in the following sections.

11.3.1.1   System Monitoring

To find any abnormalities, it is crucial to do routine system or code monitoring. The methods for finding vulnerabilities are often different for blockchain companies with massive dispersed servers and a diverse ecosystem. In order to uncover flaws, hacker engagements are sometimes accompanied with a bug bounty.

11.3.1.2   Analyzing for Potential Threats

Analyzing the possible threat is crucial when the abnormality in your blockchain code has been found. The difficulty of fixing the error or issue and, more importantly, the potential financial impact it might have on the organization are also crucial considerations.

11.3.1.3   System Improvement

The business may quickly go on to rectify the faults after successfully identifying bugs and doing proper analyses in order to ensure system improvement. The main takeaway is that the connected computer network will function at its best.

11.3.1.4 Safety Guarantee

Trusted safety may be ensured with an optimized system or blockchain network and closed flaws that could be a source of an attack.

11.3.2 Quality Assurance

Software flaws in smart contracts include reentrancy, overcharging, randomness control, and Decentralized Autonomous Organization (DAO) attack, among others. Blockchain makes certain levels of product quality achievable and maintainable. When customers put their faith in brands, they buy goods and services they know will be of a high caliber. Additionally, before a product may be sold on the market, it may need to comply with certain regulatory requirements. The terms used here are more Ethereum-centric, however the fundamental concept is applicable to any blockchain platform [41]. Ethical responsibilities are important because they are testing a system that fosters trust; where data is unchangeable and millions of dollars are on the line, testers must make a solemn commitment. Shifting to the left development environment is an essential member of the team creating the user stories and requirements should be a QA engineer. P2P Network Testing is necessary to create a framework or test strategy that takes into account the functionality, scalability, and volatility of P2P systems. Knowledge of blockchain means QA (testers) should be familiar with a wide range of blockchain frameworks and technologies. They must comprehend the fundamental distinctions between various consensus protocols (effect on performance and latency) and cryptographic methods (data encryption and decryption).

11.3.3 Malicious Behavior Detection

In addition to legitimate enterprises, blockchain may be used for nefarious actions that are difficult to identify because of its pseudonymity (i.e., anonymous blockchain addresses). However, due to the encryption of the blockchain data, it is more difficult to recognize and classify criminal behavior using simple data analytics. Additionally, the challenge is made worse by the enormous volume and heterogeneity of blockchain data as well as the variety of user behaviors [42]. Therefore, direct use of traditional classification-based approaches (such as ML methods) is not possible.

11.3.4 Blockchain Interoperability

As many companies utilize blockchain technology, a preference exists for many of them to create personalized systems using distinctive features (governance norms, blockchain technology upgrades, consensus mechanisms, etc.). These numerous blockchain are unable to operate together since at present there is no worldwide standard that would let various networks interact with one another. The skills to communicate, see, and access data between blockchain networks without the use of a mediator or centralized governance or authority is described as interoperability [43]. Interoperability issues may make broad adoption nearly difficult.

11.3.5 Lack of Adoption

Organizations are cooperating more often now to form cooperative blockchain working groups to discuss common issues and get a solution that might help everyone without revealing the personal information. For instance, in preparation for the COVID-19 pandemic, a number of significant pharmaceutical firms worked with Deloitte to develop a blockchain for the Clinical Supply Chain Industry Working Group. The team created KitChain, an application using blockchain, in collaboration with LedgerDomain. The application's capability is to track packaged medicine shipment; other benefits include supply chain security, a decrease in the need for paper records, and protection of patients' trial data confidentially.

11.3.6 Trust among Users

The sixth important restriction to broad acquisition of blockchain technology is the absence of trust between the consumers. Organizations may have trust issues regarding the security of the technology itself, and, perhaps, they will not rely on other contributors in a blockchain network, thus resulting in a dual difficulty. The blockchain looks to offer a safe, private, and verifiable way for all transactions. This is true even in the case where the network gets decentralized and there is no central authority to grant approval and substantiate the transactions. Consensus algorithms, which encourage general consensus in relation to the current state of the distributed ledger for the entire network, play a crucial part of every blockchain framework. It ensures that each new node participating is the sole, and only, version of the information accepted by all of the blockchain's nodes [44]. Business executives have found that private blockchains with no known users may be more reliable.

11.4 AI-BASED SECURE COMPUTING

Data is known to be essential to its respective owner and several kinds of data may get formed by modifying the unprocessed data to suit various purposes and conditions. For instance, it is feasible to extract and reorganize a user's health data from Private Data Collections (PDC) to produce organized medical data that is considered to be extremely helpful for its buyers from hospitals, research organizations, and health application developers. All of any entity's information in cyberspace is stored in PDC since it is a digital clone of the real thing, thus the owner places a high priority on the security of that information. In order to safeguard data, SecNet adds an Antenna System Controller (ASC) component to each PDC's OSS. AI is one of the main components of PDC [44]. There are multiple sorts of ML techniques that have been created for different AIs, including pattern matching, computer vision, and self-driving vehicles. Different AI techniques are now being developed to handle different data types. These data-specific AI tasks may be viewed as a substantial collection of the "solution islands" since both the academic and commercial communities have created a variety of unique software tools and systems that individually handle various faces of intelligence [45]. PDC serves as an operating system of AI, integrating many AI components into a more complete, unified intelligence system. In PDC, a number of AI capabilities combine to create an intelligent system. In order to offer a secure and intelligent OSS for PDC and create more potent and evolving security rules, ASC may include the Generative Adversarial Network (GAN) module from the very beginning of secure computing. The OSS of PDC would become significantly more intelligent and powerful after several iterations of generating and categorizing by the GAN module, and fake access requests for data would have minimal impact. To mislead and perplex the OSS of a PDC, the GAN module of PDC produces Fraudulent access requests for certain confidential data that "look like genuine" requests. Thanks to blockchain technology, several organizations may trade their computer results with one another while maintaining their security, improving performance, and using less energy [44].

11.4.1   How Blockchain Can Transform AI

The area of AI research describes itself as the survey of "intelligent agents," or any technology that takes activities to increase its probability of success in achieving goals and perceives its surroundings [46]. The majority of AI systems now being developed are typically specialized expert systems that reach conclusions by consulting a knowledge base. Many researchers are concentrating on the creation of AI systems that may employ highly smart decision-making algorithms to resolve a particular set of difficulties; some of these researchers may have a positive impact on our daily life. By combining AI with blockchain technology and options, applications and algorithms for decentralized AI may be designed with access to the same record security, reliable, shared platform of data, logs, knowledge, and other resources. On such a platform, a reliable audit trail of all the data that the AI algorithm acquired before and during the learning and decision-making process may also be maintained. AI systems rely on data or information for learning, inference, and selection. The ML algorithm works better when data is collected through a platform or data repository that is reliable, safe, trustworthy, and reputable. Because of the remarkable integrity and resilience of blockchain technology, it can't be changed [47].

11.4.1.1   Enhanced Data Security

Data storage via blockchain is extremely safe. Blockchain is renowned for securely containing confidential and delicate information into a disk array of surroundings. The only "respective private keys" that need to be kept secure are those for the data that are digitally signed and stored in blockchain databases [48].

As a result, AI models can work with protected data and make decisions that are more dependable and trustworthy.

11.4.1.2   Improved Trust on Robotic Decisions

Every decision generated by AI agents that users or consumers find challenging to comprehend and trust become dysfunctional. Blockchain technology is well-recognized for recording payments in point-by-point decentralized ledgers that make it easier to accept and recognize the decision made with assurance that there have been absolutely no modifications to the records throughout the user-involved assessing process [48]. In order to encourage transparency and increase public trust in the general public's capacity to comprehend robotic judgments, the way an AI system makes decisions may be published on blockchain [49].

11.4.1.3   High Efficiency

Multiuser business procedures, including individual users, corporate forms, and governmental organizations, are essentially inefficient since several stakeholders must authorize business transactions. Due to the incorporation of AI with blockchain technology, smart DAOs may be utilized for automatic and speedy acceptance of data, value, and transfer of assets between diverse customers [50].

11.4.1.4   Decentralized Intelligence

Multiple agents are needed to perform various subtasks that have permission to use the common data, when a decision of the highest level needs to be made. Thus, each individual cybersecurity AI agent can be combined to offer a fully coordinated security across the underlying network and to address issues related to scheduling (e.g., supervised learning) [51].

11.4.1.5   Collective Decision-Making

In a robotic group environment, each of the agents must work together in order to accomplish the swarm goal. Without the need for a centralized authority, distributed and decentralized decision-making algorithms have gotten deployed in the robotics field. Voting robots make decisions and the outcomes are chosen by the majority. As blockchain is available to all robots, it may be used to verify the results of the elections. Each robot has the authority to emit a vote, which takes the form of a transaction [52].

11.4.2   Decentralized AI Applications

11.4.2.1   Automatic Computing

AI applications have several objectives. One fundamental objective is to allow multiple intelligent agents (i.e., tiny computer programs) to perceive their separate surroundings, maintain their internal states, and conduct specific actions in line with those perceptions and states. The blockchain architecture can make it easier to create fully decentralized autonomous systems by enabling operational decentralization and tracking an enduring record of communication between users, apps, data, devices, and systems [53].

11.4.2.2 Planning

Planning approaches are used by AI applications and systems to coordinate along other applications and systems to address intricate issues in unique contexts. Well-planned strategies improve the efficiency, in terms of operation, and sturdiness of AI applications and systems by carrying out a variety of algorithms that are logical and rule based to achieve preliminary goals while taking into account the current input state. Distributed AI planning solutions focused on blockchain are necessary to deliver more effective strategies with long-term monitoring and provenance history since centralized planning is perceived as a challenging and inefficient task. The blockchain has the potential to produce an essential and unchangeable blueprint for strategic applications and operational systems [54].

11.4.2.3 Optimization

One of the key properties of AI-enabled applications and systems is the finding of a set of optimal solutions of all feasible options. The environments in which recent AI applications and systems function range from ubiquitous and pervasive (like edge computing systems), geographically bounded (like personal area networks, wireless local area network, etc.) and centralized, hugely parallel, and distributed (like cloud computing systems). The optimization methodologies are effective in constricted contexts depending on the application level and objectives at system level. These techniques make it easier to locate the finest solutions, like choosing the most pertinent sources of data in pervasive systems, the finest edge or cloud servers for data processing and applications, or allowing resource-effective data management in massive distributed computing environments. The execution of present optimization tactics under centralized management while taking system- and application-wide optimization objectives leads to the processing of unnecessary and unrelated data and lower quality systems and applications performance [55–58].

11.4.2.4 Perception

Monolithic data collection results from the ongoing collection, interpretation, selection, and organization of data from ambient surroundings by AI programs and applications using intelligent agents and bots [59]. Decentralized perception system can make it simpler to gather data from several points of view. Tracking perceptual trajectories, transferring collected data securely, and storing data in an unalterable manner all are made simpler by decentralization based on blockchain technology. Decentralized perception approaches are helpful since applications and systems don't necessarily need to acquire streams of data for efficient and high standard insight.

11.4.2.5   Search

Since AI applications must perform in extremely large search spaces, efficient search algorithms are the foundation of AI technology (large data sets or multivalued, high-dimensional data streams). Completeness, complexity (i.e., time and space), and optimally are only a few of the factors that are taken into consideration while designing the search algorithms. In non-linear data structures like tree and graphs, where the algorithms begin in one phase and eventually extend until they find the necessary variable or have fully traversed search space, these approaches frequently make use of a massive framework that is simultaneously centralized and dispersed in order to boost operational efficiency. Nevertheless, a critical analysis of their utilization of decentralized infrastructure deployment is necessary. The goal is to replace traditional search algorithms with blockchain technology and decentralized infrastructure in order to reliably and permanently record the successful search trails and traveling paths that might one day result in the most efficient search result for similar jobs.

11.4.3   Blockchain-based AI Applications

11.4.3.1   Decentralized Data Storage and Management with AI

The fusing of AI with blockchain technology has permitted the process of various resilient programs that permits the communication of numerous agents, offering a great framework for securely organizing, storing, and exchanging data. Several of important systems that employ this association are covered in this section.

Mamoshina et al. [60] present the biomedical research and healthcare sectors as advanced by blockchain and AI technology. They have provided a model, decentralized way to evaluate the values corresponding to time and the significance of distinctive data. This chapter gives an overview of AI and blockchain technologies that may be applied to increasing the analysis of biomedical, enhancing the predictive analysis report, enabling patients with new tools for managing and controlling their own data, and assisting them in monetizing the unique distinctive data with incentive benefits to engage in ongoing health monitoring. Recursive cortical networks, capsule networks, and other advancements in computer vision and natural language processing are just a few examples of prospective ML techniques that are now being used and explored. However, techniques like supervised learning, recurrent neural networks, and generative adversarial networks are becoming more and more popular for the use in decentralized, blockchain-powered personal data marketplaces.

Lofti et al. [61] presented emerging features of AI and blockchain which are having the potential to be highly beneficial to the healthcare sector. Socially intelligent machines can aid with elder care. Given the increasing need for elder care and storage of skilled nurses, robots that are socially dependable are among the most feasible and effective technologies that may serve as a gateway for communication and ascertain the requirements of critically ill patients or elderly people. Such robots focus on improvement by encouraging the patients and elders to exercise, maintain their stress level with some breathing exercises, and take care of themselves. The goal is to improve the user experience, and encourage patients and elders to improve quality of life [61].

The handling of enormous amounts of data, the exponential expansion of computer power, and the enormous rise in public acceptance of linked equipment and apps to record activities all have become major research goals in AI and ML [62]. Woods et al. [62] underline the significance of merging AI methods with blockchain framework to address the reliability and safety issues posed by web access, where interactions between humans and bots or bots-to-bots have expanded due to bots producing 52% of all online traffic. This is concluded that in the upcoming time, bot-to-bot communication will surpass bot-to-human communication due to rising bot traffic. Before engaging in conversation, bots will be capable of asking each other for identity and checking the backstory of the ratings and records. A better degree of security and transparency may be attained by storing the query data and information on a blockchain throughout an audit process [62].

Raja et al. [63] proposed a blockchain powered by AI that offers an automatic coding function for smart contracts, therefore converting it into an intelligent contract. Additionally, it expedited transactions verification and optimized energy usage. The findings demonstrate that, when a variety of different circumstances are taken into account, intelligent contracts offer superior security than smart contracts.

Cao et al. [64] discussed the conceptual framework, research challenges, and technology prospects of block intelligence and autonomous AI. Additionally, they focused on the interaction and meta-synthesis of centralized and decentralized AI. They further evaluated how autonomous AI and edge intelligence may support, empower, and advance smart blockchain, Web3, the metaverse, and overall decentralized technology.

Yin et al. [65] suggested a revolutionary distributed trustworthy computing and networking architecture referred to as HyperNet to address the problem of data loss. The platform called Unique Device Identification (UDI), which permits for an identifier-drive routing mechanism and protected digital identifier management, is part of HyperNet and consists of the high-tech PDC, which is regarded as the digital version of a human being, by using blockchain, every other entity can make a decentralized trustworthy connection between them, as well as smart contracts, and the UDI platforms. In addition to having the capacity to change the existing information that relies on the communication network into the future information society generally focused on collected data, HyperNet has the power to defend data sovereignty.

11.4.3.2 Decentralized Infrastructure for AI

Three innovative elements that blockchain technology introduced to traditional distributed systems are unchangeable literature cases, decentralized and distributed access, and instinctive asset exchange [66]. The framework of blockchain provides clients with new data models with better performance, distributed management throughout the training of data by AI models with better data reliability when utilized in combination with AI approaches. Blockchain offers the enormous data sets that AI needs to improve its data models. This section covers the framework and decentralized infrastructure presently in use for AI applications.

Yu et al. [67] created a blockchain platform with better performance for smart devices. This platform uses technologies, including decentralized network framework, intelligent device and block mapping, and some consensus algorithms like PBFT_DPOC for providing a reliable communication between devices during the block-to-block mapping process. A novel Delegated Proof of Contribution (DPOC) technique is proposed by Yu et al. [67] to enable any block to function as a blockchain producer (BP). In order for each node to participate in the voting process using this technique, each contender must provide a hardware framework of their own, together with processing power, storage, and bandwidth. A miner's weight-sum seniority rating and votes are used to establish the final ranking. Several mega blocks and substitute blocks are created throughout this voting process. By creating blocks using PBFT algorithm, the super-nodes arrive at consensus. Every block has to bear the signature that is digital of the rest of the BP nodes.

Huang et al. [68] presented a decentralized software-defined infrastructure design where data owners can deploy their own rules to the application systems where the data are created for further governance operations. This approach resembles the well-liked Software-Defined Networking, where users may set switch rules and modify use. The present data governance activities may be drastically changed into a decentralized topology due to gilding infrastructure architecture. Data owners have the entire authority to choose where their data should be stored and how the data may be shared, and on the one hand, data can be isolated from the program that creates it. As a result, infrastructure can set up a new generation of decentralized responsive data governance that can encourage data connecting innovation to better suit the needs of many users and the open environment.

Soker et al. [69] discussed Chain Intel to encourage people toward the development of distributed and decentralized AI agents that operate on open-source platforms, responsible for working of distributed AI and decentralized blockchain together. The purpose of Chain Intel is to implement and models of AI in decentralized applications (DApps) can be used. This platform seeks to support and distribute the AI model implementation throughout the network, allowing scalable, reliable, and intelligent applications. Currently, Chain Intel is trying to enable decentralized AI model performance, whereby a remote device can operate some components of a deep neural network while others do so on a collection of nodes that are active in Chain Intel P2P network.

These existing works are summarized in Table 11.2.

Table 11.2 Summary of Contributions

References	Year	Major Contribution
Mamoshina et al. [60]	2018	Presented the biomedical research and healthcare sectors as advanced by blockchain and AI technology
Lofti et al. [61]	2018	Presented the emerging features of AI and blockchain which have the potential to be highly beneficial to the healthcare sector
Woods et al. [62]	2018	Underline the significance of merging AI methods with the framework of blockchain to address the reliability issues posed by web access
Raja et al. [63]	2020	Proposed a blockchain powered by AI that offers an automatic coding function for smart contracts, thereby converting it into an intelligent contract
Cao et al. [64]	2022	Discussed the conceptual framework, research challenges, and technology prospects of decentralized AI and edge intelligence
Yin et al. [65]	2018	Suggested a revolutionary distributed trustworthy computing and networking architecture referred as HyperNet to address the problem of data loss
Yu et al. [67]	2018	Created a blockchain platform with better performance for smart devices. This platform uses technologies, including decentralized network framework, intelligent device, and block mapping, and some consensus algorithms like PBFT_DPOC
Huang et al. [68]	2019	Proposed a decentralized software-defined framework design where the owners of data can deploy their preferred rules to the application software where the data are created for further governance operations
Soker et al. [69]	2017	Discussed Chain Intel to encourage people toward the development of distributed and decentralized AI agents that operate on open-source platforms, responsible for working of distributed AI and decentralized blockchain together

11.5 CONCLUSION AND FUTURE SCOPE

This chapter examined and evaluated the state of the art with regard to suitability and application based on blockchain properties considering AI. The study illustrates the summary of blockchain applications for AI. Decentralized storage depicts how it might improve and address important AI-related problems. In addition, this chapter provides a comprehensive taxonomic analysis and comparisons of traditional blockchain in relation to decentralized AI operations and their implementation, different kinds of blockchain, its architecture, and consensus protocols, in order to empower AI with the support of blockchain for secure data management in a trust-less environment as well as to use AI and blockchain together to address the problem of missing data. Regarding the framework for AI and decentralized data handling, a thorough investigation for blockchain applications in intelligent multi-agent systems are examined. Moreover, several AI and blockchain characteristics are reviewed in the literature and summarized.

REFERENCES

[1] Haleem, A., Javaid, M., & Khan, I. H. (2019). Current status and applications of Artificial Intelligence (AI) in the medical field: An overview. *Current Medicine Research and Practice*, vol. 9, no. 6, pp. 231–237.

[2] Borana, J. (March 2016). Applications of artificial intelligence & associated technologies. *Proceeding of International Conference on Emerging Technologies in Engineering, Biomedical, Management and Science [ETEBMS-2016]*.

[3] Jiang, F., Jiang, Y., Zhi, H., et al. (2017). Artificial intelligence in healthcare: Past, present and future. *Stroke and Vascular Neurology*, vol. 2. doi: 10.1136/svn-2017-000101.

[4] Rezazade Mehrizi, M. H., van Ooijen, P., & Homan, M. (2021). Applications of artificial intelligence (AI) in diagnostic radiology: A technography study. *European Radiology*, vol. 31, pp. 1805–1811.

[5] Amodei, D., Olah, C., Steinhardt, J., Christiano, P., Schulman, J., & Mané, D. (2016). Concrete problems in AI safety.

[6] Hagendorff, T., & Wezel, K. (2020). 15 challenges for AI: Or what AI (currently) can't do. *AI and Society*, vol. 35, pp. 355–365.

[7] Oseni, A., Moustafa, N., Janicke, H., Liu, P., Tari, Z., & Vasilakos, A. (2021). Security and privacy for artificial intelligence: Opportunities and challenges.

[8] Soni, S., & Bhushan, B. (2019). Use of machine learning algorithms for designing efficient cyber security solutions. *2019 2nd International Conference on Intelligent Computing, Instrumentation and Control Technologies (ICICICT)*. doi: 10.1109/icicict46008.2019.8993253.

[9] Petrovic, V. (2018). Artificial intelligence and virtual worlds—toward human-level AI agents. *IEEE Access*, vol. 6, pp. 39976–39988.

[10] Jadon, S., Choudhary, A., Saini, H., Dua, U., Sharma, N., & Kaushik, I. (2020). Comfy smart home using IoT. *SSRN Electronic Journal*. doi: 10.2139/ssrn.3565908.

[11] Gulati, P., Sharma, A., Bhasin, K., and Azad, C. (May 14, 2020). Approaches of Blockchain with AI: Challenges & future direction. *Proceedings of the International Conference on Innovative Computing & Communications (ICICC)*.

[12] Mehta, S., Bhushan, B., & Kumar, R. (2022). Machine learning approaches for smart city applications: Emergence, challenges and opportunities. In: Balas, V. E., Solanki, V. K., Kumar, R. (eds) Recent Advances in Internet of Things and Machine Learning. Intelligent Systems Reference Library, vol. 215. Springer, Cham. https://doi.org/10.1007/978-3-030-90119-6_12

[13] Garcia, A. R. (2020). AI, IoT, Big Data, and technologies in digital economy with Blockchain at sustainable work satisfaction to smart mankind: Access to 6th dimension of human rights. In: Lopes, N. (eds) Smart Governance for Cities: Perspectives and Experiences. EAI/Springer Innovations in Communication and Computing. Springer, Cham.

[14] Bhowmik, T., Bhadwaj, A., Kumar, A., & Bhushan, B. (2022). Machine learning and deep learning models for privacy management and data analysis in smart cites. In: Balas, V. E., Solanki, V. K., Kumar, R. (eds) Recent Advances in Internet of Things and Machine Learning. Intelligent Systems Reference Library, vol. 215. Springer, Cham. https://doi.org/10.1007/978-3-030-90119-6_13

[15] Dharmaraj, V., & Vijayanand, C. (2018). Artificial Intelligence (AI) in agriculture. *International Journal of Current Microbiology and Applied Sciences*, vol. 7, no. 12, pp. 2122–2128.

[16] Arai, Y., Sato, T., & Himura, Y. Electronic transaction device, electronic transaction verification device, electronic transaction method, and data carrier.

[17] Bhushan, B., Sahoo, C., Sinha, P., & Khamparia, A. (2020). Unification of Blockchain and Internet of Things (BIoT): Requirements, working model, challenges and future directions. *Wireless Networks*. doi: 10.1007/s11276-020-02445-6

[18] Kashyap, S., Bhushan, B., Kumar, A., & Nand, P. (2022). Quantum Blockchain approach for security enhancement in Cyberworld. In: Kumar, R., Sharma, R., Pattnaik, P. K. (eds) Multimedia Technologies in the Internet of Things Environment, Volume 3. Studies in Big Data, vol. 108. Springer, Singapore. https://doi.org/10.1007/978-981-19-0924-5_1

[19] Treleaven, P., Gendal Brown, R., & Yang, D. (2017). Blockchain technology in finance. *Computer*, vol. 50, no. 9, pp. 14–17. doi: 10.1109/MC.2017.3571047

[20] Mannaro, K., Pinna, A., & Marchesi, M. (2017). Crypto-trading: Blockchain-oriented energy market. *2017 AEIT International Annual Conference*, pp. 1–5.

[21] Bhushan, B., Kadam, K., Parashar, R., Kumar, S., & Thakur A. K. (2022). Leveraging Blockchain technology in sustainable supply chain management and logistics. In: Muthu, S. S. (eds) Blockchain Technologies for Sustainability. Environmental Footprints and Eco-Design of Products and Processes. Springer, Singapore. https://doi.org/10.1007/978-981-16-6301-7_9

[22] Xu, J., Wang, S., Zhou, A., & Yang, F. (April 2020). Edgence: A blockchain-enabled edge-computing platform for intelligent IoT-based dApps. *China Communications*, vol. 17, no. 4, pp. 78–87, doi: 10.23919/JCC.2020.04.008

[23] Gorkhali, A., Li, L., & Shrestha, A. (2020). Blockchain: A literature review. *Journal of Management Analytics*, vol. 7, no. 3, pp. 321–343.

[24] Savi, M. et al. (2020). A Blockchain-based brokerage platform for fog computing resource federation. *2020 23rd Conference on Innovation in Clouds, Internet and Networks and Workshops (ICIN)*, pp. 147–149. doi: 10.1109/ICIN48450.2020.9059337

[25] Farah, N. A. A. (2018). Blockchain technology: Classification, opportunities, and challenges. *International Research Journal of Engineering and Technology*, vol. 5, no. 5, pp. 3423–3426.

[26] Yang, R., Wakefield, R., Lyu, S., Jayasuriya, S., Han, F., Yi, X., . . . & Chen, S. (2020). Public and private blockchain in construction business process and information integration. *Automation in Construction*, vol. 118, p. 103276.

[27] Hao, Y., Li, Y., Dong, X., Fang, L., & Chen, P. (2018). Performance analysis of consensus algorithm in private Blockchain. *2018 IEEE Intelligent Vehicles Symposium (IV)*, pp. 280–285.

[28] Ferdous, M. S., Chowdhury, M. J. M., & Hoque, M. A. (2021). A survey of consensus algorithms in public blockchain systems for crypto-currencies. *Journal of Network and Computer Applications*, vol. 182, p. 103035.

[29] Li, Z., Kang, J., Yu, R., Ye, D., Deng, Q., & Zhang, Y. (August 2018). Consortium Blockchain for secure energy trading in industrial Internet of Things. *IEEE Transactions on Industrial Informatics*, vol. 14, no. 8, pp. 3690–3700.

[30] Desai, H., Kantarcioglu, M., & Kagal, L. (2019). A hybrid Blockchain architecture for privacy-enabled and accountable auctions. *2019 IEEE International Conference on Blockchain (Blockchain)*, pp. 34–43. doi: 10.1109/Blockchain.2019.00014.

[31] Bodkhe, U., Mehta, D., Tanwar, S., Bhattacharya, P., Singh, P. K., & Hong, W. C. (2020). A survey on decentralized consensus mechanisms for cyber physical systems. *IEEE Access*, vol. 8, pp. 54371–54401.

[32] Wan, S., Li, M., Liu, G., & Wang, C. (2020). Recent advances in consensus protocols for blockchain: A survey. *Wireless Networks*, vol. 26, no. 8, pp. 5579–5593.

[33] De Angelis, S., Aniello, L., Baldoni, R., Lombardi, F., Margheri, A., & Sassone, V. (2018). PBFT vs proof-of-authority: Applying the CAP theorem to permissioned blockchain.

[34] Niranjani, V., Sanjaay Kamachi, P. S., Siddhaarth, S., Venkatachalam, B., & Vishal, N. (2022). Hybrid approach to minimize 51% attack in Cryptocurrencies. *2022 8th International Conference on Advanced Computing and Communication Systems (ICACCS)*, Coimbatore, India, pp. 2100–2103. doi: 10.1109/ICACCS54159.2022. 9785161

[35] Moubarak, E. F., & Chamoun, M. (2018). On blockchain security and relevant attacks. *2018 IEEE Middle East and North Africa Communications Conference (MENA-COMM)*, pp. 1–6. doi: 10.1109/MENACOMM.2018.8371010

[36] Bahalul Haque, A. K. M., Bhushan, B., Nawar, A., Talha, K. R., & Ayesha, S. J. (2022). Attacks and countermeasures in IoT based smart healthcare applications. In: Balas, V. E., Solanki, V. K., Kumar, R. (eds) Recent Advances in Internet of Things and Machine Learning. Intelligent Systems Reference Library, vol. 215. Springer, Cham. https://doi.org/10.1007/978-3-030-90119-6_6

[37] Kaushik, A., Choudhary, A., Ektare, C., Thomas, D., & Akram, S. (2017). Block-chain—literature survey. *2017 2nd IEEE International Conference on Recent Trends in Electronics, Information & Communication Technology (RTEICT)*, pp. 2145–2148. doi: 10.1109/RTEICT.2017.8256979

[38] Vokerla, R. R. et al. (2019). An overview of Blockchain applications and attacks. *2019 International Conference on Vision Towards Emerging Trends in Communication and Networking (ViTECoN)*, pp. 1–6. doi: 10.1109/ViTECoN.2019.8899450.

[39] Mohril, R. S., Solanki, B. S., Lad, B. K., & Kulkarni, M. S. (December 2022). Blockchain enabled maintenance management framework for military equipment. *IEEE Transactions on Engineering Management*, vol. 69, no. 6, pp. 3938–3951. doi: 10.1109/TEM.2021.3099437

[40] Xinyi, Y., Yi, Z., & He, Y. (2018). Technical characteristics and model of Blockchain. *2018 10th International Conference on Communication Software and Networks (ICCSN)*, pp. 562–566. doi: 10.1109/ICCSN.2018.8488289

[41] Zheng, Z., Dai, H. N., & Wu, J. (2019). Blockchain intelligence: When blockchain meets artificial intelligence. arXiv preprint arXiv:1912.06485.

[42] She, W., Liu, Q., Tian, Z., Chen, J.-S., Wang, B., & Liu, W. (2019). Blockchain trust model for malicious node detection in wireless sensor networks. *IEEE Access*, vol. 7, pp. 38947–38956. doi: 10.1109/ACCESS.2019.2902811.

[43] Hardjono, T., Lipton, A., & Pentland, A. (November 2020). Toward an interoperability architecture for Blockchain autonomous systems. *IEEE Transactions on Engineering Management*, vol. 67, no. 4, pp. 1298–1309. doi: 10.1109/TEM.2019.2920154.

[44] Gochhayat, S. P., Shetty, S., Mukkamala, R., Foytik, P., Kamhoua, G. A., & Njilla, L. (2020). Measuring decentrality in Blockchain based systems. *IEEE Access*, vol. 8, pp. 178372–178390. doi: 10.1109/ACCESS.2020.3026577

[45] Xu, S., Guo, C., Hu, R. Q., & Qian, Y. (August 15, 2022). Blockchain-inspired secure computation offloading in a vehicular cloud network. *IEEE Internet of Things Journal*, vol. 9, no. 16, pp. 14723–14740. doi: 10.1109/JIOT.2021.3054866.

[46] Haque, A. K. M. B., Bhushan, B., Hasan, M., & Zihad, M. M. (2022). Revolutionizing the industrial Internet of Things using Blockchain: An unified approach. In: Balas, V. E., Solanki, V. K., Kumar, R. (eds) Recent Advances in Internet of Things and Machine Learning. Intelligent Systems Reference Library, vol. 215. Springer, Cham. https://doi.org/10.1007/978-3-030-90119-6_5

[47] Panarello, A., Tapas, N., Merlino, G., Longo, F., & Puliafito, A. (2018). Blockchain and IoT integration: A systematic survey. *Sensors*, vol. 18, no. 8, p. E2575.

[48] Marr, B. (2018). *Artificial Intelligence and Blockchain: 3 Major Benefits of Combining These Two Mega-Trends.*

[49] Campbell, D. (2018). *Combining AI and Blockchain to Push Frontiers in Healthcare.*

[50] Magazzeni, D., McBurney, P., & Nash, W. (2017). Validation and verification of smart contracts: A research agenda. *Computer*, vol. 50, no. 9, pp. 50–57.

[51] Brambilla, M., Ferrante, E., Birattari, M., and Dorigo, M. (2013). Swarm robotics: A review from the swarm engineering perspective. *Swarm Intelligence*, vol. 7, no. 1, pp. 1–41.

[52] Strobel, V., Ferrer, E. C., & Dorigo, M. (July 2018). Managing byzantine robots via blockchain technology in a swarm robotics collective decision making scenario. *Proc. 17th Int. Conf. Auto. Agents MultiAgent System.* International Foundation for Autonomous Agents and Multiagent Systems, Stockholm, Sweden, pp. 541–549.

[53] Rizk, Y., Awad, M., & Tunstel, E. W. (September 2018). Decision making in multiagent systems: A survey. *IEEE Trans. Cogn. Develop. Syst.*, vol. 10, no. 3, pp. 514–529.

[54] Contreras-Cruz, M. A., Lopez-Perez, J. J., & Ayala-Ramirez, V. (June 2017). Distributed path planning for multi-robot teams based on artificial bee colony. *Proc. IEEE Congr. Evol. Comput. (CEC)*, pp. 541–548.

[55] Fioretto, F., Pontelli, E., & Yeoh, W. (March 2018). Distributed constraint optimization problems and applications: A survey. *Journal of Artificial Intelligence Research*, vol. 61, pp. 623–698.

[56] Rehman, M. H. U., Liew, C. S., Wah, T. Y., & Khan, M. K. (February 2017). 'Towards next-generation heterogeneous mobile data stream mining applications: Opportunities, challenges, and future research directions. *Journal of Network and Computer Application*, vol. 79, pp. 1–24.

[57] Rehman, M. H. U., Batool, A., Liew, C. S., Teh, Y.-W., & Khan, A. U. R. (2017). Execution models for mobile data analytics. *IT Professional*, vol. 19, no. 3, pp. 24–30.

[58] Bottou, L., Curtis, F. E., & Nocedal, J. (2018). Optimization methods for large scale machine learning. *SIAM Review*, vol. 60, no. 2, pp. 223–311.

[59] Lu, H., Li, Y., Chen, M., Kim, H., & Serikawa, S. (2018). Brain intelligence: Go beyond artificial intelligence. *Mobile Netw. Appl.*, vol. 23, no. 2, pp. 368–375.

[60] Mamoshina, P. et al. (2018). Converging blockchain and next-generation artificial intelligence technologies to decentralize and accelerate biomedical research and healthcare. *Oncotarget*, vol. 9, no. 5, pp. 5665–5690.

[61] Lotfi, A., Langensiepen, C., & Yahaya, S. W. (2018). Socially assistive robotics: Robot exercise trainer for older adults. *Technologies*, vol. 6, no. 1, p. 32.

[62] Woods, J. (2018). *Blockchain: Rebalancing & Amplifying the Power of AI and Machine Learning (ML).* [Online]. Available: https://medium.com/crypto-oracle/blockchain-rebalancing-amplifyingthe-power-of-ai-and-machine-learning-ml-af95616e9ad9

[63] Raja, G., Manaswini, Y., Vivekanandan, G. D., Sampath, H., Dev, K., & Bashir, A. K. (2020). AI-powered Blockchain—a decentralized secure multiparty computation protocol for IoV. *IEEE INFOCOM 2020 — IEEE Conference on Computer*

Communications Workshops (INFOCOM WORKSHOPS), pp. 865–870. doi: 10.1109/INFOCOMWKSHPS50562.2020.9162866

[64] Cao, L. (1 May–June 2022). Decentralized AI: Edge intelligence and smart Blockchain, Metaverse, Web3, and DeSci. *IEEE Intelligent Systems*, vol. 37, no. 3, pp. 6–19. doi: 10.1109/MIS.2022.3181504

[65] Yin, H., Guo, D., Wang, K., Jiang, Z., Lyu, Y., & Xing, J. (January–February 2018). Hyperconnected network: A decentralized trusted computing and networking paradigm. *IEEE Network*, vol. 32, no. 1, pp. 112–117. doi: 10.1109/MNET.2018.1700172

[66] Wood, G. (April 2014). Ethereum: A secure decentralized generalized transaction ledger. *Ethereum Project Yellow Paper*, vol. 151, pp. 1–32.

[67] Yu, S., Lv, K., Shao, Z., Guo, Y., Zou, J., & Zhang, B. (August 2018). A high performance blockchain platform for intelligent devices. *Proc. 1st IEEE Int. Conf. Hot Inf.-Centric Network.*, Shenzhen, China, pp. 260–261.

[68] Huang, G., Luo, C., Wu, K., Ma, Y., Zhang, Y., & Liu, X. (2019). Software-defined infrastructure for decentralized data lifecycle governance: Principled design and open challenges. *2019 IEEE 39th International Conference on Distributed Computing Systems (ICDCS)*, pp. 1674–1683, doi: 10.1109/ICDCS.2019.00166

[69] Shoker, A. (October/November 2017). Sustainable blockchain through proof of exercise. *Proc. IEEE 16th Int. Symp. Netw. Comput. Appl. (NCA)*, pp. 1–9.

Chapter 12

Blockchain Technology for Cyber-physical Systems

*Dahlia Sam, Jayanthi K., Joshi A., Deepa Kanmani S.,
Adlin Sheeba, and Kameshwaran A.*

12.1 INTRODUCTION

A cyber-physical system (CPS) combines physical components with built-in computer and storage, such as smartphones or automated televisions. Through a network of connected systems and objects, CPS connects with other systems and objects. Just a few of the numerous CPS applications in use today include smart grids, M-health and E-health, enterprise management systems, industrial production, and management processes. While this is true on one side, the fact is that the rapid development of IoT systems profoundly penetrates a number of cyberattacks, which frequently have a negative impact on millions of people's lives. Since every computerized data has a significant impact on how decisions are made, maintaining data integrity, security, and authenticity are now crucial considerations.

Blockchain, a relatively new distributed computing paradigm, offers a viable answer for contemporary CPS applications. A distributed ledger that includes technologies like cryptography, smart contracts, and consensus methods offers trustworthy infrastructures. In a blockchain setting, the data is copied after being actively validated across all network nodes using a consensus mechanism. It makes use of distributed storage techniques, and the data is replicated throughout the network on each node.

However, when it comes to CPS, the blockchain's computationally expensive nature with high bandwidth overhead and delays is the most challenging component. Therefore, the creation of a strong blockchain algorithm can protect CPS systems from security threats and provide a novel angle for CPS application research.

The use of blockchain to improve CPS performance is discussed in depth in this chapter. Section 12.2 gives an introduction about cyber-physical systems followed by its applications and challenges discussed in Section 12.3. Sections 12.4 and 12.5 give an overview of blockchain technology and the challenges in adopting blockchain for CPS. The designing of blockchain-based frameworks for CPS is discussed in Section 12.6 and the lightweight scalable blockchain is elaborated in Section 12.7. Managing data trust and user anonymity for CPS

DOI: 10.1201/9781003474111-12

applications with blockchain is discussed in Section 12.8. The various applications of blockchain in CPS are given in Section 12.9. Section 12.10 concludes the chapter.

12.2   WHAT ARE CYBER-PHYSICAL SYSTEMS?

CPS or cyber-physical systems are groups of physical items (sometimes known as "hardware") that are controlled by software- and computer-based processes. CPS entails specially designed computer and communication systems that communicate with the outside world. Software, networking, and embedded computing are only a small part of CPS. There is a significant amount of calculation, communication, and control involved. In CPS, the term "physical" refers to any man-made or natural system that abides by all the rules and guidelines of physics. The best possible integration of digital and physical components is supported by scientific theories and disciplines because it maximizes their complementary effects and enables the achievement of considerable cost, performance, and overall lifecycle sustainability gains. Here, the physical and computational processes are closely entwined, and they are able to regulate the physical process while simultaneously gathering feedback from the various systems using a variety of computer systems and sensor networks. CPS offers a number of different properties, including the capacity to work in a real-time setting with highly predictable behavior and higher performance potential.

As a large-scale system that distributes tasks and roles, CPS automatically controls and monitors numerous business, scientific, and industrial activities. It requires cross-disciplinary frameworks that are reliant on power sources, computer networks, and other infrastructure. Continuous performance improvement and the ability to self-adapt and alter in "real-time" are also strengths of CPS. CPS requires strong decision-making systems that function as distributed, interconnected systems of systems. Potential CPS devices include a Linux-powered laptop, a printer with a PCI card, a serial port DB-25, a Lego programmable robot known as "Mindstorm," a phone-operated water pump, a hybrid A&D computer, a "Smart Grid" power system, smart weapons, etc.

CPS can be thought of as a discipline that focuses on technology and calls for mathematical models. CPS combine modern computer technology with abstract mathematical modeling. Following the Turing-Church model, CPS combines abstraction of dynamical systems, linear algorithms, differential equations, etc., with computer-based data processing. CPS is a hybrid discipline that combines computer science, engineering, and mathematics. According to a generally accepted definition, CPSs are systems that smoothly integrate both the hardware and software to perform prescribed functions. As these tasks are divided up among many agents and become increasingly automated, new research trends are promoting the usage of blockchain technology.

12.3   APPLICATIONS AND CHALLENGES OF CYBER-PHYSICAL SYSTEMS

The CPS is a new era of digital systems that consists of two primary functional elements: (1) enhanced connectivity that helps ensure actual information feedback from the physical realm and the Internet, and (2) smart information management, analytics, and computation power that creates the Internet [1,2]. Applications and theoretical foundations are the two main categories of CPS studies.

Research on CPS has a substantial impact on the expansion of agriculture by enhancing the efficiency of both food production and consumption through the application of technology such as precision agriculture, intelligent water management, and more effective food distribution. Mehdipour (2014) [3] developed a "Rat Deduction System" (RDS) to act as a framework for rat surveillance in the agriculture industry. The price of rodent control, the amount of crop waste, and environmental damage all can be considerably reduced, thanks to this method. In the realms of education and research, IoT concept has been used widely in order to integrate the physical engineering systems along with the cloud. The research on CPS applications in education demonstrates that analyzing each of the following topics separately is not sufficient because when we talk about a CPS, it is not their union but rather their intersection: embedded computer systems, systems theory, sensor and communication systems, physical assets, decision theory, data fusion, information retrieval, resilience, and flexible settings. In the environment that education should provide, these components must be analyzed collectively.

CPS is one type of distributed system. Even though the vast majority of CPS devices use less energy, the uncomfortable demand and supply for energy mean that there is still a substantial challenge with the energy supply. Electricity, water, and heat waste can be minimized by energy-conscious building. The electrical power grid of the future is the smart grid, which can produce, distribute, and consume power in an adaptable and optimal manner. The CPS for environmental monitoring must be dispersed across a wide and varied geographical area (forests, rivers, and mountains) and operate for prolonged periods of time without human intervention while consuming the least amount of energy possible. Thanks to a massive number of sensor nodes dispersed around the region, CPS can monitor the local environment in the event of a natural or man-made disaster and respond quickly. Investigating how CPS affects the environment is essential since natural disasters like flooding, fire, or toxic gas can damage equipment and threaten the dependability and safety of the system. In a complex CPS, a single equipment failure might lead to abnormal environmental circumstances that would jeopardize the entire system.

Even when the end users are extremely mobile, vehicle cyber-physical systems (VCPS) have shown to be one of the most effective solutions for providing cost-effective services with the least amount of delay. In order to overcome the persistent problems in intelligent transportation systems, research on CPS, including autonomous vehicles, intelligent intersection systems, wireless communication support systems for vehicle-to-vehicle (V2V) and vehicle-to-infrastructure (V2I), can be extremely important. The main areas of research on CPS in this category include smart sensor systems for real-time patient health condition monitoring and warning, telemedicine systems that enable the provision of healthcare services remotely, and semiautonomous operated home service robots that can assist patients with their daily activities. Medical-based cyber-physical systems (MCPS) are being used by hospitals more and more to provide patients with high-quality continuous care, but developing MCPS that are safe and efficient still poses many difficulties. These include integrating information technology and cybernetics into the operating room and addressing problems with context-aware intelligence, autonomy, security, and privacy. Regardless of the viewpoint, this online health solution allows hospitals to share clinical and surgical information to PHR- and EMR-based apps. Future cyber-physical medical systems should include the following features: plug-and-play compatibility with other interoperable medical equipment; broad data integration and access; full data collection and analysis; closed-loop control characteristics; and actual visualization.

Security lapses could disrupt CPS and cause significant economic and societal losses. It is particularly challenging to design secure CPS because of the vast number of attack surfaces from the cyber and physical components, as well as the frequently constrained computing and communication resources. Cybersecurity is not the same as CPS system security. The CPS security is more important than cybersecurity because the cyber components of the CPS need to follow all cybersecurity protocols in addition to the other security protocols brought in by the physical components and their interactions. CPS provides excellent opportunities for brand-new uses in the smart city and smart home with a wide range of smart building solutions. An metropolitan region is considered to be "smart" if it provides the latest in cutting-edge social, business, emergency response, healthcare, energy distribution, and transportation services [4]. In smart homes, numerous sensors are present to assess a variety of physical traits or more complex data. Numerous possible uses exist for this ecosystem. The smart house aims to do this. Giving us comfortable living spaces is the focus of the smart homes and smart cities.

Smart cities utilize smart mobility in addition to boosting overall public safety to reduce traffic. A fundamental challenge for this application sector is the requirement to integrate several geographically scattered devices into a similar software environment. Today's applications for smart homes and cities require a unique approach to blend in and be accessible to their users. The main challenges in building industrial systems are now universally considered to be adaptability, modularity, and configurability. The use of hardware and software technologies integrated into a product to boost productivity during production or service delivery is referred to as "smart manufacturing" [5]. CPS is a crucial piece of technology for implementing smart manufacturing. Automated warehouse systems, an integral part of such systems, are currently managed using hierarchical and centralized control architectures as well as protocols for automation programming.

The majority of studies focus more on modeling, conceptualization, and application techniques than actualization because CPS research in the industrial sector is still in its early phases.

Future manufacturing has a lot of potential, as promised by the German strategic plan known as Industry 4.0. Industry 4.0 is the term used to characterize the comprehensive integration of state-of-the-art information technology (like CPS) into industrial situations, solutions, and processes. The CPS perspective on the impending industrial revolution will improve security, productivity, and efficiency by integrating embedded system production technologies, opening the door for highly flexible work flows and creative kinds of collaboration. Large memory is required by the CPS system's technical specifications in order to store the data produced by embedded systems. Any CPS system's system dynamics and control algorithm must take the system's computational complexity into account. Any system's feedback loop can be used to regulate quality control. Any CPS system will face additional difficulties due to excessive information overflow in a collaborative network.

The impact of this data overabundance is an increase in noise in any system, including pop-up windows, spam folders, and contextual advertising tied to any information. Increased energy-efficient communication between cyber and physical things is the result of the IoT paradigm's growth. The way people and machines interact is crucial. Any cyber-physical system must be realized while being aware of dangers. All levels of stakeholders must undergo many degrees of security checks, and greater device communication is required for data transfer between various systems. Physical device tampering, such as improper handling of wearable body sensors, can cause severe loss, such as the loss of patient information who is severely ill.

12.4 WHAT IS BLOCKCHAIN?

Blockchain technology is a cutting-edge database system that permits open information exchange on the inside of a business network. Data is kept in blocks that are connected together in a chain and stored in a blockchain database. Due to the inability to delete or amend the chain without network consensus, the data remains chronologically reliable. In order to manage orders, payments, accounts, and other transactions, you can employ blockchain technology to establish an irreversible or immutable ledger. A common picture of these transactions is made consistent by the system's built-in features, which also stop illegitimate transaction submissions [6,7].

Users of blockchain network can reach an agreement using blockchain, the technology platform of crypto currencies, without physically having to trust one another. Academics W. Scott Stornetta and Stuart Haber originally put forth the concept of blockchain technology in 1991. They set out to demonstrate a practical technique for securely adding time stamps to digital documents, preventing their modification or retroactive updating. They came up with a method of storing the time-stamped documents employing the concept of a cryptographically protected chain of blocks. Later in 1992, Merkle Trees were incorporated into the block-chain concept [8].

Blockchain has improved as a result and can now hold several records in a single block. A "secured chain of blocks" is created as a result. The chain of columns can be used to hold a series of linked data records. The chain's whole existence will therefore be contained in the most current record.

Later in 2004, Hal Finney, a well-known scientist and supporter of encryption, developed the Reusable Proof of Work System. After creating an RSA-signed token, this creates a proof-of-work token based on Hashcash that cannot be swapped. By maintaining a record of unit ownership on a reliable server, this prevents double spending. Users from all over the world were able to rapidly confirm its authenticity and integrity, thanks to it. RPoW is a pioneering and early prototype in the development of crypto currency. The double spending security is provided via a distributed peer-to-peer system that tracks and validates each transaction in Bitcoin.

In a nutshell, we can state that Bitcoins are created by lone miners in exchange for rewards, and they are then verified by the decentralized nodes in any network. On January 3, 2009, Satoshi Nakamoto mined the first Bitcoin, bringing about the creation of Bitcoin. It offered a 50 Bitcoin reward. Hal Finney was the first receiver, and on January 12, 2009, he was given 10 Bitcoins. The architecture of blockchain is given in Figure 12.1.

Consequently, the first Bitcoin transaction ever took place. Since then, block-chain technology has developed steadily and in a very positive direction. Initially used independently by Satoshi Nakamoto, the words block and chain gradually gained popularity as a combined word, blockchain, circa 2016. The crypto currency blockchain's data file, which included the records of every transaction made on the network, has grown significantly in size from

Digital documents will be time-stamped using blockchain to make it difficult to change or retroactively date them. Without relying on a centralized server,

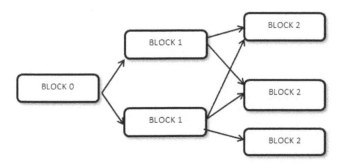

Figure 12.1 Architecture of blockchain.

blockchain is intended to overcome the problem of duplicate records. Data that has been saved inside of a blockchain is very difficult to change.

Just like we have SMTP for e-mail services, there is a software protocol called blockchain. Blockchain's, however, would not be able to function without the Internet. It consists of a variety of parts, such as a database, software, networked computers' blockchain network, that continuously add new blocks to the chain at predetermined intervals, and each network member replicates this chain. Blockchain enables portable devices to easily search the inclusion of data and also it is almost impossible to maliciously modify the chain because each block contains the hash of the blocks before it. This makes it necessary to change all of the blocks in order to change any one block's content.

In order to organize transactions, classic database techniques use a concurrency control scheme and a trusted environment. In contrast, by offering consensual, provably safe, and distributed solutions, blockchain technology can ensure security and address several common flaws. The difference between the access control guarantees in a traditional centralized architecture and the blockchain network architecture is that blockchain assumes the node will behave in a byzantine or an arbitrary way. As a result, blockchain-based systems are capable of tolerating byzantine failure and offering enhanced security as compared to incumbent database systems.

As a result of worries about data security and privacy, numerous commercial organizations and technological institutions have gradually begun to utilize the blockchain. The implementation of blockchain, however, faces difficulties with interoperability, scalability, and energy consumption. Other significant obstacles to the widespread implementation of blockchain technology include a lack of standards, a lack of legislation, and a skill scarcity.

To denote blockchain mathematically, a block B can be defined as a vector of entries. This can be denoted as follows:

$$B = (T r1, ..., T r NB) \tag{12.1}$$

In order to create a block, the entries need to be piled up.

12.5 CHALLENGES IN ADOPTING BLOCKCHAIN FOR CPS

The idea of a smart city is still developing, and despite its promising future, security issues are becoming more and more prevalent. Due to its beneficial characteristics, including auditability, transparency, immutability, and decentralization, blockchain has the potential to support the growth of smart cities.

The adoption of blockchain technology by several commercial enterprises is hampered by a number of challenges. Major problems with the application of blockchain include scalability, interoperability, energy use, a skill shortage, and a lack of standards. Bitcoin's network can only handle less than ten transactions per second, rendering it unsuitable for use in more demanding applications. Similar to this, the majority of the blockchain operates in isolated storage towers that are difficult to connect to other peer networks. They are unable to communicate with other blockchain-based systems to transfer or receive data.

The blockchain system is difficult because it requires a lot of computer power along with high cost. Additionally, there isn't yet a global standard for blockchain, which causes problems with interoperability and troublesome methods. This makes widespread adoption exceedingly challenging. There is also a serious shortage of blockchain experts and developers, which exacerbates these problems.

12.6   DESIGNING BLOCKCHAIN-BASED FRAMEWORKS FOR CPS

As the Internet gets more and more pervasive in our daily lives, at least a few MBs of data are generated. Social media has made it feasible for everyone in the modern age to work as a marketer, writer, publisher, or content producer if they have a smartphone and Internet access. It is extremely challenging to guarantee the security and copyright of social media content, including photographs, videos, and audio. Because copyright infringement occurs frequently, it should be easier to verify that the content is original and authentic. IPFS, a cutting-edge decentralized file storage system, and a secure sharing mechanism support a blockchain architecture [9]. Due to its decentralized nature, this system offers infinite opportunities for regulating copyrights of content on decentralized social media.

Although implementing blockchain has benefits for every industry, there are drawbacks as well. However, due to its numerous advantages across numerous industries, blockchain is well-known and widely used. Undoubtedly, the most important breakthrough is blockchain. The use of blockchain in the industry has significantly increased. Not only has it resulted in the change of businesses like Dropbox and Airbnb, but also of numerous others. This shift in how organizations conduct their operations will promote expansion and boost productivity. Additionally, it will assist the government in increasing employment and improving service quality. It has been crucial for businesses by offering a cheap and effective substitute for cash payments. Blockchain technology makes it possible for the payment system to work. It is also a helpful feature in a number of applications, including crowdfunding, digital identification, e-commerce, insurance, and property management.

These are a few applications of this technology. It speeds up the creation of new goods and services by businesses and industries as well as the flow of data and information, the capacity to authenticate each network transaction, and tasks that are difficult for conventional financial institutions and enterprises to complete in less than 2 seconds. Consensus is the foundation of blockchain technology, which is how the blockchain functions.

In numerous areas, blockchain has had a big impact on organizations and industries. Companies are even exploring option in blockchain implementation to create blockchain-based apps. As with any technology, blockchain has a variety of applications. It can be used to enable automated, low-latency bidding through automated contract systems or systems of record for large, complicated enterprises or to improve the efficiency and security of specific types of transactions. New blockchain applications for cyber-physical systems include applications in e-commerce, finance, transportation, and cybersecurity.

Blockchain technology is already being embraced widely due to its inherent qualities that make data decentralized and immune to fraudulent tampering. To enable intelligent transaction validation on the blockchain, numerous machine learning (ML) techniques are being used. The core of these machine learning techniques is the labor- and time-intensive process of training a model. It is challenging to make every blockchain node intelligent while utilizing the bare minimum of computing resources on the network. An entire blockchain network can be made intelligent using multilayer perceptron (MLP) [10] a single node that was trained at network formation since it has the prototype definition.

Each node becomes intelligent after the training process is over by duplicating the model and intelligence. A new node can be added to a blockchain network that is fully functional quickly.

12.7   LIGHTWEIGHT SCALABLE BLOCKCHAIN FOR CPS

Humans are interacting with the physical world in new ways owing to cyber-physical systems (CPS). Due to the complexity, limitations, and dynamic nature of the interactions, however, centralized techniques for CPS systems are unable to solve the specific issues of CPS. A decentralized strategy that takes these particular characteristics into consideration is necessary to fully utilize CPS's potential. Recently, solutions based on blockchain have been suggested to overcome CPS issues [11,12]. However, implementing blockchain for various CPS domains is not simple and comes with its own set of difficulties. Despite the benefits of blockchain for CPS applications, it is not easy to use blockchain in CPS due to scalability problems, high consumption of resources, transaction latency, poor flow, privacy concerns, and a distrust problem.

12.8   MANAGING DATA TRUST AND USER ANONYMITY FOR CPS APPLICATIONS WITH BLOCKCHAIN

In this chapter, it is proposed that clear trust-building techniques be provided using blockchain technology. A blockchain, or ledger, is a growing chain of blocks connected by cryptography that contains transactional data of various types, such as financial transactions involving the exchange of assets. As its name would imply, a blockchain is also known as a ledger. An immutable chain is created when transactions are maintained in chronological order on a blockchain, making the data there verifiable and auditable. Additionally, due to the immutability virtue of the blockchain and a creative application of cryptography and game theory, everyone in the network agrees on a single copy of the blockchain [13,14]. Figure 12.2 depicts a blockchain in a high-level picture.

Through the use of emerging technologies like blockchain, it is feasible to establish explicit methods for controlling the trust among all participants. A blockchain is a growing network of interconnected blocks that maintains transaction data of many different types, including financial transactions and the exchange of assets using smart contracts. As the name suggests, a blockchain is a network of interconnected blocks. Blockchains can help with cyber-physical system control as well. Every entry on a blockchain transaction is continuously updated, producing an irreversible chain that makes the data it contains traceable and open to inspection. The ledger is distributed among all nodes in the particular network [15]. A single copy of the blockchain is kept on each node in the network due to the immutable nature of blockchain technology, encryption, and game theory.

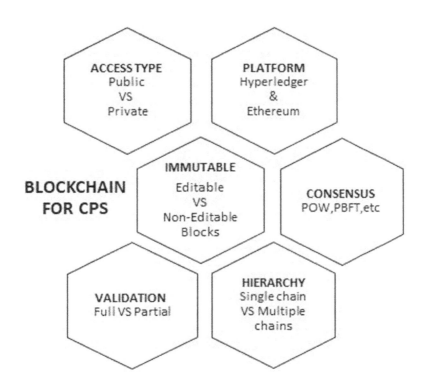

Figure 12.2 High-level view of blockchain.

In addition to being used as a ledger of records, blockchain may also be used to build smart contracts, which are autonomous entities kept on the data section of the blockchain network and encoded as a type of transaction.

A state machine with a representation of its current state on the blockchain can also be thought of as a smart contract. This is the point of communication between the physical and cyber systems. Again, when the smart contract's execution is accomplished, its new state will be broadly acknowledged by all pertinent network participants, and the blockchain will be updated to reflect this new state.

There are two primary types of blockchain, as we are previously aware. The most common form is public, where anyone may participate without needing advance authorization, like Bitcoin and Ethereum. On the other hand, a private blockchain can be created that grants each user a unique set of permissions for particular blockchain tasks, such as read, write, and access permission. The main area of interest in this cyber-physical system is private blockchain. The Hyperledger open-source project, which was founded by Intel and is managed by the Hyperledger Umbrella, is the focus of this discussion, with permission blockchain generally being given the lion's share of attention.

Traceable assembly systems will be considered as a CPS with blockchain application. In the modern world, assets are frequently used as assembly lines. It is essential to assign identities to assembly system components in order to foster trust among a group of unreliable economic actors regarding their identification and their aptitude for solving various societal and economic problems. Utilization claims include paid memberships in place of consumer ownership of assets like cars, where ownership is retained with the producer and the consumer subscribes to asset pools of varying quality, preventing the use of counterfeit parts in the automotive industry, as well as many other models of complex, decentralized ownership of assembly systems. The components may be used with confidence, which supports reuse and recycling [16,17].

A different approach by utilizing the blockchain's immutability, provenance, and consensus mechanisms is chosen. The following fundamental notion is the foundation upon which we construct a blockchain-based CPTS that offers assurance in the accuracy of identities in assembly systems and their usage data. It is presumed that physical components have digital identities that correspond to them.

Conventional identity management is unable to provide the level of confidence necessary for the identification and usage of assembly systems and other CPS in the real world. There are currently security tags on the market, such as improved RFID tags that can only be connected to actual items and cannot be removed without being destroyed. For data signing, these tags have the necessary cryptographic primitives. Additionally, we assume that assembly systems include IoT devices for usage data collection and that they are enhanced by cryptographic primitives for data signing.

In order to strengthen confidence in the accuracy of identities and usage data for assembly systems based on these presumptions, we were able to develop a demonstrator that makes use of a blockchain-based CPTS. The demonstrator offers a permissioned blockchain constructed using the Hyperledger Sawtooth architecture, which connects into a larger business logic and interacts with real items via fictitious security tags.

12.9 BLOCKCHAIN APPLICATIONS IN CPS

As computer acceptance has increased over the past few decades, records have mostly moved from being tangible paper documents to digitized ones created and controlled on computers—one of the many uses for computer security that computers have made feasible. Even though these records are made and kept on computers, a human still enters the information. Just a few examples include financial transactions, health information, and insurance information. Humans continued to be the main source of data collecting in these applications as a result. Sensors have replaced humans as the main data collection source in many systems in recent years, powered by the upsurge of IoT and pushed by the emergence of sensing applications.

In order to build an integrated system capable of abstraction, design, and analysis, CPS systems incorporate physical processes, software, and communication. Embedded systems, real-time communication, computers, networking, and physical system dynamics are just a few of the disciplines that the technology integrates. The application of blockchain technology to financial transactions has been extensively studied and documented. Innovations in this field have made it possible to deliver money directly to authorized recipients without the need for command execution. The possibility of delays, repression, or other outside effects is decreased by the implementation of blockchain-based smart contracts.

It offers complete financial security, keeps track of the conditions of the contract, and is unbreakable. Additionally, it makes it simpler to track and monitor online identities utilizing blockchain technology. The usage of blockchain as a low-cost notary system can prevent numerous frauds by creating unique certificates that are simple to validate.

12.9.1 Blockchain and IoT

Today's IoT already includes more than a billion intelligent, linked gadgets. With the expected proliferation of hundreds of billions more, the world is on the cusp of a revolution that will have an impact on a wide range of businesses, including the electronics industry. Thanks to the growth of IoT, industries can now gather data, gain insight from the data, and make decisions based on the data. As a result, there is a great deal of "confidence" in the knowledge acquired. Do we really understand where these data came from, and should we really base our decisions and conduct our business on unreliable information?

IoT can provide data that has been collected through sensors. The essential concept is to identify objects as soon as they are created so that their identity can be recognized and validated using blockchain throughout their existence. Through the use of a device identification protocol, which enables each device to have a unique blockchain public key and send encrypted challenge and response messages to other devices, it is made sure that a device maintains control over its identity. The reputation or history that a device with an identity builds can likewise be tracked by a blockchain.

The business logic of a blockchain network is expressed by smart contracts. These smart contracts operate independently when a transaction is suggested, adhering to the rules established by the network. Smart contracts can be extremely important in IoT networks since they automate coordination and authorization for transactions and interactions. IoT was first intended to surface data and provide timely, actionable insight. For instance, everything may be connected, and smart houses are a reality today. In fact, these IoT devices can even respond when something goes wrong with IoT, such as ordering a new part. Smart contracts are a terrific method to control how these devices function, which is something we need to be able to accomplish.

12.9.2   Blockchain for Automotive Industry

Blockchain technology has applications in the automotive sector, which has a large number of internal and external stakeholders (such as dealers, retailers, OEMs, insurance companies, financial institutions, fleet management services, or government agencies) from different industries and countries with different regulations. These stakeholders transmit value across their business networks (e.g., data, transactions, processes, and workflow) and have particular needs in terms of trust, security, or time (e.g., real-time access), as well as in terms of transaction and operating expenses. The usage of blockchain can help this business network in a number of areas in the automotive industry:

- *Immutable data management:* Proof of ownership can be used to safeguard intellectual property (such as patents), prevent identity-related frauds, offer a car's history of traceability, improve supply chain procedures, ensure the authenticity of cars or spare parts, and retain audit trail data.
- *Digital logbook:* A blockchain can be used to securely store, update, and validate tamper-proof data such as vehicle maintenance or ownership history. As a result, blockchain can offer a shared ledger among the various involved and authorized businesses, such as automakers, dealers, and independent repair shops. Smart contracts, which may collect data from numerous sources and then design a payment mechanism for accessing vehicular data, can be used to automate processes.
- *Operations management:* Blockchain can track the provenance of parts or vital assets in the supply chain.

- *Supply chain traceability:* To increase business productivity by lowering the cost of monitoring crucial assets, making sure warranties are upheld, and simplifying maintenance or recycling chores.
- *Fraud prevention:* By collecting, storing, and time stamping mileage data via a blockchain, odometer fraud can be prevented.
- *Financial management:* Cross-border payments, incentives, peer-to-peer payments, insurance claims, auto auctions, maintenance, and repairs all can be sped up and automated using blockchain technology.
- *Processing insurance claims:* In the event of an accident, a shared ledger can also be used to show fault. This application makes it possible to streamline and expedite the insurance and claim procedures by automatically completing a claim and sending the information to the insurance provider via a smart contract. Furthermore, data on braking habits or speed can be utilized to detect fraud or produce customized insurance quotes.
- *Incentives:* Blockchain enables the creation of individualized reward and experience systems.

12.9.3 Blockchain in Supply Chain Management

Three potential areas of value addition by blockchain technology in the supply chain industry are as follows:

- *Replacing labor-intensive, manual processes:* Despite the fact that supply chains are currently capable of handling large, complex data sets, many of their processes, especially those in the lowest supply tiers, are slow and only rely on paper, as is still frequently the case in the shipping sector.
- *Improving traceability:* Consumer and regulatory demand for provenance information is already driving change. By lowering the expensive expenses of quality problems like recalls, reputational damage, or lost sales from goods sold on the black or gray markets, boosting traceability also adds value.
- *Reducing supply chain IT transaction costs:* This advantage is now more theoretical than actual. Bitcoin compensates users to validate every block or transaction, in addition to asking those who propose a new block to include a fee in their request. Such a levy would undoubtedly be unaffordable given the massive magnitude of supply chains.

12.10 CONCLUSION

In the situation of today, CPS functions as a disruptive approach that substitutes cutting-edge CPS infrastructures for conventional power systems. Cyber-physical systems are continuously transmitted from centralized to distributed systems, requiring reliable, secure, and effective infrastructures. Because of the crucial nature of CPS, which has a high degree of heterogeneity, complexity, and resource-constrained attributes, the risk of a secure fault-tolerant robust computer system is enhanced.

For CPS, blockchain serves as the underlying technology, providing a fault-tolerant, dependable, secure, and effective computing infrastructure. The block-chain, which enables a wide range of exciting new technological applications in cyber-physical systems, including the Internet-of-Things (IoT), manufacturing, transportation, and supply chain, among many other sectors, can be used to build a secure, decentralized public ledger.

This chapter presents a thorough analysis and discussion of a variety of CPS applications that have made use of blockchain. Blockchain technology has several uses, including those in healthcare, transportation, and cybersecurity. Without a doubt, the blockchain with its built-in combination of algorithms, distributed storage, and improved security protocols can be the most effective solution for modern CPS applications.

REFERENCES

[1] Lee, EA (2015). The past, present and future of cyber-physical systems: A focus on models. Sensors (Switzerland), 15(3), 4837–4869. doi: 10.3390/s150304837.

[2] Lee, J, B Bagheri and H-A Kao (2015). A cyber-physical systems architecture for industry 4.0-based manufacturing systems. Manufacturing Letters, 3, 18–23.

[3] Mehdipour, F (2014). Smart field monitoring: An application of cyber-physical systems in agriculture. In 2014 IIAI 3rd International Conference Advanced Applied Informatics (IIAIAAI), (pp. 181–184), IEEE, Otago Polytechnic, Japan.

[4] Cassandras, CG (2016). Smart cities as cyber-physical social systems. Engineering, 2(2), 218–219. doi: 10.1016/J.ENG.2016.02.012.

[5] Gunes, V, S Peter, T Givargis and F Vahid (2014). A survey on concepts, applications, and challenges in cyber-physical systems. KSII Transactions on Internet and Information Systems, 8(12), 4242–4268. doi: 10.3837/tiis.2014.12.001.

[6] Sam, D, K Jayanthi, R Tiwari, AS Ebenezer, SD Kanmani and A Sheeba. Block-chain in internet of entities—issues and challenges; https://doi.org/10.1016/B978-0-323-91850-3.00012-3

[7] Bhushan, B, P Sinha, KM Sagayam and JA Onesimu. Untangling blockchain technology: A survey on state of the art, security threats, privacy services, applications and future research directions; https://doi.org/10.1016/j.compeleceng.2020.106897

[8] Bhushan, B, A Khamparia, KM Sagayam, SK Sharma, MA Ahad and NC Debnath. Blockchain for smart cities: A review of architectures, integration trends and future research directions; https://doi.org/10.1016/j.scs.2020.102360

[9] Kripa, M, A Nidhin Mahesh, R Ramaguru and PP Amritha (2020, May). Block-chain framework for social media DRM based on secret sharing. In International Conference on Information and Communication Technology for Intelligent Systems (pp. 451–458). Springer, Singapore.

[10] Nayak, A, D Chowdhury, S De, S Bhattacharyya, K Muhammad and S Gorbachev (2022). A novel intelligent blockchain framework with intelligence replication. In

Advanced Computational Paradigms and Hybrid Intelligent Computing (pp. 661–672). Springer, Singapore.

[11] Mehdipour, F, KC Nunna and KJ Murakami (2013). A smart cyber-physical systems-based solution for pest control. In Green Computing and Communications (GreenCom), 2013 IEEE and Internet of Things (iThings/CPSCom), IEEE International Conference and IEEE Explore, IEEE Cyber, Physical and Social Computing (pp. 1248–1253). Washington, DC.

[12] Dedeoglu, V, A Dorri, R Jurdak, RA Michelin, RC Lunardi, SS Kanhere and AF Zorzo (2020, January). A journey in applying blockchain for cyberphysical systems. In 2020 International Conference on COMmunication Systems & NETworkS (COMSNETS) (pp. 383–390). IEEE Xplore, Bengaluru, India.

[13] Lee, EA and SA Seshia (2017). Introduction to Embedded Systems—A Cyber-Physical Systems Approach, Second Edition, MIT Press.

[14] Framework for Cyber-Physical Systems, Release 1.0 (2016). Cyber Physical Systems Public Working Group, USA, National Institute of Standards and Technology, U.S. Department of Commerce.

[15] Matsumoto, S and RM Reischuk (2017). IKP: Turning a PKI around with decentralized automated incentives. In 2017 IEEE Symposium on Security and Privacy (SP) (pp. 410–426). IEEE TCSP, San Jose, CA.

[16] Beckmann, A, A Milne, J-J Razafindrakoto, P Kumar, M Breach and N Preining (2019, December). Blockchain-based cyber physical trust systems (pp. 265–277)

[17] Rathore, H and M Guizani. Blockchain enabled cyber-physical systems; https://encyclopedia.pub/entry/22213

Chapter 13

Cyber Forensics for Cyber-physical System

Sonia Chhabra, Shweta Mayor Sabharwal,
Manpreet Kaur, and Ahmed J. Obaid

13.1 INTRODUCTION

Recent technological developments have made it easier to integrate computing and communication capabilities into physical systems that interact and react to environmental cues. Networked computing technology has been developed recently. Cyber-physical systems (CPS) are a result of these embedded technologies. Cyber-physical systems are the consequence of the fusion of concepts from embedded systems, real-time systems, and control theory. CPS are large-scale, heterogeneous systems that are capable of monitoring and regulating the physical world [1]. To sense and keep track of physical entities, embedded components like actuators and sensors are used. The engineered system in CPS, which consists of both cognitive and material resources, is crucial to many applications. Physical phenomena that need monitoring and regulation are a part of physical processes. All of the cutting-edge embedded technology that analyzes data and conducts communication with a dispersed environment is included in cyber systems. A network of interfaces, including sensors, actuators, and analog to digital converters (ADC), will be employed to connect the physical and digital worlds.

The convergence and exchanges between the physical and digital worlds are made possible by cyber-physical systems [1]. CPS provides innovative technology that enhances a wide range of physical-based applications across numerous domains. CPS can be employed for improved productivity, efficiency, precision, safety, and dependability in manufacturing processes [2,3]. It can be applied to healthcare applications to offer both patients and healthcare providers practical real-time services [4,5]. CPS can be employed in big residential and commercial buildings to enhance energy efficiency and residing conditions [6,7]. It can also be applied to transportation systems to increase safety and effectiveness [8]. A few innovations, highlights, and ideas from network, circulated information bases, sensor, implanted gadgets, programming frameworks, including equipment parts, microcontrollers, and actuators are used and coordinated by CPS. CPS likewise coordinates various disciplines, including mechanical, biomedical, design, frameworks, and designing, alongside the spaces of medical services, transportation, and energy to upgrade applications in reality [9].

While CPS can give various cunning enhancements for upgrading designs and strategies, they are defenseless to cyberattacks and crime like some other advanced

DOI: 10.1201/9781003474111-13

and appropriated framework. Security blemishes in different frameworks might bring about huge actual mischief not withstanding harm to equipment, programming, and information. Actual mischief can appear as human fatalities and wounds, infrastructural harm, asset misfortune, and hardware disappointments or breakdowns. An assortment of safety efforts is pondered and included to shield the CPS applications when they are quickly created and conveyed in various fundamental spaces. CPS should likewise highlight fitting and productive legal sciences capacities to work with examinations concerning online protection dangers or crime. The creating field of CPS criminology is depicted in this concentrate alongside its deterrents and a few proposed arrangements. The report additionally examines a few forthcoming future reviews and improvement ways that could prompt better CPS crime scene investigation techniques and capacities.

This chapter focuses on aspects of the CPS cyber forensic concept in the manner shown. Section 13.2 gives foundation information on CPS such as its objectives, capabilities, and risks. A summary of the CPS investigation is provided in Section 13.3 from the perspectives of innovation, hierarchy, and legitimacy. The techniques for empowering CPS legal examination are discussed in Section 13.4. Section 13.5 deals with devices for better cyber-crime scene investigation followed by criminology apparatus suggestions in Section 13.6. Section 13.7 discusses about some cyber techniques and Section 13.8 about the potential future innovative work topics. Section 13.9 concludes the chapter.

13.1.1 Foundation

The predictable and trustworthy collaborations among its physical and innovative parts put aside arranged implanted CPS frameworks [9]. CPS are being utilized increasingly more wherever to improve the actual spaces. CPS offers significant help for shrewd, mindful, and crucial applications [10]. The interconnected application area utilizes the oversight and control abilities given by CPS to achieve foreordained objectives. Regularly, programming made complex calculations are utilized in the digital domain to make control decisions. In opposition to ordinary implanted frameworks, CPS are arranged installed frameworks with appropriated parts and handling power. Among these parts are microcontrollers, sensors, and actuators. These gadgets are connected together by wired or remote organizations and have a profound association with their actual environmental factors. Any CPS is made out of three fundamental stages: sensor checking, insightful programming direction, and actuator execution [11]. These three urgent stages are connected together in a criticism circle, as found in Figure 13.1. Distributed computing is utilized by frameworks known as "digital actual cloud frameworks" to run the frameworks and do modern calculations.

Numerous applications can profit from making and executing CPS arrangements; however, they convey significant dangers assuming that they are presented to cyberattacks. These risks might deteriorate to where they cause fatalities, foundation harm, and negative financial repercussions. The primary CPS applications are summed up in Table 13.1, along with their critical goals and related perils.

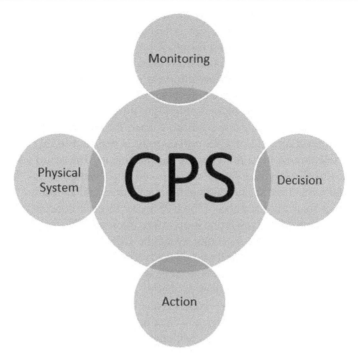

Figure 13.1 CPS closed steps.

Table 13.1 Primary CPS Applications

CPS Applications	Objectives	Issues
Smart buildings	Monitoring and treatment	Loss of resources and live
Smart water networks	Water production and water quality	Damages, life loss, pollution
Vehicle safety	Reduced congestion, traffic, accidents	Life loss, infrastructure damages
Smart manufacturing	Production, product quality, safety	Damages, safety reduction, live loss, economic impact
Energy production	Max power generations, better capabilities	Infrastructure damage, reduction in production

13.2   CPS INVESTIGATION

Computerized criminology has progressed essentially during the couple of years. Computerized legal sciences arrive in different structures. These incorporate virtual machine occasions, versatile gadgets, organizations, cloud administrations legal sciences, and computerized crime scene investigation [12]. CPS legal sciences is an original subset of PC crime scene investigation that is immature, contrasted with different subsets, and requires additional thought. Computerized criminology and CPS are consolidated in the field of CPS legal sciences (digital and actual frameworks). It can likewise be viewed as a particular part of criminology that interfaces with network legal sciences since CPSs are habitually organized frameworks. The efficient act of catching, endlessly examining network traffic and correspondences, is known as organization legal sciences [13]. CPS examinations additionally incorporate parts from every one of different classifications, contingent upon the degree of its use and the parts utilized. For example, in the event that the CPS utilized these administrations, cloud criminology would be pertinent; by the by, the fuse of framework offices or test patients would require the utilization of actual criminal legal sciences.

We will research the CPS crime scene investigation utilizing the techniques illustrated by Ref. [14] for assessing cloud legal sciences. The mechanical, hierarchical, and lawful parts of this system should be thought of in every way. We will feature a couple of key CPS legal sciences–related issues in every one of these classifications.

13.2.1   Scientific Angle

The related administrative incorporates the techniques, strategies, techniques, and devices expected to complete criminology methods in CPS situations. Among these are the social occasion of information, the advancement of displayed, reproduced, and virtual conditions, as well as the incorporation of deterrent measures. Information assortment is the method involved with finding, grouping, and acquiring crime scene investigation information. Since advanced violations might quickly affect the climate, CPS criminology assembles data about both the computerized parts and the encompassing actual climate, rather than different strategies for advanced legal sciences [15]. A few devices are utilized to remove criminological proof from the CPS, in view of the innovation that was utilized to deliver the CPS. The data source will be considerably unique in relation to current frameworks since there will be various sources with different attributes. Subsequently, the information gathering frameworks should be suitable for these conditions.

The exchange between both the physical and the advanced conditions is one of the primary principles of CPS. Thus, the CPS examination instruments should likewise envelop the actual pieces of the framework. Along these lines, virtualization, imitation, and reproduction approaches can empower CPS criminology. Making a proactive move can likewise make CPS criminology examinations a lot simpler. The criminology tasks in case of an assault, for example, can be helped by catching the correspondences that are moved, the control orders, and the entrance exercises. Moreover, the actual assessments that can be led on these CPS stages should be here and there viable (or free) with the PC legal sciences that are being applied.

One fundamental component of laying out CPS protection and CPS examinations is the utilization of interruption recognition techniques that might be executed into CPS subsystems [16]. Various interruption recognition methods have been grown explicitly for CPS frameworks [17]. These procedures attempt to address security issues and different issues with CPS applications. Using interruption identification through CPS programs empowers the assortment and examination of various statistics on CPS physical activities as well as exclusive facts pertinent to the cooperation among exclusive subsystems. This data would give computerized follow-ups in case of an attack, aiding the examination. It likewise helps in surveying how the ongoing security situation is doing. Besides, more information can be acquired and explored to more readily comprehend how the CPS's few parts are applied in reality. As well as working with CPS legal sciences systems, this data can be utilized to improve future CPS plans and brace security obstructions against new assaults.

13.2.2 Institutional Perspective

In lieu of the CPS proprietors, in some CPS applications, clients or associations from outside the CPS may very well have influence over CPS parts. Client's shrewd meters for contrast give data on power utilization to a savvy lattice that helps it run all the more effectively and control the creation, conveyance, and cost of energy. Another model is the utilization of outsider administrations in some CPS executions to give the CPS state-of-the-art highlights. It is feasible to incorporate organization and correspondence frameworks as well as cloud- and haze-based registering administrations. It is fundamental to characterize the division of assets and obligations between clients, outside organizations and associations, and CPS proprietors in these frameworks to defend the information trustworthiness. The criminology processes utilized shouldn't disregard any guidelines or regulations that are relevant to all gatherings included.

Administration is a significant test with regard to CPS criminology. At the point when an attack happens, the decision body stretches out to all framework parts, alongside the CPS, its environmental factors, and any basic foundation, and goes with choices in regard to freedom, classification issues, and access challenges [18]. In any case, truly, most CPS are created and carried out with the help of various associations and nearby suppliers. Straightforward entry to review logs, past utilization information, and other applicable legal sciences information should be composed by all partners. All parts of information insurance, including classification, uprightness, and security, should be maintained, and the legitimate conventions and regulations should be noticed.

13.2.3 Legislative Angle

The legitimate side of CPS criminology is broadening the scope of regulations and guidelines to cover its exercises and data. CPS crime scene investigation thoughts, techniques, and rules ought to be created to ensure that endeavors to lead criminology negate no regulations or guidelines. Consequently, CPS crime scene investigation will save client's security and protection rules for any frameworks drawing in outside clients all through CPS legal sciences exercises. This is to some degree related toward the administration part given that freely kept up with and possessed CPS can be audited and criminology data can be acquired inside. Nonetheless, in light of the fact that there are various associations which manage and regulate a CPS, there will be legitimate worries with circuits of locale, captures, and different limitations. Nonetheless, in the event that the proof is to be utilized in criminal allegations, inside strategies expected by the lawful cycle should be followed.

CPS crime scene research might motivate multijurisdictional worries assuming the CPS parts are dispersed throughout various states or international locations. For instance, while cloud frameworks in a single kingdom may give admittance to cloud advantages, the primary pieces of a given CPS management are probably arranged in any other. The cloud stages being utilized now and again are reachable from various nations. In specific designs, CPS information could be kept in one country while other distributed computing administrations might be given in another. Any help that is given in one more nation may likewise be utilized by a cloud supplier. Thus, while carrying out analytical activities in such frameworks, multijurisdictional practice and legitimate errors should be thought about.

13.3   APPROVING CPS LEGAL EXAMINATION

Because of the intricacy of CPS, legal examinations are exceptionally convoluted strategies. Some exploration is being finished on creating components and means to incorporate criminology standards and attributes through the development and execution of CPS to help legal sciences examination methods. This approach is known as the crime scene investigation by-plan system. This procedure is being utilized in the clinical CPS to help legal sciences examinations for deceitful clinical conditions based on clinical CPS viewpoints (innovation, innovation, clients, and so on) [19].

The idea to utilize the crime location examination approach for digital actual cloud frameworks is another model [20]. Utilizing this worldview, the creators of this study included measurable guidelines into the CPS creation and execution stages. The significance of this examination rests in the way that while distributed computing can give CPS various advantages, its joining suggests conversation starters in regard to how to guarantee the protection, precision, and openness of information. Because of the broad usage of frameworks, actual parts, and organizations in the improvement of CPS, they are particularly helpless to potential cyberattacks. Assaults might begin from the parts of the CPS, the organizations that interface the CPS to the assistance, or even the actual cloud. Six necessities are illustrated in the proposed system for a CPS to some way or another be affirmed as fitting for criminology examinations. These incorporate regulations and laws, CPS equipment and programming necessities, prerequisites, episode dealing with necessities, legal sciences readiness prerequisites, risk of the board methodology and thoughts, and industry-explicit necessities. The significance of approval was likewise stressed by the creators as a method for guaranteeing the steadfastness of the turn of events and plan of CPS examinations.

As a rule, the criminological insightful methodology might help in finding security breaks, particularly their sorts and sources. Also, it screens, examines, and makes inferences from the proof. Therefore, it is more straightforward to respond to different criminology-related questions. The scientific undertaking system is likewise a significant stage since it gives a construction to the CPS insightful methods. In contrast with other conventional cycles that have a huge choice of business assessments instruments and programming that can be utilized for security occurrences, creating legal sciences strategies for CPS can be very challenging. Thus, utilizing the proposed criminology by-plan framework is very gainful. Despite the fact that it could raise speculation expenses and improve-ment intricacy, utilizing this strategy will accelerate legal sciences examinations and safeguard the CPS. The CPS's ability to create a high return on initial capital investment all through exercises is supposed to profit from this. These advantages are additionally of most noteworthy significance in light of the fact that the greater part of CPS is utilized for basic applications and applications influencing human prosperity. These situation's defects, assaults, and control could bring about fatali-ties, huge wounds, framework misfortunes, and information breaks, among other possible outcomes. A couple of models incorporate canny assembling, water-sav-ing frameworks, shrewd transportation organizations, and keen designs.

13.4   DEVICES FOR COMPUTERIZED CRIME SCENE INVESTIGATION

This section comprises the different devices required for the cyber-crime scene investigation of cyber-physical system.

13.4.1   Computerized Legal Sciences

Computerized legal sciences include the crime scene examination devices and different techniques required for the investigation.

13.4.1.1   EnCase

This business stage contains various examination devices and techniques [21]. It cautiously concentrates on document recuperation from cancellation, record asso-ciation and audit, hash code examination, exhibition appraisal, vault evaluation, investigation of marks, and examination of web history. With the assistance of the bookmarking instrument, enCase sorts out the material and produces a report that is incredibly clear and easy to figure out, stressing significant information.

13.4.1.2   Examination

This open-source program can perform measurable procedure on Windows and Unix-based working frameworks [22]. The recovery of online antiquities, hashed filtration, web examination, sequential investigation, catchphrase searches, and results on record types should be in every way possible with dissection for analytical purposes.

13.4.1.3   Measurable Toolbox

Measurable Toolbox [23] is a piece of Window outlines PC crime scene investigation programming made by Access Data. This device empowers information investigation, document recuperation from erasure, MD5 and SHA hashing check, record examination for FAT, NTFS, Ext2, and CDFS, and graphical record seeing. Plate imaging likewise utilizes the FTK Imager application, which is a part of the FTK Tool compartment.

13.4.1.4   Instability

Memory legal sciences, infection examination, and occurrence reaction are for the most part empowered by open-source programming named Instability [24]. Linux, Windows, Macintosh, and Android are a portion of these working frameworks. Notwithstanding RAM on 32-digit or 64-cycle PCs, Unpredictability additionally takes a gander at natural unloading, VMware unloading (vmem), debacle removal locales, virtual machine dump destinations, Firewire, Lime standard, Master proof HPAK design (fast dump), and QEMU memory deep oil drilling destinations.

13.4.1.5   Mail Watcher

Use Mail Watcher [25] to see and examine messages in Mozilla Thunderbird, Windows Store, Microsoft Viewpoint Express 4, 5, and 6, as well as other client mail programs. It has the ability to direct broad requests across the messages in general and channel through mail envelopes at the same time.

13.4.2   Network Legal Sciences

Network legal sciences involves the tool for analysis purpose by monitoring the network activities. Some of them are discussed in the following sections.

13.4.2.1   Wireshark

It [26] is an open-source, freeware point of interaction and organization analyzer that cause sudden spikes in demand for Windows, UNIX, macOS, BSD, and Linux. It has the capacity to record crude USB traffic, accumulate bundles from a genuine framework utilizing pcap, identify discourse through associations in the caught rush hour gridlock, and variety code edges to assist clients with recognizing various kinds of traffic, in addition to other things.

13.4.2.2   Xplico

Xplico is utilized to extricate the information from the recorded application, including email interchanges, convention information, and discourse over convention content [27]. Web traffic investigation, multi-stringing, adaptable information (convention decoder) and result (regulator) interfaces, port-independent convention distinguishing proof, and careful pcap information examination are among Xplico's key highlights.

13.4.3   Portable Legal Sciences

Portable legal sciences focus on the framework and hardware devices required for the cyber investigation.

13.4.3.1   XRY

Worldwide situating frameworks, cell phones, and different gadgets can be explored utilizing a computerized and versatile criminology device called XRY [28]. This is involved by associations in the military, authorization offices, law enforcement, and knowledge. XRY analyzes information by spilling RAM, bypassing the operating system, and managing it straightforwardly.

13.4.3.2   Cellebrite UFED

The Cellebrite UFED Genius scope of versatile legal hardware [29] upholds examinations by social event, unravelling, assessing, deciphering, checking, and controlling information. This tool stash's abilities incorporate the capacity to decode cloud-based proof, get ongoing information, access iOS and android gadgets, screen and survey video proof, assemble live information, do measurable imaging, and investigate encoded information.

13.4.4   Data Set Crime Scene Investigation

When we need to work on the data, we require a strong device for the cyber investigation based on legal sciences. The following sections show the data set of crime scene investigation.

13.4.4.1   SQLite Crime Scene Investigation Program

The proof used to foster a case can be made, kept up with, and assessed utilizing a data set legal sciences program called SQLite Diagnostics Program [30]. This device can make SQLite data sets, look at and survey data set objects, record data sets, add various overseer sections, do complex examinations, and concentrate information in various different record designs.

13.4.4.2 SQLCMD

A data set extraction instrument created by Microsoft can be used as an order line device to execute erratic code and programming in SQL data sets [31]. This application works with the assessment of information bases and cycle logs. A printed yield is created when SQLCMD is performed.

13.4.5   Forensics Information Examination

"Criminology information investigation" is a part of computerized legal sciences that ganders at organized information, for example, large information, information from programming projects, and data sets pertinent to monetary violations and other deceitful exercises. PC programming, data set, and organization examination procedures are utilized by criminology information examination to accomplish insightful objectives.

13.5   DIGITAL CRIMINOLOGY APPARATUSES SUGGESTIONS

Digital criminology innovations are as yet being grown widely for application in a scope of cyber examinations. The accompanying worries are considered concerning and creating specialized fields, as discussed in the following sections.

13.5.1   Portable Criminology

For the digital forensic, we first focus on the portable devices and their investigation to perform the cyber investigation. Some of the investigation processes are discussed in the following sections.

13.5.1.1 Antiquity Extraction

Most economically open portable examination devices accompany state-of-the-art usefulness. The main disadvantage to utilizing an expert instrument is its expected expense. They support examining offices in their data gathering, yet they are excessive all the time. This may be settled by means of obtaining open-source programming for Android, iOS, as well as economic plan cell telephones. Through a troubleshooting span interface, initiatives like the Linux Memory Extractor are used to get memory in Android cellular telephones. Basic cell phones can likewise have information gathered by BitPim, and gadget reinforcements can be inspected utilizing the iPhone Reinforcement Analyzer. The downsides of elements extraction instruments, separately open source and business, include their powerlessness to perceive scrambled as well as covered-up information, their failure to interpret data put away by versatile applications, and their own impediments concerning equipment similarity with specific working frameworks, for example, Paraben Gadget Seizure [32].

13.5.1.2   Reporting

Any examination technique must have the option to create a decent record of the found data and reached inferences. An instrument that creates itemized reports at the finish of the interaction is expected for that point. Hexa unloading is the course of genuinely gaining a cell phone's document frameworks. There is an error in revealing and examination of hex-unloading in cell phone legal sciences devices [33]. This disservice exists in light of the fact that these cell phone and PDA parts have not yet been shown by versatile scientific apparatuses for the motivations behind announcing design.

13.5.1.3   Cloud

While endeavoring to gather and break down information from cloud administrations relating to cell phones, Versatile Criminology arrangements go up against various hardships [34]. These legal sciences devices, which are utilized to direct cloud examinations on cell phones, are restricted in their capacity to share assets in a cloud climate, to distinguish and give subtleties on information beginnings, to determine issues with cloud access approval, and to find the sources from which the proof is being gotten, especially in a processing server. Just few applications are sent for cloud examination utilizing the principal methods, including information review and investigation, while most of portable criminology strategies accessible are disconnected-based.

13.5.1.4   Android Forensics

With the acquaintance of various models with the cell phone market and the assistance of Android gadgets, the area of portable criminology today has extended [35]. Indeed, even while there are immediate obtaining procedures and instruments like Crisis Download Mode (EDL) division, these are low-level methods that are just accessible from a limited handful makers of Android versatile gadgets and chips. Moreover, contingent upon the settings of the cell phone, the form of Android, and any dynamic encryption modes, such apparatuses probably won't have the option to obtain and remove information. For example, Android reinforcements were never encoded on cell phones before Android 9, which made it conceivable to embrace unstable information acquisitions.

13.5.1.5 Deleted Data Analysis

In light of the encryption key components used by those cell phones, it was especially difficult to reestablish and recuperate erased records [36]. The Strong State Drives (SSD) have been managed to make it difficult to recuperate information after a record has been erased. Strategies, including SSD, producing access modes are currently being investigated to recover private archives from the SSD circles. Consequently, such functionalities are being tried in criminology programs to recuperate lost records from cell phones.

13.5.1.6 Two-factor Authentication

Criminology apparatuses in some cases don't get to delicate data by impairing, a validation procedure like Two-Component Confirmation [37]. For instance, Apple gadget clients, who utilize Two-Element Confirmation to safeguard their records from unapproved access, can impair the Track Down My Insurance choice or resetting Apple Recognizable proof/iCloud secret word without giving their genuine Apple ID/iCloud secret phrase. This leads portable clients to stow away or adjust data, which can be valuable in examinations.

13.5.2 Cloud PC Crime Scene Investigation

Cloud investigation is an important aspect of digital forensic. Here we have listed some of them.

13.5.2.1 Recognizable Proof of Proof

It is annoying to have to check through logs because their accessibility is likely to obscure distributed execution models [38]. The information extraction and spot verification processes are difficult for the distributed scene of transmitted figures. It is far more difficult to access the open logs in institutions like Programming as an Organization and Stage as an Organization than in System as an Organization. Server businesses monitor client practices are carried out in communicated processing because the cloud carries information that is erratic in character.

13.5.2.2 Unstable Information

Information that will be lost when a computer is shut down is referred to as shaky information [39]. Unstable information must be protected from being altered and evaporated in conveyed figure scenes because it frequently does so throughout evaluation phases. The majority of virtual machines use dynamic RAMs, which prevent information storing and information getting work environments, and it contains unpredictable information when handled in a distributed manner. As a result, even during real-time information acquisitions for evaluations, any motorized device for legitimate sciences cannot be tested to isolate uncertain information.

13.5.2.3   Decency of Data

Analysts must protect the consistency of data in quantitative judgments while gathering information [40]. It should be the firsthand facts that the expert receives, which you may present in court and influence opinion with. Being conscious of the consistency of information quality is annoying in Cloud Genuine sciences. Dispersed handling has a nature that permeates both virtual and conveyed designs. While information is extremely static and being handled, cloud information will typically change every time. Keep in mind that when acquiring network data, meta information also changes. Current devices for genuine sciences are not capable of retrieving and examining the data in its unusual kind of state.

13.5.2.4   Cloud-enabled Huge Data

Cloud-empowered Immense Information impacts criminal appraisals as well as expected suits [41]. This happens on account of Cloud-Drew in Epic Information is being dealt with and managed in dispersed structures. Dispersed enlisting criminal science contraptions face troubles in unmistakable additional items of data related with enormous affirmation, which are supposed to have been obtained.

13.5.3   Virtualization Criminal Science

This section discusses the virtual investigation of crime scene.

13.5.3.1   Internet-based Data

Framework machines, hosts, and servers are unwound and managed as virtual machines, virtual hosts, and virtual servers in virtualization, respectively [42]. The software or hardware known as a hypervisor creates and manages virtual computers. Without knowledge of the host server or design, network traffic can occur between virtual machines or between virtual relationships. As a result, network data can be altered or destroyed. The hypervisor is accessible to overseers and criminal science devices whenever possible, but not to the virtual computers. The affiliation information that is outside the framework also cannot be followed [43]. All affiliation information will be deleted immediately when a virtual machine is destroyed.

13.5.3.2   Duplicate Mac Areas

In Ethernet-based affiliations, Mac addresses are used for communication, and they are unique for each Affiliation point Card [44]. Mac addresses are used to divide virtual machines into certain associations, but because they exist in a virtual environment, these Mac addresses generally won't be chosen as excellent Mac addresses. Since the addresses are not new, it is highly unlikely that the affiliation data will have been securely stored. The information obtained might occasionally combine a nearby Mac address that would be assigned to different hosts. This leads to the challenging situation of seeing questionable computers in the affiliation.

13.5.3.3   Virtual Machine Eradication

Fundamentally, information in virtual computers cannot be followed and obtained by assessments since it is affiliation data [45]. A virtual machine is wiped and no trace of it is left when the client destroys it. Due to the fact that information depends on volatilization, when you erase the machine, the data inside and the information stored in virtual memory both are destroyed. In addition to specially designed activity gadgets, ongoing tools are needed for the recovery of crushed data.

13.5.3.4   Following Back Records

In a specific virtualization structure known as Microsoft's Virtualization Framework [46], there are two age types of virtual machines. The main machine includes drivers built into the sharable components that grant the ability to create logs and record specifics about calculations and exercises. Real-world devices can extract information for evaluations by using stuff drivers. However, the machines of the next age don't produce such drivers; instead, planned drivers have been implemented. These don't keep any kind of records of tests or workouts. Real sciences devices fail to obtain information on those machines since there is no way to obtain data from virtual machines and no built-in support for obtaining such data in the devices.

13.5.3.5   Multitenancy

With the use of virtualization, a dynamic and flexible foundation of virtual computers can continually run [47]. Memory, network cards, and disks are among the hardware components that these virtual computers have in common. It is challenging for inspectors to correctly collect data from the "getting contraptions" on these virtual computers. To put it even more plainly, it is seeking to identify the machine of the crucial client and identify the odd activities for that client.

13.5.3.6 Settled Virtualization

Wrapping virtual machines within other virtual servers, an idea that is not yet fixed in stone, communicates the idea of established virtualization [48]. Since the virtual PC network is completely shut off from the real structure in such systems, routine data retrieving and management are irritating. With Settled Virtualization, malicious devices are not able to collect data from network traffic, logs, and wiped systems. Bad behavior that occurs online as well as through Virtual Private Networks (VPN) in Resolved Virtualization systems cannot be detected by the instruments and methods used today for evaluations.

13.5.4 Network Criminal Science

The following apparatus is required for the network criminal investigation.

13.5.4.1 Gigantic Extension PC Associations

Enormous expansion network comprises gigantic limitation of information, in which the confirmation related with a terrible way of behaving is seen to be attempting by using existing devices [49]. The essential proof is gotten while neglecting some genuine affirmation, and that infers an extensive sum to make closes. Information in massive degree networks is a test to get as they travel through the relationship at striking velocity. This makes the appraisal instruments incapable to get the most tremendous and exact data. Segments of affiliation information can be missed, and a couple of extra data can be added. In that capacity, the uprightness of the got information is at serious gamble. Criminal science instruments for gigantic augmentation networks are restricted to various contraptions, which essentially contain single-client PCs and single hung highlights [50]. These contraptions are not equipped with the most recent turn of events and planning to help the assessment of continuous affiliation wrongdoing area. Besides, the majority of them can't keep up with different plans of information in network breaking point, and managing tasks of the affiliation, which ultimately results in releasing the early phases free from the information obtained. The monetary condition of devices puts the limited scale appraisal relationship in getting them down, although they are valuable and distinct in exploring confirmation. Moreover, in the monetary level of devices, it requires a lot of cash to permit the contraptions prior to using them.

13.5.4.2 Virtualization

In equipment structures, each certifiable affiliation interaction card has a corresponding virtual alignment interface card that is used to establish a connection with a virtual affiliation [51]. The incoming and dynamic communication bundles are connected with some pNICs when a vNIC is used in a virtual machine, while also looking at an outside connection from surreptitiously used virtual machines. The affiliation information cannot be obtained by information-gathering criminal science devices in virtual designs without compromising their security and dependability. By altering affiliation data, information in a virtual affiliation can be transferred from one host to the next according to a client's fundamentals. The development of virtual computers and vNICs improves information addressing and collaboration, for example, VXLAN badly designed [52]. Properly, the getting and examining of affiliation information utilizing legal sciences devices extremely become baffled and touchy.

13.5.4.3 Programming Portrayed Association

In programming the above-mentioned associations, the majority of evaluation techniques utilized in the judicial sciences fail to pinpoint the assault's origin [53]. This often happens in association-created attacks, when the attacker utilizes switches to create false links between Association Layer Disclosure Reveal parties in order to deceive the groups. Data concerning this new association is propelled by a supervisor in the association who assumed it would be a real association. Snooping attacks have so begun at this time. Since no tools have been established or any components introduced to help determine the source and data starting points linked with an attack at any moment when it has been recognized, association criminal science is still working to figure out how to do this.

Log records and follow archives are crucial in evaluations to identify and separate the activities that took place during an assault, despite the difficulty of protecting them. Assessments in association legal disciplines in the area of criminal science are unsuccessful due to the difficulty in maintaining the correctness of log recordings once an attack has taken place. The lack of collaboration between associations and dependable, cutting-edge frameworks enables an attacker to change the substance of log reports during a vindictive show [54]. In the Association's field of criminal science, there are no procedures in place or approved elements are being used to confirm the accuracy of the gathered data and regions.

13.5.5 Robot Working Structure Criminal Science

Cyber investigation also involves the robot working structure for the examination of the evidence collected. Some are discussed in the following sections.

13.5.5.1 Uprightness of Evidence

Getting of information from Robot Working Designs (RWD) should be possible through live or far-off information-getting methodologies, as RWD in a general sense manages unstable information [55]. In live gaining methodology, information can be changed and extra data can be added to the principal confirmation considering the correspondence between the Robot Working Design and robot sensors. In distant information procurement techniques, it is seen that the information, which is being obtained from RWD through an affiliation, is titanic in size and it is challenging to move from the continuous criminological gadgets. No matter what and how there are devices, for example, FTK as well as enCase have to do static information getting, there is not any contraptions made with cutting-edge parts to get information precisely from a Robot Working Design in a decent way.

13.5.5.2   Specific Gadgets

Due to communication, security, and access control difficulties involving the reserved data, legal sciences assessments in robot working systems are at risk [56]. During evaluation, every newly or emerging bit of data that is included in the system must be entirely dismantled. According to ROS Legal Sciences Assessments, specified Crime Location Examination frameworks and Advances are required in order to collect, safeguard, and view evidence as well as to keep order, dependability, and accessibility of data while using automated gadgets.

13.6   WEB OF THINGS CRIME LOCATION EXAMINATION

This section focuses on cyber investigation over the evidence collected by Web of Things Crime scene.

13.6.1   Recognizing Evidence of Confirmation Sources

Assessments are increasingly challenging to do due to the vast amount of data created by Web of Things infrastructure. It is difficult to pinpoint the origins, bases, and sources of the information gathered, and it appears incredibly unlikely that the analysts could have gathered all the data without leaving any proof behind. It was found that there are ambiguities surrounding the location of data storage, the method of data collecting, and the method of evidence organization after consuming the borders of criminal science devices in IoT legal sciences [57]. Along these lines, specialists in respectable sciences ought to separate the verification while searching for the physical and mechanical nature of clever machines.

13.6.2   Discovery Exactness

Technology advancements like AI and deep learning computations are used in the legal sciences devices used for IoT criminology examinations [58]. These calculations are used to create informational indexes, which improve the accuracy of functionalities like information identification and highlight determination. A lot of computations are being made without taking into account real-time norms of behavior as IoT devices and frameworks handle frequent situations in daily life. Because it requires constant interruption discovery systems to be included in the computerized criminology equipment, Web of Things Legal sciences is thus at risk.

13.6.3   Preparing Information

A measurable tool needs to be accurate, reliable, and able to participate in an evaluation cycle [59]. Even though there are informational indexes created on criminology devices to separate proof in information-handling calculations based on artificial intelligence, they end up being manufactured informational indexes that are several years old. For the complex IoT Organization Criminology tests being conducted today, these informational collections are outdated. Additionally, it might be challenging to get precise results, especially when using these crime scene investigation tools to consistently organize and gather information.

13.6.4   Present-day Techniques

The proof gathering method is more complicated in cloud legal sciences due to the distributed characteristics of cloud information and the lack of actual access to sophisticated artifacts. The usual methods of interaction for recovery cannot be used by the legal representatives. Original tools are consistently supported by computerized legal sciences in order to genuinely gather evidence. These days, an additional examination field termed emergency is used. This method enables the location of collections of artifacts and the speedy identification of the most essential ones from the perspective of wrongdoing. Live and postmortem are two important applications of emergency that depend on AI technology [60].

The cooperation of software engineering skills with the real world renders CPS defenseless against vengeful attacks that go beyond the scope of conventional digital assaults. For recovering bombed framework states, this method transmits CPS checkpointing and recovery models—a clever conception of the situation.

The idea of recovery is to advance the framework to align with the benefits of internal components. By using a sliding window-based checkpointing convention, the framework states for recovery are recorded. The benefits of this novel technology are low and endless sensor overt repetition. The major Cloud Legal Sciences Challenges include information assortment, live crime scene investigation, proof isolation, virtualized climate, inner staffing, and outer reliance chains.

The Digital Forensics Recommendation Model [61] helps forensic investigators by giving them guidance as they carry out their investigations. A list of model's phases is provided in Figure 13.2.

Digital real-world systems rely on modern distant technology, like 5G, to connect with the outside world. Successful remote data changes can be made using the Cloud, IoT, or V2X foundations [62].

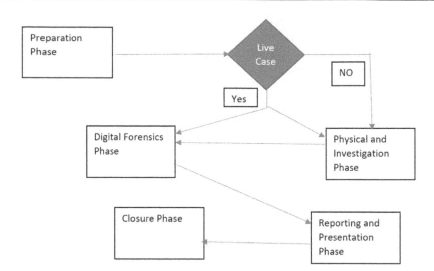

Figure 13.2 Model phases.

13.7   FUTURE CPS CRIMINOLOGY

As CPS develops and significantly more CPS frameworks are produced and distributed, approaches for CPS security and CPS legal sciences will also be expected to be spelled forth. There are numerous approaches to make improvements. This section discusses potential developments in CPS criminology in the future.

As with other logical disciplines, one pattern is for CPS legal sciences and security to be information-driven. Information can be utilized to create more precise models, which can then be applied to other survey and inspection cycles that highlight areas where CPS implementations fall short.

13.7.1   Criminology and Information-driven Security

For CPS, criminology and information-driven security might include a number of points which affect the cybersecurity system.

13.7.2   Attack Area and Assistance Using Data-driven Science

The implications of a few CPS security and criminal science systems, such as interference acknowledgment and countering systems, as well as overseeing testing CPS security conditions, such as undeniable level consistent risks and low and slow vectors [66], can be covered in this point. Setting description and sharing, recognizing assaults by thinking about them, identifying attacks using outline language structures, and differentiating attacks using stream-based plans are some potential strategies that could be employed for this point.

13.7.3 Foundations for Procedure-based Sharing and Unwavering Data Quality

There are several expected directions for data reliability, sharing, and remembering unshakable quality of data for provenances, formal course assessment, and reproducibility of security tests. This will necessitate reliant strategies that can disperse and maintain awareness of trust associations between the many CPS applications' components and various structures connecting with them. Blockchain technology is one potential method for reimagining trust and securing transactions [63].

13.7.4 An Approach Based on Risk for Controlling Security Estimations

This viewpoint incorporates many categories for examining security dangers, such as showing attacks, client and association hazards, defensive measures, and game speculation models for thorough bet evaluations [63].

13.7.5 Collection and Extraction of the Evidence

Following the collection and extraction of the evidence, the reconstruction phase entails doing network analysis, ownership and possession analysis, ownership and time frame analysis, application and file analysis, ownership and data concealment analysis, log file analysis, and ownership and possession analysis, as shown in Figure 13.3.

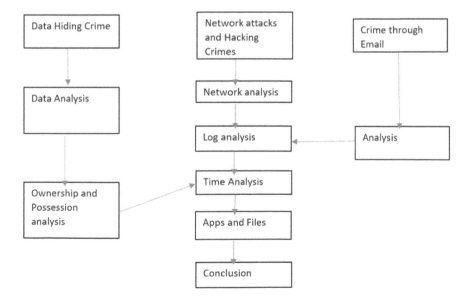

Figure 13.3 Reconstruction of data.

In addition, it is practicable to employ data-driven methods of managing to identify the link between human behaving style and vulnerability to various types of attacks for CPS applications that incorporate human participation and collaborative efforts [59]. This has a significant impact on how distinct CPS applications are organized because it uncovers a few shadowy elements through insights and comprehensive data analysis. Due to the detachment of the necessary data sets, it was difficult to create such apps two or three years ago. However, it is now conceivable as many applications and systems gather a significant amount of data as they function. As a result, we now have more information on the many CPS applications to evaluate and gain insightful knowledge from. It is possible to uncover numerous discernments connected to CPS security attacks by reusing data-driven methodologies. There are numerous applications for these discernments:

- They can be used as a data source by CPS improvement associations to assist them in planning their future security measures and organizations for various CPS applications.
- Government security organizations can utilize them to outline its CPS wellness initiatives, requirements, standards, and plans.
- Different associations and affiliations that use CPS applications can use them to demonstrate their security practices and fend off potential security bets.

Taking on some of these procedures will assist in reducing the application and usage of better security and legal sciences components and deal with any implications regarding shield of various kinds of systems, including CPS. In the upcoming years, it is expected that more research and current examination will be conducted in an effort to identify appropriate, conventional, and effective game strategies. These include discovering new ways to organize social gatherings, make proposals, clean-up security data, look at security data [64], and recognize more notable security noticing and risk management techniques. Additionally, faster data-driven tools will be developed to discover historical insights, including identifying zero-day assaults. Additionally, new security and criminal science strategies will be essentially advanced to provide better well-being endeavors and assessments. These strategies include human direct security strategies that solidify human approaches to acting in providing more secure CPS applications and setting careful security courses of action that combine information about the continuous environment setting in overseeing security risks.

13.7.6   Crime Scene Investigations

Another crucial future component of CPS legal sciences is the manner that many CPS crime scene investigations rely on clever calculations and AI techniques to handle powerful CPS applications and streamline operations and cycles. Intelligent buildings, self-driving cars, innovative water systems, high-level assembly, clever lattices, and astute traffic signal management are a few examples of CPS uses. These clever CPS applications make choices with the goal of benefiting from enormous amounts of acquired information in order to increase their dependability, precision, efficiency, and cost-adequacy.

These systems could be exposed to security threats as a result of becoming more vulnerable to security bets. For instance, attackers may be able to provide a few misleading details that adversely affect the learning process and reduce the display of these astute structures. It is crucial to protect the computer-based intelligence computations from any threats, such as those that could affect their effectiveness or security. Security risks against the arrangement stage and security risks against the testing/gathering stage are the names of these dangers. The hurting attack, which disrupts the availability and dependability of the simulated intelligence processes by familiarizing poorly constructed models with the planning instructive record, is one significant security risk against the arrangement stage. Attacks that cause harm can be divided into two groups: attacks that cause harm without modifying any components or checks and attacks that cause harm while changing features or names.

13.7.7 Countermeasures

There are variety of controlled ways for advanced computing and artificial intelligence. These tactics can either be proactive securities or open shields. Consolidating the countermeasures utilized in the readiness stage and the testing/understanding stage, different countermeasures were studied in Ref. [65]. Anyways, to accomplish this, CPS will need to develop valid scientific tools and components that are useful for monitoring computations involving automated thought and artificial intelligence. In these circumstances, it may also be possible to use artificial intelligence and man-made thinking procedures to detect and prevent security breaches and provide superior scientific mechanical assembly to CPS lawful sciences if attacks do actually occur. Additionally, it is crucial to look into how these practices might be used to prepare for and reduce the harm caused by security assaults while still providing adequate legal support to follow and handle actual attacks.

13.8 CONCLUSION

Experts and analysts, who are associated with coherent assessment and computerized bad behavior assessments, have recognized various hardships in advanced quantifiable contraptions. Open-source devices can be actively and strategically acquired, but commercial mechanical assembly must be purchased. A corporate tool would be much more effective and precise in recovering results from evaluations than an open-source tool. In the field of automated criminal science, obstacles are found in fields like flexible, association, cloud, virtualization, robot working systems, and Web of Things legitimate sciences. Problems with these devices have arisen as a result of a lack of most remote points of data acquisition, obtaining network information, appraisal, advancement assortments, similitude, and receiving reliable confirmation. These challenges achieve poor high-level legitimate sciences assessments, and give incorrect verification, which can't be recognized and consumed to take decisions. Thus, at the present time, several mechanical assemblies are recognized to be at progress stage in executing deals with the disadvantages.

In this chapter, we characterized and examined another sort of criminology, digital actual frameworks legal sciences (CPS crime scene investigation). We examined CPS criminology standards and issues as far as innovative, hierarchical, and legitimate perspectives. Given the continuing research in this area, we recognize that there are opportunities to further locate this point and provide effective CPS criminology measures. Endeavors to foster reasonable approaches, methodology, instruments, guidelines, and arrangements for this significant legal sciences type are critical. One potential methodology that offers some encouraging commitment is the legal sciences by design approach, where criminology endeavors are empowered as implicit abilities in CPS and CPCS consolidated all through the improvement cycle. Subsequently, when an event happens, the CPS outfitted with these methods will have underlying measures to give agents the important information for the crime scene investigation process. The chapter likewise examined future turn of events and exploration bearings for further developing CPS security and criminology abilities and cycles.

REFERENCES

1. K. Nickolaos, N. Moustafa and E. Sitnikova, "Forensics and deep learning mechanisms for botnets in internet of things: A survey of challenges and solutions", *IEEE Access*, vol. 7, pp. 61764–61785, 2019.
2. B. K. Sharma, M. A. Joseph, B. Jacob and L. C. B. Miranda, "Emerging trends in digital forensic and cyber security-an overview," *2019 Sixth HCT Information Technology Trends (ITT)*. IEEE, pp. 309–313, Nov. 2019.
3. D. Suryawanshi, "Image recognition: Detection of nearly duplicate images", *Repository.library.csuci.edu*, 2019, [online] Available: http://repository.library.csuci.edu/handle/10211.3/203471
4. M. Keshavarzi and H. R. Ghaffary, "I2CE3: A dedicated and separated attack chain for ransomware offenses as the most infamous cyber extortion", *Computer Science Review*, vol. 36, May 2020.
5. N. Mohamed, J. Al-Jaroodi and S. Lazarova-Molnar, "Leveraging the capabilities of industry 4.0 for improving energy efficiency in smart factories", *IEEE Access*, vol. 7, pp. 18008–18020, 2019.
6. Q. Liu, P. Li, W. Zhao, W. Cai, S. Yu and V. C. Leung, "A survey on security threats and defensive techniques of machine learning: A data driven view", *IEEE Access*, vol. 6, pp. 12103–12117, 2018.

7. C. Iwendi, Z. Jalil, A. R. Javed, T. Reddy G. R. Kaluri, G. Srivastava, et al., "Key-SplitWatermark: Zero watermarking algorithm for software protection against cyber-attacks", *IEEE Access*, vol. 8, pp. 72650–72660, 2020.

8. A. R. Javed, M. O. Beg, M. Asim, T. Baker and A. H. Al-Bayatti, "AlphaLogger: Detecting motion-based side-channel attack using smartphone keystrokes", *Journal of Ambient Intelligence and Human Computing*, pp. 1–14, Feb. 2020.

9. S. Goyal, N. Sharma, B. Bhushan, A. Shankar and M. Sagayam, "Iot enabled technology in secured healthcare: Applications, challenges and future directions", *Cognitive Internet of Medical Things for Smart Healthcare*, pp. 25–48. doi: 10.1007/978-3-030-55833-8_2.

10. A. Tiwari, V. Mehrotra, S. Goel, K. Naman, S. Maurya and R. Agarwal, "Developing trends and challenges of digital forensics", *2021 5th International Conference on Information Systems and Computer Networks (ISCON), 2021*. doi: 10.1109/ISCON52037.2021.9702301

11. A. R. Javed, Z. Jalil, W. Zehra, T. R. Gadekallu, D. Y. Suh and M. J. Piran, "A comprehensive survey on digital video forensics: Taxonomy challenges and future directions", *Engineering Applications of Artificial Intelligence*, vol. 106, Nov. 2021.

12. M. A. Alsmirat, R. A. Al-Hussien, W. T. Al-Sarayrah, Y. Jararweh and M. Etier, "Digital video forensics: A comprehensive survey", *International Journal of Advanced Intelligence Paradigms*, vol. 15, no. 4, pp. 437–456, 2020.

13. P. Purnaye and V. Kulkarni, "A comprehensive study of cloud forensics", *Archives of Computational Methods in Engineering*, vol. 29, pp. 33–46, Jan. 2022.

14. S. N. Joshi and G. R. Chillarge, "Secure log scheme for cloud forensics", *Proc. 4th Int. Conf. I-SMAC (IoT Social Mobile Analytics Cloud) (I-SMAC)*, pp. 188–193, Oct. 2020.

15. Schlepphorst, Sebastian & Choo, Kim-Kwang Raymond & Le-Khac, Nhien-An. (2020). *Digital Forensic Approaches for Cloud Service Models: A Survey*. 10.1007/978-3-030-47131-6_8.

16. Shukla, U., Mandal, B., Kiran, K.V.D. (2018). Perlustration on mobile forensics tools. In: Smys, S.Palanisamy, R., Rocha, Á., Beligiannis, G.N. (eds) *Computer Networks and Inventive Communication Technologies*. Lecture Notes on Data Engineering and Communications Technologies, 58: 1225–1231. Springer, Singapore. https://doi.org/10.1007/978-981-15-9647-6_97

17. M. Varshney, B. Bhushan and A. K. M. B. Haque, "Big data analytics and data mining for healthcare informatics (HCI)", in Kumar, R., Sharma, R. and Pattnaik, P. K. (eds) *Multimedia Technologies in the Internet of Things Environment*, vol. 3. Studies in Big Data, vol. 108. Springer, Singapore, 2022. https://doi.org/10.1007/978-981-19-0924-5_11

18. N. R. Mistry and M. S. Dahiya, "Signature based volatile memory forensics: A detection-based approach for analyzing sophisticated cyber-attacks", *International Journal of Information Technology*, vol. 11, no. 3, pp. 583–589, Sep. 2019.

19. S. Y. Lim et al., "Dropbox forensics: Forensic analysis of a cloud storage service", *International Journal of Engineering Trends and Technology (IJETT)*, no. 2020, pp. 45–49, 2020.

20. V. R. Silvarajoo, S. Y. Lim and P. Daud, "Digital evidence case management tool for collaborative digital forensics investigation", *2021 3rd International Cyber Resilience Conference (CRC)*. doi: 10.1109/CRC50527.2021.9392497

21. Awad, Rima Asmar, Juan Lopez, and Mike Rogers. "Volatile Memory Extraction-Based Approach for Level 0–1 CPS Forensics." *2019 IEEE International Symposium on Technologies for Homeland Security (HST)*. IEEE, 2019.
22. S. Kalle, N. Ameen, H. Yoo and I. Ahmed, "Clik on plcs! attacking control logic with decompilation and virtual plc", *Binary Analysis Research (BAR) Workshop Network and Distributed System Security Symposium (NDSS)*, 2019.
23. H. Yoo and I. Ahmed, "Control logic injection attacks on industrial control systems", *IFIP International Conference on ICT Systems Security and Privacy Protection*, pp. 33–48, 2019.
24. Okereafor, Kenneth & Djehaiche, Rania. (2020). *A Review of Application Challenges of Digital Forensics.*
25. Grispos, George & Bastola, Kiran. (2020). *Cyber Autopsies: The Integration of Digital Forensics into Medical Contexts.* 10.1109/CBMS49503.2020.00102.
26. A. Dimitriadis, N. Ivezic, B. Kulvatunyou and I. Mavridis, "D4I-Digital forensics framework for reviewing and investigating cyber-attacks", *Array*, vol. 5, pp. 100015, 2020.
27. J. G. Nortjé and D. C. Myburgh, "The search and seizure of digital evidence by forensic investigators", *South Africa Potchefstroom Electronic Law Journal (PELJ)*, vol. 22, no. 1, pp. 1–42, 2019.
28. H. Griffioen, T. Booij and C. Doerr, "Quality evaluation of cyber threat intelligence feeds", *Applied Cryptography and Network Security*, vol. 12147, pp. 277–296, 2020, [online] Available: http://link.springer.com/10.1007/978-3-030-57878-7_14
29. J. Cha, S. K. Singh, Y. Pan and J. H. Park, "Blockchain-based cyber threat intelligence system architecture for sustainable computing", *Sustainability*, vol. 12, no. 16, pp. 6401, Aug. 2020, [online] Available: www.mdpi.com/2071-1050/12/16/6401
30. R. Rathi, N. Sharma, C. Manchanda, B. Bhushan and M. Grover, "Security challenges & controls in cyber physical system", *2020 IEEE 9th International Conference on Communication Systems and Network Technologies (CSNT)*. doi: 10.1109/csnt48778.2020.9115778
31. A. Dizdarević, S. Baraković and J. Baraković Husić, "Examination of digital forensics software tools performance: Open or not?", *Advanced Technologies Systems and Applications IV -Proceedings of the International Symposium on Innovative and Interdisciplinary Applications of Advanced Technologies (IAT 2019)*, vol. 83, pp. 442–451, 2020, [online] Available: http://link.springer.com/10.1007/978-3-030-24986-1_35
32. N. Serketzis, V. Katos, C. Ilioudis, D. Baltatzis and G. Pangalos, "Improving forensic triage efficiency through cyber threat intelligence", *Future Internet*, vol. 11, no. 7, p. 162, Jul. 2019, [online] Available: www.mdpi.com/1999-5903/11/7/162
33. D. Schlette, F. Böhm, M. Caselli and G. Pernul, "Measuring and visualizing cyber threat intelligence quality", *International Journal of Information Security*, vol. 20, no. 1, pp. 21–38, Feb. 2021, [online] Available: https://doi.org/10.1007/s10207-020-00490-y
34. D. Bhamare, M. Zolanvari, A. Erbad, R. Jain, K. Khan and N. Meskin, "Cybersecurity for industrial control systems: A survey", *Computers & Security*, vol. 89, pp. 1–18, Nov. 2019.
35. A. Iqbal, F. Mahmood and M. Ekstedt, "Digital forensic analysis of industrial control systems using sandboxing: A case of WAMPAC applications in the power systems", *Energies*, vol. 12, no. 13, pp. 1–15, Jul. 2019.
36. A. Dimitriadis, N. Ivezic, B. Kulvatunyou and I. Mavridis, "D4I—Digital forensics framework for reviewing and investigating cyber-attacks", *D4I—Digital Forensics Framework for Reviewing and Investigating Cyber-Attacks*, vol. 5, pp. 1–8, 2020.

37. W. Ashford, "Cyber-attacks targeting industrial control systems on the rise", *ComputerWeekly.com*, Mar. 2019, [online] Available: www.computerweekly.com/news/252460353/Cyber-attacks-targeting-industrial-control-systems-on-the-rise
38. S. Ghosh and S. Sampalli, "A survey of security in SC AD a networks: Current issues and future challenges", *IEEE Access*, vol. PP, no. 99, pp. 1–1, 2019.
39. H. Villar-Vega, L. Perez-Lopez and J. Moreno-Sanchez, "Computer forensic analysis protocols review focused on digital evidence recovery in hard disks devices", *Journal of Physics Conference Series*, vol. 1418, p. 012008, 2019.
40. B. Bhushan, "Middleware and security requirements for internet of things", in Sharma, D. K., Peng, S. L., Sharma, R. and Zaitsev, D. A. (eds) *Micro-Electronics and Telecommunication Engineering*. Lecture Notes in Networks and Systems, vol. 373, 2022. Springer, Singapore. https://doi.org/10.1007/978-981-16-8721-1_30
41. A. Iqbal, F. Mahmood and M. Ekstedt, "Digital forensic analysis of industrial control systems using sandboxing: A case of WAMPAC applications in the power systems", *Energies*, vol. 12, no. 13, p. 2598, 2019.
42. E. Ateş, G. E. Bostanci and M. Guzel, "Security evaluation of industry 4.0: Understanding industry 4.0 on the basis of crime big data internet of things (IoT) and cyber physical systems", *Güvenlik Bilimleri Dergisi*, vol. 9, pp. 29–50, 2020.
43. O. Bongomin, G. G. Ocen, E. O. Nganyi, A. Musinguzi and T. Omara, "Exponential disruptive technologies and the required skills of industry 4.0", *Journal of Engineering 2020*, pp. 1–17, 2020.
44. M. Stoyanova, Y. Nikoloudakis, S. Panagiotakis, E. Pallis and E. Markakis, "A survey on the internet of things (IoT) forensics: Challenges approaches and open issues", *IEEE Communications Surveys and Tutorials*, vol. PP, no. 99, pp. 1–1, 2020.
45. B. R. Yogeshwar, M. Sethumadhavan, S. Srinivasan and P. P. Amritha, "A light-weight cyber security implementation for industrial SCADA systems in the industries 4.0", *Information and Communication Technology for Intelligent Systems*, pp. 463–472, 2021. doi: 10.1007/978-981-15-7062-9_46
46. W. Dai, P. Wang, W. Sun, X. Wu, H. Zhang, V. Vyatkin, et al., "Semantic integration of plug-and-play software components for industrial edges based on micro services", *IEEE Access*, vol. PP, no. 99, pp. 1–1, 2019. doi: 10.1109/ACCESS.2019.2938565
47. R. S. Khalaf and A. Varol, "Digital forensics: Focusing on image forensics", *2019 7th International Symposium on Digital Forensics and Security (ISDFS)*. doi: 10.1109/ISDFS.2019.8757557
48. F. Khan, "A detailed study on Security breaches of digital forensics in cyber physical system", *2019 Sixth HCT Information Technology Trends (ITT)*. doi: 10.1109/ITT48889.2019.9075094
49. N. Serketzis, V. Katos, C. Ilioudis, D. Baltatzis and G. Pangalos, "Improving forensic triage efficiency through cyber threat intelligence", *Future Internet*, vol. 11, no. 7, p. 162, Jul. 2019.
50. N. Mohamed, J. Al-Jaroodi and I. Jawhar, "Cyber-physical systems forensics", *2020 IEEE Systems Security Symposium (SSS)*. doi: 10.1109/SSS47320.2020.9174199
51. M. Hina, M. Ali, A. R. Javed, F. Ghabban, L. A. Khan and Z. Jalil, "SeFACED: Semantic-based forensic analysis and classification of e-mail data using deep learning", *IEEE Access*, vol. 9, pp. 98398–98411, 2021.
52. A. Khamparia, P. K. Singh, P. Rani, D. Samanta, A. Khanna and B. Bhushan, "An internet of health things-driven deep learning framework for detection and classification of skin cancer using transfer learning", *Transactions on Emerging Telecommunications Technologies*, 2020. doi: 10.1002/ett.3963

53. V. Fernando, "Cyber forensics tools: A review on mechanism and emerging challenges", *2021 11th IFIP International Conference on New Technologies, Mobility and Security (NTMS)*. doi: 10.1109/NTMS49979.2021.9432641

54. W. Ahmed, F. Shahzad, A. R. Javed, F. Iqbal and L. Ali, "WhatsApp network forensics: Discovering the IP addresses of suspects", *Proceedings of 11th IFIP International Conference New Technology Mobility Security (NTMS)*, pp. 1–7, Apr. 2021.

55. T. Wang, Y. Quan, X. S. Shen, T. R. Gadekallu, W. Wang and K. Dev, "A privacy-enhanced retrieval technology for the cloud-assisted internet of things", *IEEE Transactions on Industrial Informatics*, Aug. 2021.

56. S. Sachdeva, B. Raina and A. Sharma, "Analysis of digital forensic tools", *Journal of Computational and Theoretical Nanoscience*, vol. 17, no. 6, pp. 2459–2467, 2020.

57. Y. Li, F. Juan, L. Xiu-Li and L. Qiang, "Design of intelligent home security monitoring system based on Internet of Things [J]", *Modern Electronics Technique*, vol. 42, no. 8, pp. 55–58, 2019.

58. F. Wei and P. Li, "Public laboratory remote monitoring system based on ZigBee technology[J]", *Modern Electronics Technique*, vol. 44, no. 3, pp. 11–15, 2021.

59. Xia, Y.-Q & Yan, C. & Wang, X.-J & Song, X.-H. (2019). *Intelligent Transportation Cyber-physical Cloud Control Systems*. Zidonghua Xuebao/Acta Automatica Sinica. 45. 132–142. 10.16383/j.aas.c180370

60. X. Wang, Y. Han, V. C. M. Leung, D. Niyato, X. Yan and X. Chen, "Convergence of edge computing and deep learning: A comprehensive survey", *IEEE Communications Surveys Tutorials*, vol. 22, no. 2, pp. 869–904, 2020.

61. Y. Zeng, M. Chao and R. Stoleru, "EmuEdge: A hybrid emulator for reproducible and realistic edge computing experiments", *2019 IEEE International Conference on Fog Computing (ICFC)*, pp. 153–164, 2019. doi: 10.1109/ICFC.2019.00027

62. M. Chao, R. Stoleru, L. Jin, S. Yao, M. Maurice and R. Blalock, "AMVP: Adaptive CNN-based multitask video processing on mobile stream processing platforms", *2020 IEEE/ACM Symposium on Edge Computing (SEC)*, pp. 96–109, 2020. doi: 10.1109/SEC50012.2020.00015

63. B. Suman, S. Mohammod, S. Radu, M. Chao, H. Amran, A. Altaweel, M. Maurice and R. Blalock, "R-Drive: Resilient data storage and sharing for mobile edge computing systems", 2022.

64. J. Ormanis and A. Elsts, "Towards body coupled communication for ehealth: Experimental study of human body frequency response", *2020 IEEE International Conference on Communications Workshops (ICC Workshops)*, pp. 1–7, 2020.

65. G. Berthou, K. Marquet, T. Risset and G. Salagnac, "Accurate power consumption evaluation for peripherals in ultra-low-power embedded systems", *2020 Global Internet of Things Summit (GIoTS)*, pp. 1–6, 2020.

Index

Milton Keynes UK
Ingram Content Group UK Ltd.
UKHW031130141024
449569UK00006B/314